CORSICA

CORSICA

CONTENTS

DISCOVER CORSICA 6

Welcome to Corsica..................................8

Reasons to Love Corsica......................10

Explore Corsica.....................................14

Getting to Know Corsica.....................16

Corsica Itineraries...............................20

Corsica Your Way.................................26

A Year in Corsica..................................50

A Brief History......................................52

The GR20...60

EXPERIENCE CORSICA 70

Bastia and the North.........................72

Ajaccio and the West Coast......104

Bonifacio and the South.............128

Corte and the Interior..................150

NEED TO KNOW 172

Before You Go.......................................174

Getting Around....................................176

Practical Information..........................180

Index...182

Phrasebook...188

Acknowledgments...............................190

Left: An assortent of fishing nets
Previous page: Old houses in Bonifacio
Front cover: The ancient mountain village
of Speloncato

DISCOVER

The beautiful village of Piana

Welcome to Corsica......................................8

Reasons to Love Corsica.........................10

Explore Corsica..14

Getting to Know Corsica.........................16

Corsica Itineraries....................................20

Corsica Your Way......................................26

A Year in Corsica.......................................50

A Brief History...52

The GR20...60

WELCOME TO
CORSICA

One of the wildest islands in the Mediterranean, Corsica is a land made for adventurers, with epic mountains, deep gorges, pristine beaches and a patchwork of ancient towns and fortified cities. Whether you're seeking a relaxing coastal break or a rugged outdoor escape, this DK travel guide is the perfect companion.

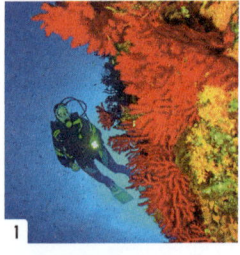

1 Scuba diving with red seafans off the west coast.

2 Ancient menhir monoliths at Cauria.

3 Dining in Bonifacio's charming old town.

4 Boats moored at Bastia's pretty harbour.

Corsica is fully deserving of its nickname – "*L'Île de Beauté*" (the Isle of Beauty) – but this isn't the kind of quiet beauty you'll find in the south of France. Few islands combine sea and summit so dramatically, with the highest peaks in the Mediterranean plunging to meet azure waters teeming with marine life. The island has been whittled over eons into two soaring granite mountain ranges, marked by jagged features like the Calanques de Piana and traversed by Europe's toughest hiking route, the infamous GR20.

It isn't only these wild landscapes that distinguish Corsica from mainland France. Abundant roadside graffiti proclaiming "Corsica is not French" speaks of the long-running struggle for the island's autonomy. In towns and cities like Bastia, Corte and the bustling capital, Ajaccio, you'll find examples of Corsica's thriving independent culture: food festivals celebrate a unique mix of Italian and French cuisines, local musicians practise polyphonic singing, and a plethora of religious traditions speak of Corsica's long Catholic past. The birthplace of Napoleon Bonaparte has a proud history as varied as the meats on its charcuterie boards, with a story stretching back to the Neolithic peoples of Filitosa.

So, where to start? We've broken Corsica down into easily navigable chapters, with helpful itineraries, expert local knowledge and comprehensive maps to help you plan the perfect visit. Whether you're staying for a weekend, a week or longer, this DK guide will ensure that you make the most of the island. Enjoy the book, and enjoy Corsica.

REASONS TO LOVE
CORSICA

Relaxing on pristine golden sands, enjoying rugged mountain hikes or exploring ancient megaliths and fortified Genoese cities. There are so many reasons to fall in love with Corsica. Here are just a few of them.

1 NAPOLEON'S LEGACY

Corsica's celebrated son looms large in his hometown, Ajaccio, the island'd capital. Explore his past at the Maison Bonaparte Museum *(p110)* or see his towering statue at Place d'Austerlitz *(p112)*.

HIKING THE GR20 *2*

One of Europe's toughest hiking trails runs from Calenzana *(p98)* in the northwest to Conca *(p67)* in the southeast. It's an epic 10–14 day hike through mountains, valleys and gorges.

3 FRESH PRODUCE

The island's rich Mediterranean diet is a perfect fusion of French and Italian influences, with local chestnuts, *figatellu* sausages, brocciu goat's cheese and honey just some of its delights.

THE SLOW TRAIN 4

The rattling slow train between Ajaccio and Bastia, known as the Trinichellu, passes through 32 tunnels and across the mountains via Corte. You won't want this spectacular journey to end.

MEGALITHIC SITES 5

Unique prehistoric megaliths known as menhirs dot Corsica's landscape, with a a particularly large grouping of statues at Filitosa *(p147)*. No one can say for sure what ritual purpose they served.

RARE WILDLIFE 6

The island is strikingly biodiverse. Thanks to the reintroduction efforts of the Parc Naturel Régional de Corse *(p44)* you can see Corsican deer and the mouflon, a rare wild sheep.

THE GOLDEN BEACHES OF PORTO-VECCHIO 7

With their soft sand, canopy pines and shallow, turquoise waters, Palombaggia, Pinarellu, Rondinara and Santa Giulia *(p140)* are among the world's most picturesque beaches.

BOAT TRIPS FROM BONIFACIO 8

The stunning port of Bonifacio *(p132)* offers a host of cruises and boat journeys to remote beaches, outlying islands and echoing caves on the wild southern coast.

9 HISTORIC CHURCHES

Corsica's Catholic history is on glorious display at an array of unusual churches, from the polychrome San Michele de Murato *(p88)* to the red-carpeted Chapelle de la Scala Santa *(p80)*.

10 BALAGNE'S MEDIEVAL VILLAGES

Between Calvi on the northern coast and Monte Grosso are the ancient stone villages of the Balagne region. Pigna *(p96)* and Sant'Antonino *(p99)* are just two stand-outs.

POLITICAL HERITAGE 11

Forged by a long history of invasion and the struggle for independence, Corsica has a proud political past. Explore it in Corte *(p154)*, the historic cradle of independence.

SNORKELLING ÎLES LAVEZZI 12

Shallow, crystal-clear waters and spectacular marine life make diving off the Lavezzi archipelago *(p137)* a truly memorable experience for both new and experienced divers.

EXPLORE
CORSICA

This guide divides the island into four colour-coded sightseeing areas, as shown on the map below. Find out more about each area on the following pages.

L'Île-Rousse

Lozari

Calvi

Calenzana

Argentella

Galéria

Haut-Asco

Girolata

Bardiana

Calacuccia

Porto

Piana

Guagno

Vico

Cargèse

AJACCIO AND THE WEST COAST
p104

Sagone

Bocognano

Tyrrhenian Sea

Tiuccia

Appietto

Bastelica

Villanova

Ajaccio

Cauro

Îles Sanguinaires

Porticcio

Grosseto

Taravo

Fozzaninco

Petreto-Bicchisano

Porto-Pollo

BONIFACIO AND THE SOUTH
p128

Propriano

Campomoro

Sartène

L'Ortolo

Tizzano

Naseo

Figari

0 kilometres   20

0 miles   20

N ↑

Bonifacio

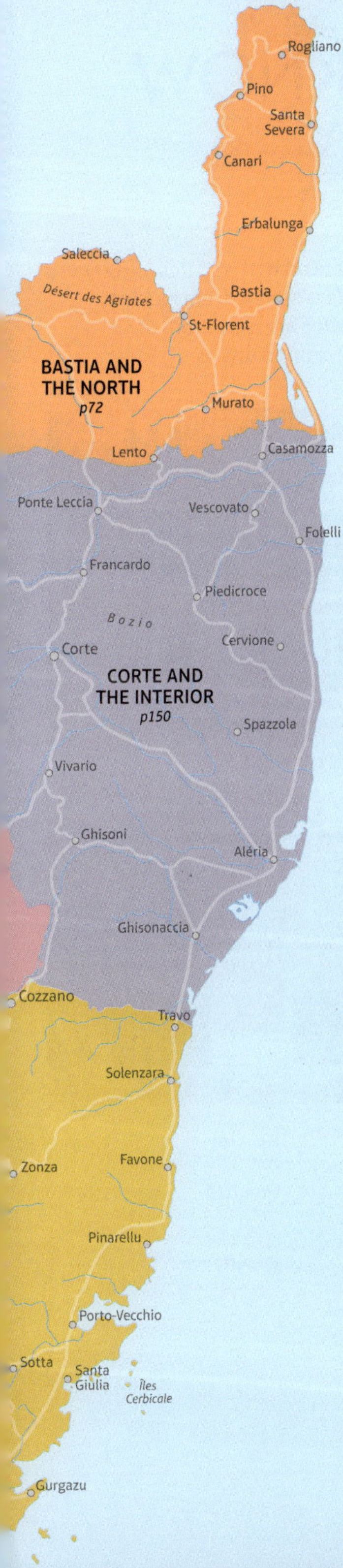

Rogliano

Pino

Santa
Severa

Canari

Erbalunga

Saleccia

Désert des Agriates

Bastia

St-Florent

BASTIA AND
THE NORTH
p72

Murato

Lento

Casamozza

Ponte Leccia

Vescovato

Folelli

Francardo

Piedicroce

Bozio

Cervione

Corte

CORTE AND
THE INTERIOR
p150

Spazzola

Vivario

Ghisoni

Aléria

Ghisonaccia

Cozzano

Travo

Solenzara

Zonza

Favone

Pinarellu

Porto-Vecchio

Sotta

Santa
Giulia

*Îles
Cerbicale*

Gurgazu

LOCATOR MAP

FRANCE

ITALY

● Corsica

Tyrrhenian Sea

ALGERIA

TUNISIA

GETTING TO KNOW
CORSICA

The fourth-largest island in the Mediterranean, Corsica has a beautifully rugged and mountainous topography that differs starkly from much of mainland France. Dotted across its hills and plains are a plethora of Neolithic sites, along with bustling cities and fortified towns.

BASTIA AND THE NORTH

PAGE 72

Corsica's main port and second-largest city, Bastia looks out east towards Italy's Tuscan coast, its cobbled streets and busy squares exuding an unmistakable Mediterranean charm. It might be presided over by the 15th-century Genoese Citadelle, but Bastia has the feel of a bustling modern city, particularly in summer. Away from the city, the north is home to the harbour of St-Florent, the hip resort of Calvi and plenty of old villages in the Balagne and Nebbio regions.

Best for
Bastia's boutique shops

Home to
Bastia, Calvi, San Michele de Murato

Experience
Exploring Bastia's Citadelle

AJACCIO AND
THE WEST COAST

Ajaccio and Napoleon Bonaparte are often mentioned in the same breath, but Corsica's largest city is so much more than the ruler's birthplace. The island's cultural wealth is on glimmering display at the Palais Fesch, while the Quai Napoléon and Quai l'Herminier brim with sea-facing cafés and bars. Leave the city, and you'll find some of the island's most incredible landscapes, including the misty pines of the Forêt d'Aïtone and the towering rocks of the Calanques de Piana.

Best for
Coastal walks

Home to
Ajaccio, Réserve Naturelle de Scandola

Experience
Spotting seabirds at the Réserve Naturelle de Scandola

→

PAGE 128

BONIFACIO AND THE SOUTH

The fortified city of Bonifacio might be ancient, but its origins are relatively recent compared to the prehistoric gems to be found across southern Corsica. Fans of the Neolithic are spoilt for choice, with sites like Filitosa and the wild Cauria plateau dotted with hundreds of mysterious menhir statues. For more contemporary pleasures, the south is home to some of the island's best tourist attractions including the busy port of Solenzara and the beach town of Porto-Vecchio.

Best for
Prehistoric adventures

Home to
Bonifacio, Aiguilles de Bavella

Experience
*Taking a guided boat ride
beneath the cliffs of Bonifacio*

CORTE AND THE INTERIOR

Overlooking the dramatic mountain chain that intersects Corsica from north to south, Corte is both the geographic and political heart of the island. It was here that the constitution for an independent Corsica was drafted, and the spirit of patriotism lives on in the town's many cultural institutions, including the Musée de la Corse. The island's interior is a must-visit for both history lovers and hardy mountaineers, with a dizzying roster of peaks just beyond Corte's border.

Best for
Mountain hikes

Home to
Corte

Experience
Driving or cycling the undulating mountain roads

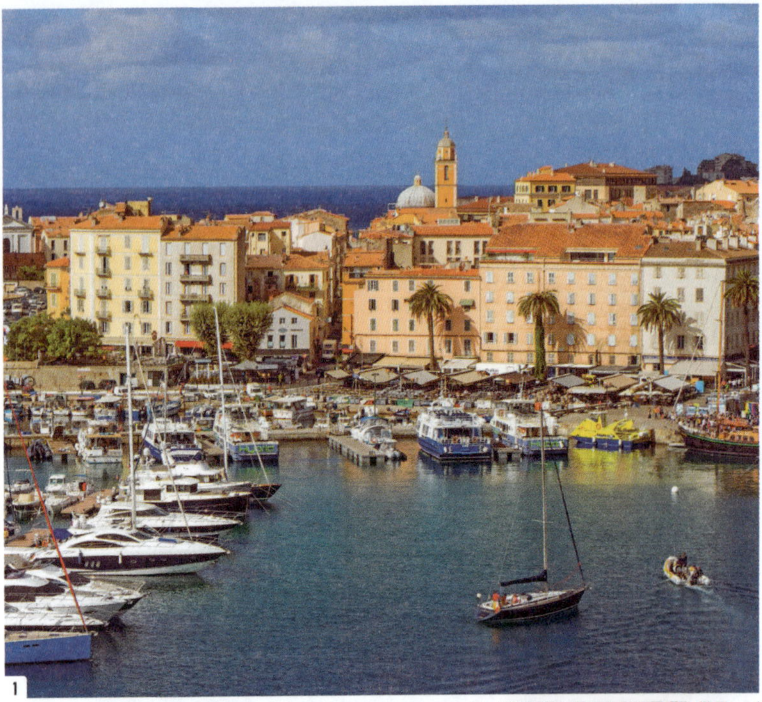

1

2

3

4

←

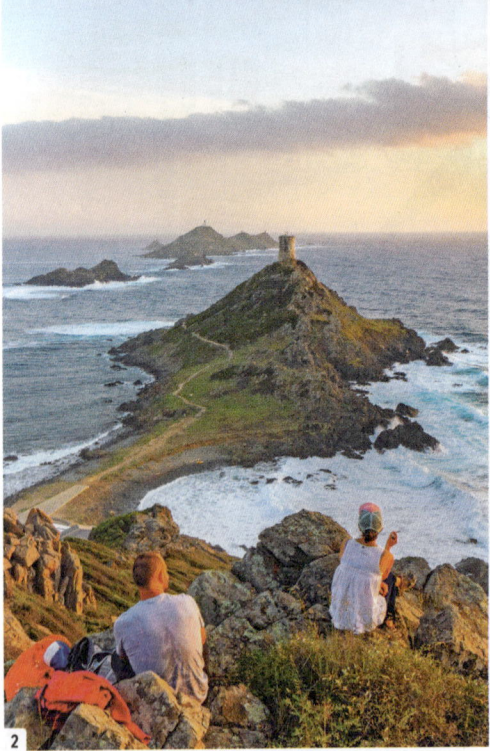

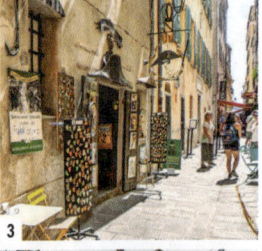

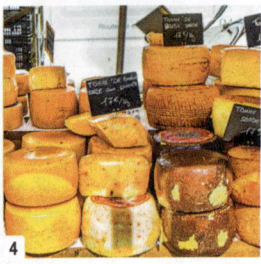

1 Yachts moored in Ajaccio's colourful marina.

2 The Genoese Torre di a Parata on the coast.

3 Ajaccio's old town.

4 Cheese at a market.

2 DAYS

in Ajaccio

Day 1

Morning Begin your exploration of Corsica's largest city with a coffee and *canistrelli* (a popular Corsican biscuit) overlooking Ajaccio's colourful marina – if you're an early riser, you can enjoy the traditional fish market which takes place here daily at 7am (*p111*). Take a stroll around the nearby Place Foch, a palm-lined square home to the Salon Napoléonien, which holds an exhibition devoted to the city's most illustrious son, Napoleon Bonaparte (*p48*). Cross the square for a visit to the Palais Fesch (*p114*), the city's fine arts museum. You can while away the rest of the morning marvelling at the world-class collection of Italian Renaissance art that includes works by Titian, Veronese and Botticelli.

Afternoon Try one of the bistros near Ajaccio's Citadelle for lunch (we recommend Le Roi de Rome, *12 Rue Roi de Rome*) before making a visit to Napoleon's birthplace, the Maison Bonaparte (*p110*), home to a museum featuring an array of exhibitions on the Bonaparte family and the history of the island. It's one of the highlights of the city's Old Town, an area defined by pastel-shaded, terracotta-tiled houses and narrow streets that have changed little in centuries. Next, take a walk along the ramparts of the Genoese Citadelle (*p108*) where there is a café and a viewing station, with art exhibitions housed in the former gunpowder room.

Evening Begin the evening with a glass of local wine at Bar à vin 1755 (*15 Rue Roi de Rome*) before taking a sunset stroll along the seafront promenade. Seafood is a speciality in Ajaccio, so enjoy some oysters and locally caught *rouget* (red mullet) or *loup-de-mer* (sea bass) at one of the many seafood restaurants on the Port Tino Rossi.

Day 2

Morning The island prides itself on its fresh delicacies, so why not start today by procuring some of the highlights? Stroll around the fresh-produce market on the Place Campinchi for a taste of local honeys, jams, *brocciu* cheese and charcuterie. Ajaccio's best shops line the city's main thoroughfare, Cours Napoléon, which is only a short stroll away. At lunch, you can enjoy some of that delicious market food *al fresco*.

Afternoon Head down to the port and catch a boat out to the îles Sanguinaires (*p118*) – numerous tour providers run daily trips. Located off the Pointe de la Parata at the southernmost tip of the Golfe d'Ajaccio, these tiny islands are crowned by lighthouses, watchtowers and designated seabird reserves – look out for the ruined Genoese tower, Torra di a Parata. Disembark on Mezzomare, the largest of the four islands, for a guided walk (most tours stop here).

Evening Back in Ajaccio, have a dip in the sea before returning to the Quartier des Étrangers for a taste of the local specialities, *civet de sanglier* (wild boar casserole) and *fiadone* (cheesecake).

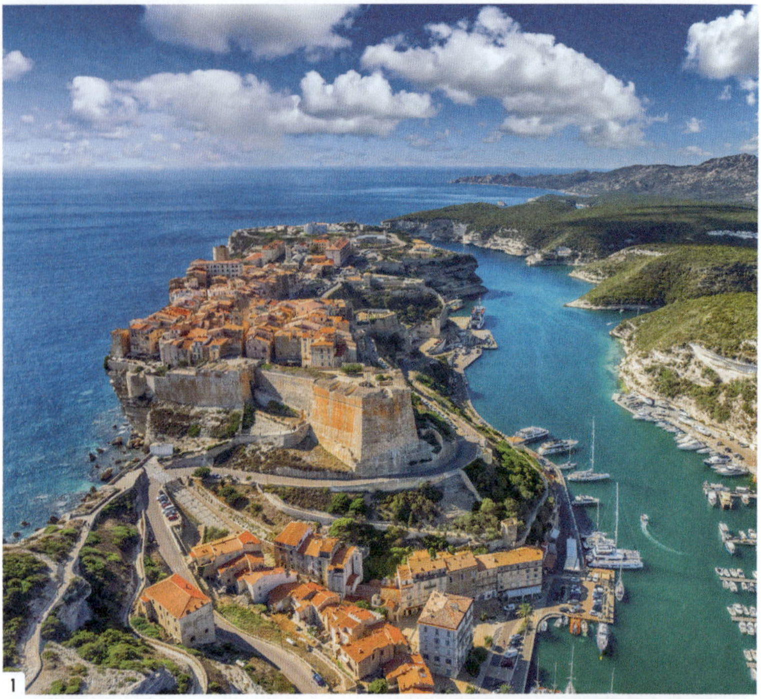

1

3

4

2

→

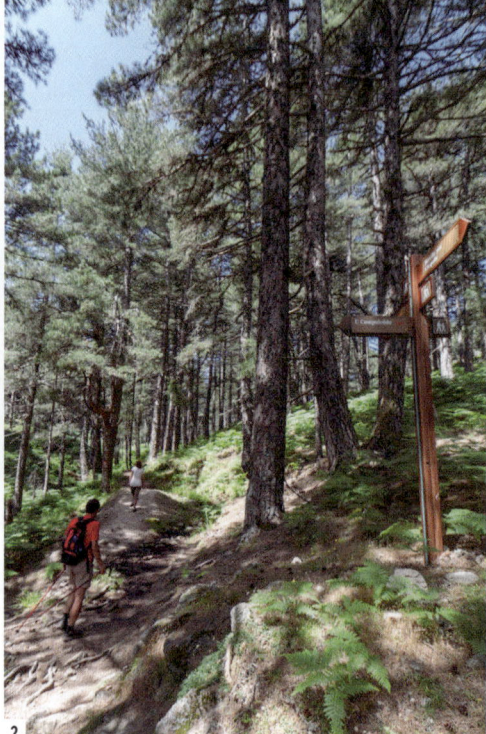

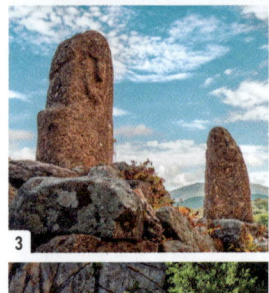

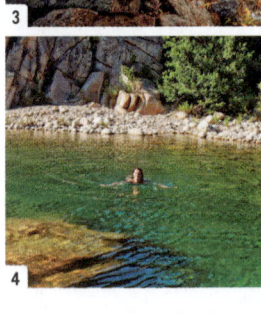

1 Bonifacio on its rugged promontory.

2 Hiking the Col de Bavella.

3 Prehistoric menhirs at Filitosa.

4 Swimming near Ajaccio.

5 DAYS
in southern Corsica

Day 1

Start your adventure through southern Corsica by taking the coast road south of Ajaccio. Keep your beach towels to hand: you'll want to swim in the azure waters of the Plage de Cupabia on your way. After a lunchtime stopover in characterful Olmeto, head inland to your main destination: Filitosa *(p147)*. The island's most important archaeological site is the best place to see incredible prehistoric menhirs. Continue to Campomoro (p146); one of Corsica's loveliest seaside villages, it's a cluster of houses overlooked by a watchtower.

Day 2

Today you'll enjoy a break from the coast by taking a short drive inland to Sartène *(p144)*, "the most Corsican of Corsican towns" according to French writer and archaeologist Prosper Mérimée. The town is best known for its Good Friday U Catenacciu ritual, a procession through the streets by hooded penitents (p51). This atmospheric fortress town is a great place to explore. The Musée Départemental de Préhistoire Corse et d'Archéologie is worth visiting to better understand the island's ancient history. Finish the day with an hour's drive south to Bonifacio *(p132)*, a beautiful town perched on a narrow chalk promontory facing the straits of Sardinia.

Day 3

Spend the morning in Bonifacio, walking through the medieval streets and vaulted passageways of the Haute Ville). Take the famous 187 steps down towards the sea – the staircase was supposedly carved into the rocks in a single night during the siege of Bonifacio in 1420 – and look out over the towering cliffs. In the afternoon, get on a boat from the marina to the Îles Lavezzi *(p137)* where you can explore the islands, enjoy the pretty beaches or go snorkelling. Take an evening boat back to Bonifacio and enjoy a gourmet meal at Del Ferro by the marina *(3 Quai Banda del Ferro)*.

Day 4

Today, the island's golden sands are beckoning. The beaches on the coast between Bonifacio and Porto-Vecchio are among the finest in Europe, with some beautiful spots like Palombaggia, Pinarellu and Santa Giulia *(p141)*. Spend the day under a parasol with a good book, before driving to the former Genoese stronghold of Porto-Vecchio *(p140)*, where you can treat yourself to fresh seafood at the restaurant Casadelmar *(casadelmar.fr)*.

Day 5

For your final day, head to the prehistoric site of Cucuruzzu *(p145)* to marvel at ruins from the 2nd millennium BCE. Your last destination is charming Zonza, a picture-postcard village with the Aiguilles de Bavella ranges *(p138)* towering in the distance. If you're feeling energized, finish by taking one of the trails around the Col de Bavella, before having a meal at Zonza's Eternisula *(leternisula.com)*.

7 DAYS
in northern Corsica

Day 1

Your tour begins in Bastia *(p76)*, the island's second-largest city and its economic capital. Begin with breakfast under the palms of the Place St-Nicolas *(p79)* – the square has countless eateries – before taking a stroll around the fresh-produce market in the Place du Marché *(p76)*. Marvel at the unique architecture of the old town hall before taking a leisurely stroll to the church of St-Jean-Baptiste *(p76)*. The Palais des Gouverneurs houses the Musée de Bastia *(p77)*, which charts the city's history as well as offering panoramic views over the harbour. When you're finished, a tricky choice awaits: where to eat? We recommend Le Mademoiselle *(lemademoisellebastia.fr)*.

Day 2

Today, you'll head north up the Cap Corse on the exhilarating Corniche Road, stopping at Macinaggio for a walk along the clifftop Sentier des Douaniers *(p91)*, once used by customs officers to control smuggling. Stop at one of the delightful fishing villages of Tollare or Barcaggio *(p90)* on the tip of the Cape for a swim and a bite to eat. Descend the Cape on the western flank to arrive in the town of St-Florent *(p94)* by evening.

Day 3

A short road trip awaits you today; it's all the better taken slowly, to soak up the charm of the north. First, drive inland through the hill villages of the misty Nebbio region, perhaps stopping to admire the views from the Col de Teghime mountain pass *(p95)*. Head on to the polychromatic Pisan chapel of San Michele de Murato *(p88)*, arguably the most beautiful Corsican church. Next, call in at one of the many vineyards surrounding Patrimonio *(p94)* for a taste of north Corsica's finest wines, before heading back to St-Florent. Finish at one of the fish restaurants by the marina.

1 The old town of Corte.
2 Playing *pétanque*.
3 Sunset over Calvi's port.
4 Patrimonio's vineyards.
5 Bastia's Palais des
Gouverneurs.

Day 4

After a leisurely morning by the marina, drive to the town of Calvi (*p84*), capital of the Balagne region, which sits upon a rocky promontory. You can explore the town's stunning Genoese Citadelle (*p86*), taking in the charming cathedral and the Palais des Gouverneurs Génois before strolling down the Quai Landry (*p84*). Or you can simply roll out a towel and plant yourself on the town's stunning beach to enjoy a perfectly restorative afternoon.

Day 5

The inland villages between île Rousse and Calvi survey the coast from a giant amphitheatre of crags and hilltops. On your journey through the villages, visit Pigna (*p96*), known for its music and craft workshops, and Sant'Antonio (*p99*), perched on an outcrop that has become a centre for lemons, almonds and wine. Take your time in the villages before spending the night in L'Île Rousse (*p96*).

Day 6

It's a spectacular drive down towards Porto (*p123*) on the rugged northeast coast, crossing red porphyry headlands that emerge from bays of cobalt blue. Walk one of the Calanque trails south of Porto before returning to the village. Still keen for adventure? Porto is a perfect base for all sorts of watersports. Then finish your day with a meal with a view at Le Panorama (*Route de la Marine 20150*).

Day 7

From Porto, the drive inland to Corte passes through the spectacular Gorges de Spelunca (*p124*). Stop for a swim in one of the many mountain streams and dry off in the Fôret d'Aïtone, perfect for a shady picnic. Continue on to Corte (*p154*) at the island's mountainous centre. Here, you can wander the cobbled streets before visiting the Musée de la Corse (*p158*). Toast the end of your trip with a fine meal at La Rivière des Vins (*5 Rpe Sainte-Croix*).

Happy Hiking

It might be justifiably famous for the epic GR20 *(p61)*, but the island is crisscrossed by numerous other hiking trails, each showcasing a different side to Corsica. There's the *Mare a Mare* path, which runs from Porto-Vecchio *(p140)* to Propriano through the rugged heart of the Alta-Rocca region. Or you could try something a little gentler with the Chemin des Crêtes, an easy ridge hike overlooking the beautiful Gulf of Ajaccio.

→

Hiking rugged mountains on the approach to Porto-Vecchio

CORSICA FOR
ADVENTURES ON LAND

Corsica's wild terrain offers some of Europe's most thrilling outdoor adventures, whether you hike the coast, ride the hills or soar over the island's peaks. So lace up those boots: there are trails waiting.

Take to the Skies

To truly experience the unique landscape of Corsica, it helps to admire it from above. Book a paragliding or parachuting session with Altore *(altore.com/parapente)*, which runs tandem flights; we recommend starting in St-Florent *(p94)*.

←

Coming into land over beautiful St-Florent

Chasing Rivers

A varied network of rivers cuts right across the island, cleaving deep gorges and tumbling into ice cold lakes. And the best thing? With little industrial activity, these are some of the cleanest waterways in Europe. For a unique adventure, you can combine a river walk with a spot of Corsica's favourite hobby: angling. The Cavu river *(p141)* offers fishing in crystal-clear waters – anglers can catch species such as barracuda, dorado and various types of snapper. Head to the small village of Tolla, which boasts an artificial lake known for its trout fishing. Corsica is also home to no less than 45 lakes at high altitude, each stocked with freshwater salmon and fario trout that have been swimming these waters for over 15,000 years. Summer is the most popular time for angling, but in winter you can fish for the large denti at sites across southern Corsica.

← Angling at a lake in southern Corsica

Travel on Two Wheels

You've heard of the GR20, but what about the cyclist's equivalent, the GT20? The "Great Crossing" spans 550 km (340 miles) of winding roads, heading from Capi to Bonifacio. A word of warning, though: these hills require some seriously strong quads (or an electric bike). For those who prefer to veer off the paved road, the Balagne region *(p96)* is ideal for mountain bikers. The La Serra loop starts in the hills above Calvi *(p84)* and offers some epic descents and technical climbs.

> 💬 INSIDER TIP
> **Biking Routes**
>
> The Balagne website *(en.balagne-corsica. com)* has a long list of mountain bike circuits. It's best to stick to these, as cycling off marked trails is not permitted.

Mountain biking on a road near the Col de Bavella ↑

Gourmet Meals

Corsican chefs take humble French dishes and turn them into elevated wonders - no wonder there are five Michelin star restaurants across the island. Perhaps the most celebrated is Porto-Vecchio's Casadelmar *(Casa delmar.fr)*, with a menu centred around seafood (try the cannelloni with crab). At Calvi's fine La Signoria *(hotel-la-signoria. com)*, you can enjoy a carefully curated journey through Corsica's culinary history, or at Bonifacio's Kissing Pigs you can eat cuts of *nustrale* (Corsican pork).

←

Small plates on display at La Signoria

CORSICA FOR
FOOD LOVERS

By combining flavours from two of the world's favourite national cuisines – French and Italian – and drawing on abundant local produce, Corsican chefs whip up all manner of delights. From cured meats and goat's cheeses to fresh chestnuts, food is sure to be a favourite part of your island adventure.

Food Fairs

Islanders celebrate their culinary heritage at a variety of food festivals held across Corsica throughout the year. The A Fiera di U Casgiu *(fromages-corse.org)* is an annual contest for the best local cheese – it's a great place to sample the native Corsican goat's cheese, *brocciu*. A Fiera di l'Amandului, held in August in the tiny village of Aregno *(p98)*, is a celebration of the culinary produce of the Balagne region, with a particular focus on local almonds.

→

A cheese stall at a food fair in Ajaccio

Seafood on the Beach

When dining in Corsica, where you eat is just as important as what you're eating. Take, for example, seafood: it's best enjoyed straight from the source, so seek out a seafood shack right by a beach. Bonifacio's La Cabane du Pêcheur (restaurant poissons bonifacio.fr) offers the finest catches from the nearby bay. Another great beachside shack is attached to Villa Mandarine in Calvi (calvi-location-villa.com). Local boats catch fresh lobster daily, which can be taken away to the beach in compostable dishes.

↑ Enjoying a fresh picnic on the beach

Divine Delicacies

Corsica has an abundance of home-grown delights. Look out for the humble chestnut, which has been a mainstay here since the Genoese planted trees across the interior. Another local treat is *sanglier*, or wild boar. It's served best in Corisca's signature stew, the deliciously hearty *civet de sanglier*.

A fresh batch of chestnuts, harvested in autumn

Did You Know?

Local *brocciu* cheese is the main ingredient in fiadone, a decadent Corsican cheesecake.

Family Beaches

Buckets and spades at the ready! Lounging on Corsica's golden sands or dipping in shallow waters is a winner for kids and adults alike. Calvi's beach *(p84)* has everything you need for an ideal day at the seaside: a long bay lapped by warm, shallow waters, with a host of restaurants just a short walk away. The main town beach in St-Florent *(p94)* can be reached by a short walk from the port. Here, you'll find an array of water sports, with sailing, canoeing and diving lessons designed for younger learners. For a spot of quiet snorkelling, visit Campomoro *(p146)* on the west coast.

CORSICA FOR
FAMILIES

Corsica's dramatic mountains, hidden beaches and fabled forests are sure to set young imaginations racing. And the best thing? Most of the island's resorts and activities are designed with kids in mind, meaning Corsica is sure to be a new family favourite.

Gentle Hiking

It might be renowned for its arduous hikes, but Corsica has plenty of gentler walks, too. The dense canopy of the Forêt d'Aïtone *(p125)* hides a number of enchanting footpaths, with routes leading past trickling waterfalls. Older children will love exploring the jagged pinnacles of the Aiguilles de Bavella *(p138)*.

←

Hiking through the Aiguilles de Bavella

💬 INSIDER TIP
The GR20

Keen to give the kids a taste of the GR20? The Bocca di Guagnerola section, starting at Col de Vergio, is a relatively easy stretch with epic views of the Capu Tafunatu mountain.

Bathing at one of the quiet beaches on Corsica's west coast

TOP 3 FAMILY DAY TRIPS

Turtle Sanctuary
At the A Cupulatta turtle and tortoise sanctuary (p109) near Ajaccio you can see giant Galapagos and Seychelles tortoises.

Asco Adventure
This adventure course (interracorsa.com) in the Vallée de l'Asco has a host of suspended bridges, rope swings and climbing frames.

Kayaking
The calm waters of Lake Tolla (p120) are the perfect place for a spot of family paddling.

Days Out

You'd need a good few months in Corsica to exhaust the seemingly limitless list of family day trips. Chartered boat trips from Porto to the Scandola peninsula (boattrip scandola.com) offer kids the chance to dive in and have a paddle. Or why not whisk them back in time at the mysterious Neolithic site of Filitosa (p147)? There's every chance they'll have their own theories about the strange menhirs dotting the plains.

Enjoying Corsica's warm coastal waters on a family holiday

Adrenaline-fueled Adventures

Bored of making sandcastles? Kids demanding something a little more exciting? The Parc Aventure de Solenzara (corse-canyoning-parc.com) on the east coast offers a range of thrilling activities: canyoning, paintballing, kayaking and archery. Or there's Parc Aventure de Porto-Vecchio (parc-aventure-porto-vecchio.fr), an adventure park set in the heart of a splendid eucalyptus forest.

Canyoning with the family near Solenzara

Ugo Casalonga crafting
instruments at his
workshop in Pigna ↑

CORSICA FOR
ARTS AND
CRAFTS

Keen to take home a small piece of the island? In workshops across Corsica, talented ceramicists, instrument-makers, knife-makers and jewellers create bespoke crafts using age-old methods and local materials.

Jewels of the Sea

Corsica's beaches aren't just great for sunbathing – jewellers also comb the sands to find shells and coral to work into beautiful designs. In Bonifacio, La Boutique du Corailleur *(corail-rouge.com)* crafts fine pieces from rare red coral. Many jewellers also sell necklaces decorated with the operculum shell. Known as the "Eye of Saint Lucia", the circular, red-tinted shell is a symbol of the island.

→

Red coral jewellery
on display in a
jeweller's window

Strings Attached

Corsica has a rich musical tradition, and the island is home to an array of unique stringed instruments, each lovingly made by skilled craftspeople. For decades, artisan Ugo Casalonga has been crafting the Corsican *cetera* (similar to a mandolin) and other instruments from his small workshop in the village of Pigna *(p96)*. His shop *(casa-liutaiu.com)* is a living repository of musical history, with instruments dating back to the early Renaissance. Keen to hear these instruments played? The Patrimonio guitar festival *(festival-guitare-patrimonio.com)*, held in June, is a celebration of the island's musical heritage.

Knife-Makers

Perhaps the most distinctively Corsican craft of all is the practice of knife-making. The tradition began when the ancient Romans developed the first folding knife on the island, before shepherds' knives were given to those working the land as part of an initiation rite. Today, you can pick up exquisite bespoke blades at makers like Ceccaldi in Porticcio *(couteaux-ceccaldi.com/en)*.

← A variety of Corsican knives on display, including the island's famous Vendetta design

ARTISANS' ROAD

There are few better ways of appreciating Corsica's artisans than by driving the Strada di l'Artigiani, the Artisans' Road *(p100)*. This serpentine drive between the villages of La Balagne was conceived in 1993 to celebrate the region's artisanal heritage. At small villages along the route, you'll find local studios with craftspeople creating everything from ceramics, honey and wine, to leather goods, music boxes, wooden flutes and guitars.

Sublime Ceramics

The history of ceramics in Corsica pre-dates the Iron Age. In Balagna, you can visit the studio of ceramicist Jacques Quilichini *(20220 Pigna)*, or you can pick up some beautiful Corsican pottery at Nebbio Pottery *(Route d'Oletta, 20232)*.

↑ Quilichini's workshop in the village of Pigna

Fireworks over
the harbour during
Calvi on the Rocks ↑

CORSICA FOR
MUSIC AND
FESTIVALS

In Corsica, there's barely a week in the calendar without a festival or cultural gathering. From huge contemporary music events to celebrations of the season's bounty, these parties are the social heart of the island.

Rural Gatherings

The Corsican calendar is structured around a series of village events and gatherings. Many of these celebrate food and drink, including the small celebration of Corsican cheese, A Fiera di u Casgiu *(fromages-corse. org)* in Venaco. Other local festivals include one of France's favourite heritage car festivals, Tour de Corse Historique *(tourdecorse-historique.fr)*, which sees classic cars race through rural villages.

Racing classic cars
at the Tour de
Corse Historique ↑

The Big Hitters

Many of Corsica's smaller festivals may look back at the island's remarkable heritage, but the island plays host to some defiantly modern parties, too. In July, Calvi is home to Europe's largest open-air club, as thousands of global indie and electronic artists play at Calvi on the Rocks (*calviontherocks.com*). The entire town and its surrounding beaches welcome revellers who come to enjoy six days of cutting-edge music and culture. Meanwhile, in Patrimonio, Les Nuits de la Guitare has been hosting an international guitar festival in July for over 20 years. In addition to local musicians, the festival has seen some of the biggest names in rock music, including Patti Smith, Jeff Beck and Led Zeppelin's Robert Plant.

← A stage on the beach at Calvi on the Rocks

THE POLYPHONIC REVIVAL

Visit any music festival in Corsica and you'll likely hear the stirring hymn-like strains of a polyphonic chorus. Rooted in religious or folk practices, polyphonic music, or *pulifunie*, has been a central part of Corsican culture and identity since the 15th century. It involves *a cappella* singing, with between four and nine voices relaying tales of faith, love or tragedy in perfect harmony. Since the 1970s, the genre has been revived as musicians have sought to safeguard Corsica's heritage, with groups like I Muvrini and A Filetta breathing new life into the genre.

HIDDEN GEM
Church Concerts

St-Dominique Church (*p134*) in Bonifacio is a perfect place to hear traditional music. Visit *bonifacio.co.uk* for listings and a chance to book tickets.

→ Performers at Ajaccio's Jazz In Aiacciu festival

Traditional Sounds

Corsicans have long documented the history of their island through song, and this musical heritage is kept gloriously alive at hundreds of small music festivals. You can hear the island's famous polyphonic singing at the Polyphonic Song Festival (*rencontres polyphoniques.com*), which takes place in Calvi in September. The village of Pigna, meanwhile, hosts the Festivoce (*voce.corsica*), a celebration of folk music, while the island's long-standing love affair with jazz is on full display at Ajaccio's Jazz In Aiacciu (*jazzinaiacciu.com*).

Mysterious Menhirs

Entirely unique to Corsica's ancient culture, menhirs are stone monoliths carved from granite, many of which have anthropomorphic faces and features. Most were built in around 1500 BCE, but little is known of their purpose; some experts see the stones as phallic symbols for use in fertility rites, while others see them as a means of warding off evil. The best places to see these ancient stones are at Filitosa *(p147)* or dotted across the wild planes of Cauria *(p148)*.

Mysterious prehistoric menhirs at the ancient site of Cauria ↑

CORSICA FOR
ANCIENT SITES

Corsica's earliest societies are shrouded in mystery, with evidence of civilizations dating back over 8,000 years. As such, the island is home to some of the most celebrated ancient sites in Europe, and archaeologists are still unearthing wonders, adding ever older chapters to Corsica's tale.

BRONZE AGE *TORRI*

During the Bronze Age, Corsica was home to the mysterious Torrean civilization, which was characterized by its distinctive *torri*, or towers. These tall stone structures, the remnants of which can still be seen at Araggio and Casteddu du Tappa, were designed to watch the coast and the surrounding hills. In peacetime, they were likely used as storehouses for the village's provisions and possessions. *Torri* resemble the *nuraghe* built in Sardinia.

Military Structures

Centuries of naval invasion have meant Corsica has always defended its coastal borders. The impressive Neolithic site of Casteddu du Tappa consists of a number of fortified dwellings. Not far away is the ruined Bronze Age fortress of Araggio *(p141)* with walls so thick as to be almost impregnable. A hike to the fortress makes for an eerie journey back in time.

→ Ruins at the historic fortress of Araggio

↑ Ancient ruins on display at the Roman site of Aleria

The Roman Empire

In 260 BCE, at the end of the First Punic War, Corsica became a Roman province along with neighbouring Sardinia. The most impressive reminders of the era can be found in the first Roman settlement of Aléria *(p163)* – here you'll see remnants of the Roman town, including the villa and necropolis. The ancient town of Corte *(p154)*, meanwhile, was fortified by the Romans. Artifacts from this occupation have been discovered in the mountains and are displayed at Corte's excellent Musée de la Corse *(p158)*.

Did You Know?

Corsica became a destination of exile for political opponents of ancient Rome's political rulers.

Prehistoric Settlements

Corsica offers a thrilling insight into the domestic lives of the ancients. Head to the famous site of Filitosa *(p147)* for an overview of 8,000 years of history, spanning from the Neolithic era to the Romans. Tools, weapons and other finds are found at the site museum. Or there's Castello di Cucuruzzu *(p145)*, near Levie, a fortress village dating back to the Bronze Age.

→ Filitosa, Corsica's most famous ancient site

Vineyard Tours

Corsica's vineyards occupy some of the most beautiful terrain on the island. Start your tour in the southern Sartène wine region with a visit to Domaine Saparale (*lesvinsdesaparale.com*). The vineyard makes a wonderfully fresh white from Vermentino grapes, which have been cultivated in Corsica since the 14th century. In the north, try Clos Culombu (*closculombu.fr*), an organic vineyard near Calvi. The vineyard's winemakers shed light on the nuances of the terroir as you sample their fine cuvées.

→

Neatly ordered vineyards overlooking the Mediterranean

CORSICA
BY THE GLASS

The island's joint history of Italian and French rule, coupled with its varied soil and sunny climate, make it a winemaking destination *par excellence*. Some of Europe's most prized vineyards are dotted across the mountainous terrain, with local grape varieties winning the wine world's best awards.

Grape Festivals

It would be a gargantuan undertaking to visit all of Corsica's vineyards. Thankfully, the island's illustrious wine festivals bring the best grapes to you. Fiera di u Vinu (*fieradiuvinu. corsica*), formerly held in the village of Luri, now tours the island's grape-growing heartlands, with a new location every May. The In Aleria festival (*inaleria.com*), held in September, is a bacchanalian celebration of Corsica's best food and wine.

A selection of Corsica's finest local wines on offer at a festival stall

Did You Know?

Corsica has been pouring wine since Phoenician settlers planted vines in the 6th century BCE.

TOP 3 — CORSICA'S BEST GRAPES

Vermentino
One of the most important white grapes in Corsica's long winemaking history, Vermentino is grown in chalk and limestone soils all over the island.

Sciacarello
This red grape is used in some of Corsica's finest red wines. Sciacarello wines are lightly coloured with red fruit characters and herby, peppery notes.

Nielluccio
Commonly used to make rosé but also used in the reds from Corsica's Patrimonio region, Nielluccio produces fruity, full-bodied wines that improve with age.

← Red grapes ready for harvesting in Corsica

Hip Bars

To soak up Corsica's chic side, head to one of the island's many wine bars, where you can enjoy a perfect glass alongside local cheese or charcuterie. Tucked beneath a stone vault dating back to the 13th century, Le Caravelle *(hotelcaravelle.fr)* in Bonifacio offers a wide selection of wines and spirits as well as a range of small plates. In Ajaccio, La Cave du Cardinal *(lacavedu cardinal.corsica)* is a bar and bottle shop as famed for the expertise of its staff as it is for its vast cellar. For something more raucous, Le Patio *(patio portovecchio. com)* in Porto-Vecchio is one of the island's hotspots, with live DJs.

↑ Drinking in one of Calvi's many outdoor bars

Plain Sailing

Corsica's coast has long lured experienced seafarers and novice sailors alike. There are few better experiences at sea than drifting slowly into Bonifacio *(p132)*, the town rising above you on its rugged coastal shelf. Or you can sail from Macinaggio around the Cap Corse *(p90)*, cruising past Genoese towers and secluded bays. Either sail in your own boat or take a guided tour with Les Voiles de Bonifacio *(voilesdebonifacio.com)*.

→

Sailboats moored in the azure waters near Bonifacio

CORSICA FOR
ADVENTURES ON WATER

The island is at its wildest and most beautiful where the land meets the sea. With over 1,000 km (600 miles) of sublime coastline dotted with cliffs, coves and golden beaches, a world of Mediterranean adventures awaits.

Canoes and Kayaks

Gently paddling around the island's wild border is always memorable. One of the best spots is the UNESCO-recognized Reserve Naturelle de Scandola *(p116)*, where red and orange-hued rocks rise from the Gulf of Girolata, or you can push off from Bastia *(p76)* as old church bells chime from the harbour.

↑ Gentle kayaking through sea caves near Bastia

Wild Swimming

Where to start with Corsica's glimmering abundance of golden beaches? Almost every stretch of sand is divine, but there are certain areas that are more suitable for a casual swim. When choosing your beach, note that the island's Haute-Corse region to the north is home to wilder beaches with fewer amenities compared to the family-friendly spots in the south. Just south of Porto-Vecchio, Palombaggia *(p141)* is known for its clear blue waters and white sands, with welcome shade provided by a smattering of pine trees. For a more secluded experience, try the Ghignu beach in the wild Désert des Agriates region *(p96)* – you'll need to arrive by boat or 4WD. But the island isn't only great for sea swimming – head inland to find a mosaic of pools, rivers and lakes. The Gorges du Tavignano *(p165)* is home to a massive pool fed by a series of trickling waterfalls, while the Solenzara valley *(p142)* offers dreamy river bathing.

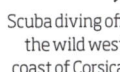

Snorkelling in a quiet lagoon near the beach at Palombaggia

Deep Diving

In Corsica, what you see above the water is only a small part of the story; beneath the waves, you'll find a teeming world of marine life. Experienced divers (level 2) can take in the eerie wreck of a B-17 bomber near Calvi, that has been submerged since 1944 and is now home to scorpionfish and eels. In the Gulf of Propriano are rocks shaped like needles, reaching deep under the water *(divingcalvi.fr)*.

→

Scuba diving off the wild west coast of Corsica

Did You Know?

The Bouches de Bonifacio Nature Reserve is the largest marine reserve in France.

Forest Forays

Corsica might be more readily associated with beaches and mountains, but the island is France's most forested region. Beneath the mist-shrouded canopy of the Aïtone forest (p125) you'll find wild trails leading past native Corsican pines, plunging waterfalls and deep pools.

↑ Hiking a trail through the pines in the dense Aïtone forest

 GREAT VIEW
Wild Waterfalls

A 10-minute walk from the village of Evisa (p124), you'll find the Aïtone waterfall trail. Each cascade falls into a natural pool framing the dense canopy.

CORSICA FOR
NATURAL WONDERS

They don't call Corsica the *Île de Beauté* (Isle of Beauty) for nothing. This is a land of wild extremes: misty forests cloak the Mediterranean's highest mountains, which plummet to meet golden beaches. Prepare to dive in.

Mighty Mountains

Corsica's towering ranges run in dramatic flurries down the island's spine, with 120 peaks exceeding 2,000 m (6,500 ft). But perhaps more impressive than their dizzying height is the mountains' unique shape. Northwest of Porto-Vecchio, the Aiguilles de Bavella (p138) is a jagged cluster of granite needles rising sharply from the watershed, and one of the island's most dramatic roads leads through the Bavella massif. Hardy climbers, meanwhile, make for Monte Cinto (p166), the tallest peak, which looms above the wild Asco Valley.

→

Sunrise over the jagged needles of the Bavella massif

Calanques and Gorges

The island's wild west is a land defined by elemental forces. Among the most impressive natural features are the 250-million-year-old Calanques de Piana *(p116)*, granite towers sculpted into abstract cavities by wind and rain. The region is also home to dramatic gorges carved out by torrents crashing from the mountains. Visit the Gorges de Spelunca *(p124)* to find a land of plunging canyons and sweeping seaward vistas.

→

The strange red-tinted granite rocks of the Calanques de Piana

A Storied Coast

Corsica is defined by its glorious coastline, with some of Europe's finest sands in areas like Piana *(p122)*. Above the beaches, famously craggy cliffs offer a stirring reminder of the ocean's force. Visit Capo Pertusato *(p136)*, Corsica's southernmost point, to see colossal chalk caves.

←

Perfect golden beach overlooking the Golfe de Porto near Piana

---

TOP 3 PEAKS AND CLIFFS

Bonifacio cliffs
The cliffs around Bonifacio *(p132)* are best admired from the sea, all the better to see the stark furrows and sharp belvederes.

Monte d'Oro
A strenuous 7-hour hike leads to the summit of this peak in the startling Cascade des Anglais range *(p162)*.

Monte Rotondo
This mountain peak overlooks a wild valley, home to the Gorges de Restonica *(p160)*.

PARC NATUREL RÉGIONAL DE CORSE

The Corsican Regional Natural Park covers around two-thirds of the island's territory and comprises many of Corsica's most beautiful features, from mountains to historic villages. The park was established to conserve the island's unique biodiversity, but its mission also extends to protecting local ways of life that rely on Corsica's bountiful ecosystem. From its headquarters in Corte *(34 Cours Paoli)*, and through its website *(pnr.corsica)* and education centres, the park endeavours to maintain Corsica's abundant wildnerness, while inspiring locals and visitors alike.

HISTORY OF THE PARK

In 1970, a union of conservationists, politicians, farmers and locals came together to discuss plans for the park. Their initial charter was grand in its ambition, with a proposal to conserve Corsica's natural sites and to renovate the rural economy by promoting sustainable live-stock farming. The initiatives also included devising the first legs of the GR20 hiking route and the refuges used by hikers *(p61)*. Within two years, the bill to establish the park had been ratified. Since then, the park's governors have had a great many successes, from curating Europe's toughest

↑ Hiking near Monte Cinto on a route maintained by the park

hiking route to reintroducing wild deer to the island in 1985. The park now governs many of Corsica's beloved landscapes, including the peaks of Monte Cinto, Rotondo and the Aiguilles de Bavella, the forests of Aïtone and Vizzavona and the rugged gorges of Spelunca and l'Asco. The park is traversed by all of the island's main hiking paths, including the GR20.

THE PARK TODAY

Visitors to Corsica can make the most of the park in a number of ways. The park runs Casa di a Natura in Vizzavona *(p161),* a pioneering centre dedicated to ecological education, and curates a busy schedule of events at various sites across the island, including acclaimed summits on threatened species like the bearded vulture. The park also maintains a helpful website, with information on hikes and wildlife.

RESPECTING THE LANDSCAPES

Many of the parks most beautiful and popular sites are now dealing with the problem of overtourism. To offset the effects of high visitor numbers, a series of strategies have been developed. Wild camping is banned across the island to ensure the hinterland remains pristine, but there is an abundance of designated campsites for those looking to explore the outdoors. Mountain biking off trails is strictly prohibited and hiking routes are well waymarked to preserve delicate habitats.

TOP 4 PROTECTED SPECIES IN THE PARK

Corsican deer
This deer has thrived since being reintroduced in the 1980s.

Bearded vulture
The park guards this bird of prey to protect a dwindling population.

Mouflon
This distinctive wild sheep came to Corsica 7,000 years ago with the Neolithic people.

Hermann's tortoise
This rare and now threatened tortoise is protected by dedicated reserves run by the park across the island.

↑ European mouflon, a rare ancestor of domestic sheep

← A mountainous stretch of the GR20 hiking route

Genoese Relics

The Genoese conquered Corsica following the defeat of the Pisans in 1284. Over their five centuries of rule, they built many of the island's most impressive forts, squares and towns, but it's their coastal watchtowers that are most striking. These 67 towers were built in the 15th and 16th centuries to monitor naval invasions, with the best examples at Girolata *(p124)* and Campomoro *(p146)*. For further evidence of the Genoese style, look out for striking footbridges like the one at Altiani *(p123)*.

→

Genoese watchtower overlooking the Gulf of Porto

CORSICA FOR
HISTORY BUFFS

A Mediterranean melting pot, Corsica has seen waves of settlers anchor on its rugged shores, leaving behind a fascinating collage of monuments and relics. The island was equally influenced by French and Italian rule, creating a unique fusion of European styles and designs.

Grand Churches

Rulers have often saved their grandest architectural styles for religious buildings, and this is certainly true in Corsica. To see the beautiful excesses of the Italian Baroque, visit La Porta's Saint-Jean-Baptiste *(p164)*, with its soaring bell tower, constructed in 1648. The largest church in Corsica is Bastia's Saint-Jean-Baptiste *(p76)*, while the most striking is the San Michele de Murato *(p88)*, a checkerboard church built by the Pisans in the 12th century.

Saint-Jean-Baptiste church overlooking Bastia's port

Imposing Citadelles

Centuries of conquest have left a legacy of fortified structures across Corsica. Foremost among these are the Citadelles of Corte *(p154)*, Calvi *(p84)* and Bastia *(p76)*. The former, sat on its rocky spur, predates the arrival of the Genoese, though it was heavily fortified with huge bastions in the 13th century. Bastia's Citadelle, meanwhile, was constructed in the 16th century with thick ramparts.

→

The Citadelle of Corte commanding a view across the mountains

Napoleonic Ajaccio

Corsica's favourite son is everywhere in the city of his birth, Ajaccio. The Maison Bonaparte *(p110)*, the ruler's ancestral home and now a museum, is the best place to start, but to see the full extent of Napoleon's formidable legacy, take a stroll down Cours Napoléon *(p112)*, past Café Napoléon towards the huge statue of ... you get the idea.

←

A cabinet of Napoleon ceramics at Maison Bonaparte

NAPOLEON IN CORSICA

In Corsica's capital, Ajaccio, the influence of Napoleon Bonaparte looms large. Born in the city in 1769, he only lived on the island until he was 10 years old, but his life remains irrevocably bound up with Corsica's fortunes. Having left for the mainland, Napoleon rose to prominence during the early days of the French Revolution and would go on to lead military campaigns across Europe in what became known as the Napoleonic Wars (1796–1815). He led the French Republic as First Consul before becoming Emperor from 1804 to 1815. But how did one of France's most famous leaders rise from his Corsican origins, and why is he seen by many on the island as a controversial figure?

BIRTH AND EARLY YEARS

Long before Napoleon was born, the Bonaparte family was prominent in Corsican high society, with their ties to the island stretching back over 200 years. As power on the island shifted from the Genoese to the French in the decades before Napoleon's birth, the Bonaparte family were quick to ally with French powers on the mainland, ensuring their ongoing wealth and influence in Corsica.

Napoleon was born on 15 August 1769 in Ajaccio, the second of eight children. His early years were lived in the shadow of Corsica's complex political landscape, with the French seeking to maintain power on the island in the face of rising objections from Corsican nationalists. From the outset, Napoleon's identity was divided between his family's French sympathies and his Corsican roots, with the young Napoleon idolizing Corsican nationalist leader Pascal Paoli *(p58)*.

Napoleon was sent to mainland France to receive a formal education at a military academy, and in 1785, he graduated from

Napoleon and his troops fighting for French control of Corsica

TOP 3

NAPOLEONIC SIGHTS IN CORSICA

Maison Bonaparte
The family home of Napoleon *(p110)* has been converted into a museum with original items providing insight into his early years.

Place d'Austerlitz
A huge statue of Napoleon dressed in the uniform of the Colonel of the Garde dominates Place d'Austerlitz *(p112)*, with a smaller statue in Place Foch *(p111)*.

Palais Fesch
This museum *(p114)* was established by Napoleon's uncle, Cardinal Fesch, and includes portraits and other items related to the Bonaparte family.

the École Militaire in Paris. The stage was set for his rapid political ascent.

REVOLUTIONARY PERIOD

When the French Revolution erupted in 1789, the political and social landscape of France was altered forever. Napoleon

Napoleon's statue in Place Foch, Ajaccio

embraced the revolutionary ideals of liberty, equality and fraternity, and in 1793, he played a key role in the Siege of Toulon, which led to a significant victory against royalist forces and his promotion to general at just 24 years old.

It wasn't long before Napoleon was led back to Corsica. Following Pascal Paoli's attempt to take control of the island with the help of the English in 1794, Napoleon intervened, restoring power to France. It was a definitive moment in his relationship with Corsica and with Paoli, his boyhood hero: no longer was Napoleon sympathetic to the appeals of Corsican nationalists. Paoli would die in London in 1807, while Napoleon would go on to become emperor of the French.

LEGACY IN CORSICA

He might be Corsica's most famous son, but Napoleon is a controversial figure on the island. During his time in power, he invested heavily in Corsica's infrastructure, but nationalists have long denounced him as a traitor. In any case, there's no getting away from his towering influence.

A YEAR IN
CORSICA

JANUARY

△ **St Anthony the Great Procession** (*first Sunday after 17 Jan*). Locals in Aregno ask the priest to bless oranges to protect their property from fire and keep them in good health.

Restonica Trail Blanc (*end Jan*). A series of running events take place around Niolu.

FEBRUARY

Italian Film Festival (*mid-Feb*). Bastia celebrates Italian cinema, past and present, with a fortnight of screenings, documentaries and prizes.

△ **A Tumbera food festival** (*first weekend of Feb*). A celebration of pork, ham, *figatelli*, sausages and other meat-based cuisine takes place in the southern village of Renno.

MAY

A Fiera di u Casgiu (*early May*). The annual fair in Venaco is dedicated to cheese and the many artisanal crafts made in Corsica.

△ **Festimare** (*early May*). L'île Rousse hosts an ocean-focussed festival for young people with workshops and talks on the science of the seas.

JUNE

△ **Corsica Raid** (*start of Jun*). Five days of trail running, sea swimming, mountain biking and other epic outdoor activities that attract competitors from all over the world.

Saint-Erasme (*early Jun*). The patron saint of fishers is celebrated in Ajaccio's Port Tino Rossi.

SEPTEMBER

△ **Les Rencontres de Chants Polyphoniques** (*mid-Sep*). Calvi hosts the five day festival of Corsica's polyphonic singing in the Cathédrale St Jean-Baptiste and Saint-Antoine Oratoire.

Pascal Paoli Pétanque Challenge (*end of Sep*). Île Rousse hosts the international *boules* competition for teams of two and three.

OCTOBER

△ **Tour du Corse Historique** (*start of Oct*). Classic cars from 1947 to the late 1990s compete in five days of rally-racing along the winding roads of Corsica.

Arte Mare (*mid-Oct*). The Mediterranean Cultures film festival has been based in Bastia since 1982, hosting a large selection of films and exhibitions dedicated to cinema.

MARCH

A Festa di l'oliu novu (*mid-Mar*). A two-day olive festival in Sainte Lucie de Tallano.

Holy Week processions (*end Mar-early Apr*). Religious processions take place all over Corsica with the most famous, the Procession de la Cerca, passing through the Brando region.

△ **U Catenacciu** (*Good Friday*). Sartène's representation of Christ's journey to Calvary sees a local resident wearing a hood and chains.

APRIL

△ **Les Agrumes en Fête** (*early Apr*). A festival celebrating locally grown citrus fruit in Bastelicaccia.

Les Rencontres de la Bande-Dessinée (*early Apr*). Also known as BD à Bastia, this festival takes place over four days and is a celebration of everything to do with comics and illustrations.

JULY

△ **Calvi on the Rocks** (*early Jul*). A five-day indie and electronic music festival in and around the Citadel in Calvi.

Les Nuits de la Guitare (*end of Jul*). A guitar festival in Patrimonio, running for over 30 years.

AUGUST

Festival du Film de Lama (*end Jul/start Aug*). Lama's film festival has been going since 1994 and attracts over 10,000 people to open-air screenings.

Fêtes Napoleoniennes (*13-15 Aug*). Three days of conferences, dancing and music devoted to Napoleon in Ajaccio, the city of his birth

DECEMBER

Foire de la Châtaigne (*first weekend of Dec*). Bocognano has been hosting its Foire de la Châtaigne (chestnut festival) for over 40 years, gathering together over 150 local producers. Chestnuts are among the island's most popular local produce.

Animation de Noël (*Dec*). Ajaccio pulls out all the stops at its Christmas fair with games, rides, chalets and a temporary ice rink.

NOVEMBER

△ **Festival d'Autunnu di A Ruralità** (*early Nov*). The Corsican rural autumn festival is a celebration of vineyards and other local produce.

San Martinu Festival (*mid-Nov*). This small festival honours the patron saint of winemakers and welcomes the first wines of the season.

A BRIEF HISTORY

Phoenicians, Romans, Genoese, French: a plethora of rulers have controlled Corsica over its history, contributing to the island's unique cultural identity. But no occupying power ever dampened Corsicans' powerful sense of independence and autonomy, a pride that remains alive to this day.

An Ancient Island

The prehistoric skeleton now known as the "Lady of Bonifacio" is one of the earliest pieces of human evidence in Corsica, dating from 7500 BCE. Around this time, Neolithic settlers left their mark in the form of unique stone monoliths. These early settlers dwelt in peace until the 5th century BCE, when Phoenician arrivals founded the city of Aléria. It wasn't long before the Romans conquered the island around 260 BCE.

1 Map of Corsica (c 1771).

2 Roman Emperor Hadrian hunting wild boar in Corsica.

3 Woodcut of Genoa in the Middle Ages (c 1870).

4 The naval battle of Meloria between Genoa and Pisa.

Timeline of events

8000 BCE
The first humans settle in Corsica.

7500 BCE
The Lady of Bonifacio dies near the present-day town.

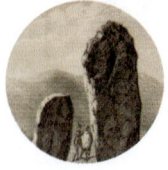

3500 BCE
Corsican megalithic monuments known as menhirs are built.

750-500 BCE
The city of Alalia is founded by Greek settlers.

Fall of the Romans

After the decline of the Roman Empire, the island was subject to raids from the Vandals, Goths and Byzantines, among others, and Corsica's population comprised a disparate collection of clans. In 754, powerful feudal lords (many of them from nearby Tuscany and Liguria) intervened in this power struggle, carving up the island before passing control to the Pope and the Kingdom of Pisa.

Genoese Control

The Pisan era was marked by skirmishes with the Genoese. By 1187, Genoa took possession of Bonifacio and, in 1268, founded the city of Calvi. Following the Battle of Meloria in 1284, the Genoese took control of the whole island – they built vast citadelles, dotted the coast with towers, and ushered in a period of great wealth and thriving agriculture.

THE BATTLE OF MELORIA

In 1284, a Genoese fleet sailed into the waters opposite Porto Pisano. Startled by this move, the ruling Pisans attacked from the cliffs of Meloria. The battle was violent and the outcome uncertain, until the arrival of yet another group of Genoese galleys, which caught their enemies by surprise and ultimately handed control to Genoa.

260 BCE
The First Punic War turns the island into a Roman province.

1060
Skirmishes begin between Pisa and Genoa.

1284
The Battle of Meloria results in Genoese rule.

4th–3rd centuries BCE
The Etruscans arrive in Corsica.

754
After the fall of Rome, numerous civilizations vie for Corsica.

The End of the Genoese

The relative prosperity of the early Genoese era was marred first by the Black Death in the 14th century – over two-thirds of the island's population lost their lives – and then by French invasion just a century later. French forces landed on Corsica in an attempt to gain a firm foothold in the Mediterranean, and Genoese strongholds fell one after the other until a peace treaty obliged the French to withdraw. Genoese power was reinstated, but ordinary Corsicans were increasingly disenfranchised with their rulers. After new taxes were imposed in the 18th century, a series of revolts were to change the course of the island's history.

Did You Know?

The last recorded case of the bubonic plague in Corsica was as recent as 1945.

Brief Independence

In 1735 in the town of Corte, the Corsicans drafted a constitution for an independent sovereign state. The following year, Corsica elected a king, Baron Theodor von Neuhof, but he abandoned the throne after only eight months. In 1745, Corsican politician Jean-Pierre Gaffori became the leader of a major insurrection, followed by 30-year-old political leader Pascal Paoli in 1755. Paoli succeeded in establishing a constitutional state, founded the University of

Timeline of events

1348
The plague decimates the island's population.

1553
The French arrive on the island.

1735
Corsican nationalists declare independence.

1755
Pascal Paoli is elected head of the resistance.

Corte and created a local army. For just 14 years, the island was independent under Paoli's rule, but the French had their sights set on the island. Paoli lost the Battle of Ponte-Novu, and French rule began.

Turning Tides

Sentenced to death by French revolutionaries, the Jacobins, Pascal Paoli appealed to the English for help in taking Corsica back from the French. The English complied with his requests, and their intervention on the island led to the birth of the brief Anglo-Corsican kingdom (1794–6). In 1796, French troops were sent out to retake the island, and they were led by a young Ajaccio-born officer, Napoleon Bonaparte *(p48)*.

After Napoleon's fall in 1815, the 19th century in Corsica was one of relative calm under French rule. A secure economic scene and a wave of infrastructural development improved accessibility and general standards of living on the island. In the late 19th century, Corsica's tourism industry developed. The Industrial Revolution saw a period of decline, however, as the island lagged behind the productive mainland, with Corsica confined to predominantly rural ways of living.

1 Corsican patriots join Pascal Paoli in 1793. ↑

2 Napoleon and his military staff on the battlefield.

3 Illustration of French troops arriving in Corsica.

4 Illustration of Ajaccio, capital city of Corsica.

1769
Birth of Napoleon Bonaparte in Ajaccio.

1790
Paoli returns from exile.

1815
Hundred Days War culminates in Napoleon's exile and eventual downfall.

1821
Death of Napoleon.

War and Emigration

Despite improvements in living standards, dire poverty afflicted the island in the early 20th century, forcing thousands of Corsicans to emigrate. The island's dwindling population was to pay a high toll during World War I, with 20,000 losing their lives. The 20th century was set to bring more turbulence to the island: during World War II, Mussolini's forces conquered Corsica, but the Italians were met with heavy resistance from locals. In October 1943, Corsica became the first French territory to become liberated from Fascist control, a huge boost for the Allied forces.

The Independence Movement

At the end of World War II, the many Corsicans who had gone abroad were repatriated and there were renewed calls for Corsican autonomy (p58). In the 1960s, there was a new presence in the elections, the Front Régionaliste Corse (FRC). In 1973, the FRC, together with the Action Régionaliste Corse (ARC), demanded full political control for Corsica, a de-centralized government and protection for Corsican land

1 Ruined tents after a Nazi aerial attack on an airfield. ↑

2 Nationalist protests in Ajaccio.

3 Ajaccio, the centre of Corsica's modern tourism industry.

Did You Know?

Corsica became an important base for the US Air Force during World War II.

1942

Mussolini's forces occupy Corsica.

1943

The Allies liberate the island.

1960

The FRC enters the political scene.

1976

The FLNC forms to advocate for Corsican independence.

3

against tourist development. The independence movement was punctuated by occasional acts of violence: in 1975, demonstrations ended in the shooting of two police officers. Following this, the Front de Libération Nationale de la Corse (FLNC) was founded, which committed more acts of terrorism, including the shooting of French politician Claude Érignac in 1998. Violence became less common following the 1990s, but the nationalist movement remains very much alive.

Corsica Today

In 2018, Corsica was granted the status of *collectivité territoriale unique* (single territorial collectivity), which gives the island more legislative powers than other regions of France. Since 2015, Corsica's governing party has been Pè a Corsica (For Corsica), a nationalist party formed by a coalition of the two nationalist parties, Femu a Corsica and Corsica Libera. The Corsican language, which went into decline in the mid-20th century, is undergoing a revival (39 per cent of the population now speak Corsican as well as French). Tourism remains the island's key industry, supporting a burgeoning culinary scene.

TOURIST INFRASTRUCTURE

Corsica's politically active citizens have often reacted against the construction of major tourist infrastructure. Though the island is twice the size of Mallorca, no high-rises or vast holiday complexes exist, and much of the island remains wild. This lack of accomodation is one reason why Corsica has a reputation for being expensive.

2003
Referendum to increase regional autonomy is rejected.

2013
Corsica hosts the first three stages of the 100th Tour de France.

2015
The French government permits a regional assembly.

2024
French and Corsican officials strike a deal in a "decisive step" towards the island's autonomy.

CORSICAN LANGUAGE AND CULTURE

Wherever you travel on the island, you're likely to see flags and stickers bearing the Moor's Head – the symbol of an independent Corsica for over three centuries. Originally used by Aragonese kings to celebrate their Christian victory in the 13th century, the symbol was ceded to local clan leaders before being adopted by Pascal Paoli. Nowadays, the Corsican flag is used as a proud reminder of the island's independent culture, language and customs. Corsicans have always had a strong regional identity, with their own dialects, religious traditions and festivals. Here's a short guide to the island's rich culture.

CORSICAN LANGUAGE

Proponents of independence have long viewed language as a matter of great importance. In the northeast, the Corsican language, Corsu, is soft and musical, with an inflection and many words that are similar to Tuscan dialects. When Pascal Paoli was drafting his constitution for an independent Corsica, he proposed that Italian was adopted as the official language, recognizing the similarities

→
Revolutionary leader
Pascal Paoli

A rally for Corsican
independence in the 1970s,
with the Corsican flag ↑

↑ Ajaccio's popular
Napoleonian Days festival

CORSICAN CUSTOMS

Most Corsicans are Catholic and the local traditions that have been preserved through the centuries are mostly of a religious nature. The most fascinating are the processions held during Easter Week *(p50)*, for example in Bonifacio, Calvi and Sartène. Local saints' days are widely celebrated in the cities and villages, as are ceremonies for the dead, accompanied by solemn processions to the cemeteries or to the unusual and impressive mortuary chapels along the roads of Cap Corse and the west coast. However, the best-known "custom" in Corsica is the vendetta *(p113)*.

PRESERVING THE CULTURE

Today, calls for greater sovereignty are rooted in a belief that taking back control from Paris will revitalize the island's rich heritage and customs. Corsica's regional parliament, currently in the hands of leaders who support greater autonomy from France, has been directing resources to new language projects and cultural education programmes – an indicator of their success is that these projects have long waiting lists, as young people look to reconnect with their island's culture.

between the regional dialect and that spoken in Tuscany. The Corsican language is deeper and more crisp in the south-west, bearing influences of neighbouring Sardinia. The "double d" is used heavily in the south; for example, the word for "beautiful" in Bastia is *bellu*, while in Ajaccio it becomes *beddu*.

Recognized as a regional language in 1974, Corsu is now enjoying a revival thanks to courses at the island's university and increased access to language classes.

Did You Know?

There are an estimated 180,000 Corsu speakers, a number that is set to rise.

THE GR20

The GR20 is talked about in reverential tones, both by past and future hikers. The origins of the route can be traced back to the 1950s, when local walkers planned a long-distance path stretching down the island's spine. It wasn't until the establishment of the Parc Naturel Régional de Corse in 1972 *(p44)* that the path became a reality. With local approval, a 180-km (112-mile) route between Calenzana in the north and Conca in the south was tirelessly waymarked, and a series of abandoned shepherd huts along the route were renovated to form hikers' refuges. The project quickly took on a political dimension; as the route passed through rural areas long overlooked by politicians and decimated by depopulation, the GR20 was seen as a symbol of commitment to the island's rural life and landscapes.

Since the 1990s, the route has become one of Europe's most popular, and the ubiquitous red and white flags (which mark all of France's GR – *Grande Randonnée* – routes) guide some 18,000 hikers a year along the route. It's notoriously one of Europe's most challenging routes, too. Many walkers opt for either the northern or southern parts, as the route in its entirety can take around two weeks to complete. Some sections of the trail require scrambling, with iron rungs and cords to help walkers up or down the rock face. With a decent level of fitness and the right amount of planning, however, the GR20 is a truly unforgettable outdoor experience.

STAGES 1–5

Crossing Corsica from northwest to southeast, the GR20 (Grande Randonnée 20) runs at an average altitude of 1,000–2,000 m (3,300–6,600 ft), linking Calenzana, in the Balagne region, with Conca, in the Porto-Vecchio hinterland. Though some choose to hike the route from south to north, the majority of hikers start in Calenzana. The GR20 is divided into 15 stages, with most hikes taking almost an entire day on terrain with altitude differences as much as 800 m (2,600 ft). Stages 1 to 5 have spectacular but difficult stretches, the most notorious being Cirque de la Solitude, a route fitted with fixed ladders, chains and cables.

Stage 1 of the walk starts in Calenzana (275 m/902 ft), and finishes at the Ortu di u Piobbu refuge (1,570 m/5,151 ft). The leg is 10-km (6-miles) long and takes an average of 7 hours to complete.

↑ Camping at the Ortu di Piobbu refuge

REACHING THE TRAILHEADS

Whether you arrive in Corsica by boat or plane, reaching both the northern and southern trailheads is relatively straightforward. Most hikers who plan to hike north-to-south arrive in Calvi before catching a 30-minute bus to the village of Calenzana. Those looking to start in Conca in the south typically arrive in Figari before catching a two-hour bus to the village. Note that buses run regularly during the summer season, but services may be less frequent in the winter months.

START
Calenzana

Ruisseau de l'Ondo

La Figarell

Capu Taita
1,836 m (6,024 ft)

Ruisseau de Moghine

Ruisseau de Cavicchia

Capo Rossu
2,158 m (7,080 ft)

Capo alle Giargiole
2,105 m (6,906 ft)

Capu di Guagnarola
1,967 m (6,453 ft)

Punta a e Cricche
2,057 m (6,749 ft)

Did You Know?

The Sentier de Spasimata, a path near Cirque de Bonifatu, is famous for its narrow footbridge.

GR20: Stages 1-5
GR20: Stages 6-10
CORSICA
GR20: Stages 11-15

Locator Map

For **Stage 2**, you'll leave the Ortu di u Piobbu refuge and finish 8 km (5 miles) later at the Carrozzu refuge (1,270 m/4,167 ft). The climbs are hard abd the leg takes around 6.5 hours to complete.

From the Carrozzu refuge, **Stage 3** sticks to the high peaks and finishes at the Asco Stagnu refuge (1,422 m/4,665 ft). The leg is 6 km (4 miles) and takes around 6 hours.

Stage 4 involves rocky climbs around the Cirque de la Solitude. It runs for 8 km (5 miles) and finishes at Bergeries de Ballone (1,440 m/4,724 ft).

Monte Cinto is the tallest peak in Corsica and dominates the third and fourth stages of the path.

Stage 5 is a longer 13-km (8-mile) stretch finishing at Castel de Verghio (1,404 m/4,606 ft). The terrain is slightly flatter, and the legs takes an average of 7 hours to complete.

Capo al Dente
2,029 m (6,657 ft)

Ortu di u Piobbu refuge
1,520 m (4,986 ft)

Capu Rasino
1,604 m (5,262 ft)

Refuge de Carozzu
1,270 m (4,167 ft)

Passerelle de la spasimata

Haut Asco to Refuge

Monte Cinto
2,706 m (8,878 ft)

Refuge de Tighiettu
1,683 m (5,522 ft)

Bergerie de Ballone

Punta Licciola
2,235 m (7,333 ft)

Le Golo

Castel de Vergio
FINISH

0 kilometres   3
0 miles   3

N

The treacherous Spasimata footbridge over a mountain stream

STAGES 6–10

Stage 7 of the GR20 is one of the toughest stretches, but hikers are awarded with some of the best views of the entire route. It doesn't climb any peaks, but it crosses the GR20's highest pass, the Breche de Capitello, at 2,225 m (7,300 ft). The easiest part is the eighth stage, a shaded route without steep slopes.

GREAT VIEW
Lakes Like Lace

Lac de Nino (Lake Nino) is a glacial lake that feeds the Tavignano river. It forms a marshy area called Pozzine ("the wells") that looks like lacework from the trail above.

Le Golo

START
Castel de Vergio

Ruisseau d'Aïtone

Forêt de Valdu-Niellu

Capu a Rughia 1,712 m (5,617 ft)

Capo alle Pertiche 2,130 m (6,988 ft)

Lac de Nino

Capu a e Furcelle 2,062 m (6,765 ft)

Refuge de Manganu 1,601 m (5,252 ft)

Another long stretch, **Stage 6** runs for 14 km (9 miles) to the Manganu refuge (1,601 m/5,253 ft). Taking 5.5 hours on average, the leg is relatively flat, with beautiful views.

Monte Sant'Eliseo 1,511 m (4,957 ft)

Stage 7 is harder than the previous leg. It finishes at Petra Piana refuge (1,842 m/6,043 ft). The leg is 10 km (6 miles) and takes around 6 hours.

U Fiume Grosso

↑ Hiking a high-altitude stretch near the Manganu refuge

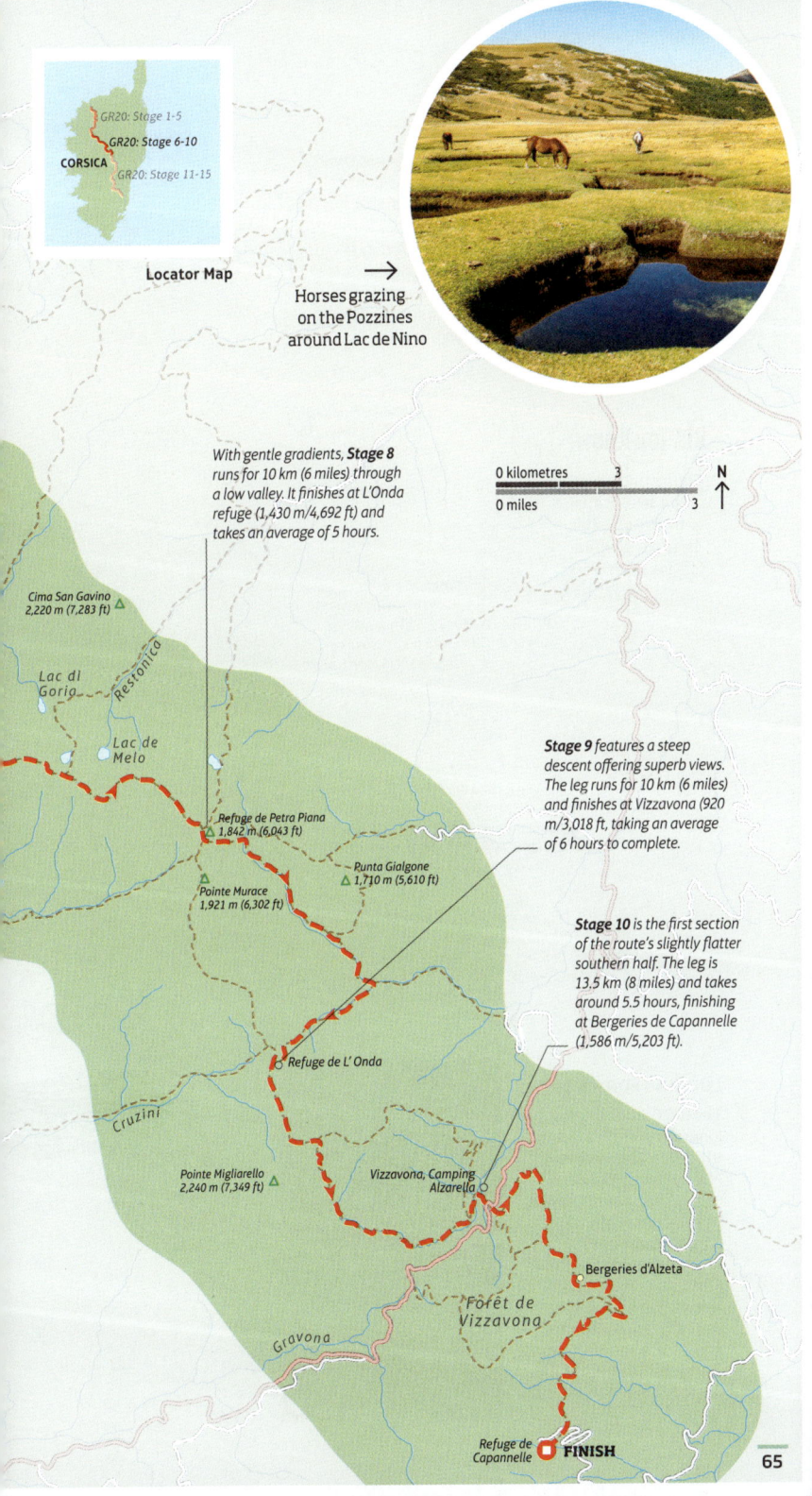

Locator Map

GR20: Stage 1-5
GR20: Stage 6-10
GR20: Stage 11-15

CORSICA

→ Horses grazing
on the Pozzines
around Lac de Nino

With gentle gradients, **Stage 8**
runs for 10 km (6 miles) through
a low valley. It finishes at L'Onda
refuge (1,430 m/4,692 ft) and
takes an average of 5 hours.

0 kilometres   3

0 miles   3

N

Cima San Gavino
2,220 m (7,283 ft) △

Lac di
Goria

Restonica

Lac de
Melo

Stage 9 features a steep
descent offering superb views.
The leg runs for 10 km (6 miles)
and finishes at Vizzavona (920
m/3,018 ft), taking an average
of 6 hours to complete.

Refuge de Petra Piana
1,842 m (6,043 ft) △

Punta Gialgone
1,710 m (5,610 ft) △

△ Pointe Murace
1,921 m (6,302 ft)

Stage 10 is the first section
of the route's slightly flatter
southern half. The leg is
13.5 km (8 miles) and takes
around 5.5 hours, finishing
at Bergeries de Capannelle
(1,586 m/5,203 ft).

○ Refuge de L' Onda

Cruzini

Pointe Migliarello
2,240 m (7,349 ft) △

Vizzavona, Camping
Alzarella ○

Bergeries d'Alzeta ○

Forêt de
Vizzavona

Gravona

Refuge de
Capannelle   □ **FINISH**

STAGES 11–15

The last stages of the GR20 offer little respite to those who have ventured this far. Almost all stages have their difficult stretches, with rugged terrain and some steep climbs, but they make up for this with spectacular views, especially in the area around the famous Aiguilles de Bavella (*p138*). Around five days should be enough to walk these last stretch, and Conca is the perfect place for a well-deserved celebration (and long rest) upon completion. Not far from Conca, the fine beaches and sea-facing restaurants of Favona and Tarco await.

Did You Know?

The mouflon (wild sheep) was once near extinction but has been a protected species since 1956.

Stage 11 starts at Bergeries de Capannelle and finishes at Prati (1,820 m/5,970 ft). One of the longest stretches, it runs for 16.5 km (10 miles) and takes around 6.5 hours.

Stage 12 finishes at the Usciolu refuge (1,750m/5,741 ft). It takes around 5 hours to walk these 9 km (6 miles).

The second half of **Stage 13**, which runs to the Asinau refuge (1,530 m/5,020 ft), is a lot steeper than the first. The whole leg is 14.5 km (9 miles), taking a good 8 hours.

The penultimate leg, **Stage 14** runs around the Aiguilles de Bavella and finishes at the Paliri refuge (1,055 m/3,461 ft). Leave a good 7 hours to walk the 13 km (8 miles).

Map labels

START
Bergeries de Capannelle

U Fium'Orbu

D69

Col de Verde
1,250 m (4,101 ft)

Prati
1,820 m (5,971 ft)

Punta di a Cuperchiata
1,937 m (6,355 ft)

Palneca

Ciamannacce

D28

D69

Usciolu refuge
1,750 m (5,741 ft)

Le Taravo

Punta di l'Arleda
1,254 m (4,114 ft)

Punta Sistaja
1,724 m (5,656 ft)

Monte Incudine
2,134 m (7,001 ft)

Asinao refuge
1,462 m (4,797 ft)

Punta di a Funtana Spartuta
1,631 m (5,351 ft)

Prugna

D268

LOOKING FOR MORE?

The GR20 is not the only long-distance hiking route in Corsica. There are two *Mare e Monti* ("between seaand mountains") paths: the first links Calenzana to Cargèse in ten easy stages, and the second goes from Porticcio to Propriano in five stages, overlooking the cliffs. There are also three *Mare a Mare* ("from sea to sea") paths.

Punta Cutina
1,268 m (4,160 ft)

Punta Alta
1,053 m (3,455 ft)

Punta Lattonaccia
1,710 m (5,610 ft)

L'Abatesco

Monte Malo
1,847 m (6,060 ft)

Punta Nera
1,527 m (5,010 ft)

D268

Paliri refuge
1,054 m (3,458 ft)

Punta Pinzuta
814 m (2,670 ft)

Punta di Quercitella
1,461 m (4,793 ft)

Punta Piana
496 m (1,627 ft)

FINISH   Conca

D168

GREAT VIEW
Soaring Summit

The Punta Paliri is a huge peak that looms over the Bavella forest. Admire the view as you enjoy the final high-altitude stage of the hike before the arduous descent back to the village of Conca.

GR20: Stages 1–5
GR20: Stages 6–10
CORSICA
GR20: Stages 11–15

Locator Map

↑ Approaching the Prati refuge

0 kilometres   5

0 miles   5

N
↑

The final leg of the journey, **Stage 15** leads you to the village of Conca (252 m/827 ft). This leg is 12 km (7 miles) and features beautifully diverse forests and peaks. It takes around 5 hours.

PLANNING YOUR HIKE

The GR20 is not an adventure to be undertaken lightly, and it's not a trail recommended for first timers. Many sections require scrambling that verges on full-blown climbing. There are scree descents and ascents that obliterate the knees as well as relentless climbs that last for hours. Most unpredictable of all is the weather in the Corsican mountains, which can be a particular challenge if you plan to camp during your hike. But an adventure of this magnitude is also one that attracts a lot of footfall, and thousands of hikers set out on the trail, meaning camaraderie is high. This short guide contains a few handy tips and tricks to ensure your experience runs smoothly.

BEFORE YOU GO

Book your accommodation as early as possible if staying in refuges (large cabins along the route, many with kitchens and dining areas). Refuge reservations open around March (although the refuges themselves don't open until May) and can be made at *pnr-resa.corsica*. Since spaces are limited (often just 30 or so beds) they fill up rapidly. Bivouac spots, located close to refuges, can be reserved last minute, often as late as the day before.

Decide on the direction you're going to hike. There's no right way, but far more people choose to walk from north to south, most likely because the northern section rightly has the reputation as the harder section, so most people prefer to hike it first. On the other hand, if you choose to hike south to north, you'll warm up to the hardest section.

With very few shops for vast stretches of the hike, you'll likely need a stove to cook, but don't get caught out without camping gas. Note that French canisters use a twist seal, which isn't compatible with all camping stoves.

Get the season right. If you set off in May or June or the latter half of September, there'll be fewer crowds, but there's a higher chance of encountering snow. If hiking in July or August, refuges are full to bursting. When hiking out of season, most refuges are left open to shelter hardy adventurers, but you'll have no electricity, no gas and no water.

↑ One of many tricky ascents on the route

DURING YOUR HIKE

A hiker's prime consideration is almost always food. Organized hiking tours (often the self-guided kind) will often include a half-board basis at refuges (breakfast and dinner) meaning that you'll only need to organize your own lunch each day. This makes for a much lighter pack, but it's the most expensive way of doing the trek. Vegetarians may also struggle – always let the refuge know in advance.

If you're packing your own food, you don't need to bring enough to last you the whole hike. The best place to resupply is Vizzavona, where there are *épiceries* (grocery stores). If you're really low on supplies, you can take a rest day and catch the train to Corte to do a full restock.

Take much more cash than you think you'll need: refuges don't accept card and you won't pass any cash points en route. However much food you've brought, it's difficult not to be tempted by a chilled Pietra (Corsican lager) or chocolate at the refuge, no matter how inflated the prices.

Completing the GR20 in one trip is a huge achievement, but if it gets too much, don't

↑ GR20 waymarkings on the route; the entire hike is well waymarked

worry. Even the most experienced hiker can be scuppered by an accident or extreme weather, and there are a number of exit routes back to lower ground if you want to cut things short. Even better, Corsica has many other fantastic shorter hiking routes on offer across its varied terrain.

↑ Campsite overlooking the mountains outside the Petra Piana refuge

EXPERIENCE

Walking the coast near Calvi

Bastia and the North 72

Ajaccio and the West Coast 104

A Bonifacio and the South 128

Corte and the Interior 150

BASTIA AND THE NORTH

Geographically closer to Italy than to France, Bastia and northern Corsica have long been a fusion of cultures. Traces of prehistoric inhabitants are fewer in the north than in the island's south, though the Romans built large conurbations here, founding the ancient city of Mantinon, which was mentioned by the geographer Ptolemy.

The region's fortunes were made with the arrival of the Genoese in the 13th century. They built the main citadelles of Calvi and Algajola, expanded the small town of Bastia and planted the olive trees that are found across the region. The proximity to and close relations with Italy left a mark on the region's language and architecture, too, with a Tuscan inflection to the dialect and buildings that resemble those of Italy's Ligurian coast.

Northern Corsicans have always relied on the sea for their livelihoods. Firewood, oil, cork and other local products were loaded on to ships and taken to the mainland. So too was the region's famed wine, still produced in the many vineyards that spread out through the hills around Bastia.

More recently, the proximity to Italy has made the region a popular stopover for cruises, with tourists enjoying the beaches, olive orchards and old villages. Today, the main tourist localities in the region lie along the west coast, beyond the Col de Teghime: St-Florent features a lovely yacht harbour, Calvi is renowned for its nightlife and Bastia is the island's economic hub.

BASTIA AND THE NORTH

Must Sees
① Bastia
② Calvi
③ San Michele de Murato

Experience More
④ Erbalunga
⑤ Cap Corse
⑥ Pietracorbara
⑦ Macinaggio
⑧ Centuri
⑨ Île de la Giraglia
⑩ Pino
⑪ Canari
⑫ Nonza
⑬ Patrimonio
⑭ St-Florent
⑮ Nebbio
⑯ Oletta
⑰ Désert des Agriates
⑱ Pigna
⑲ L'Île Rousse
⑳ Algajola
㉑ Calenzana
㉒ Lama
㉓ Aregno
㉔ Speloncato
㉕ Sant'Antonino

Mediterranean Sea

Marseille

0 kilometres   8

0 miles   8

N

Vado Ligure

Plage de
Guignu

Cima d'Ifana
479 m (1,571 ft)

Plage de
l'Ostriconi

Piobetto

Monetta

T30

Guardiola   Lozari

Curzo   L'ÎLE
           ROUSSE
        ⑲

Monticello

Punta di Parasu
396 m (1,299 ft)

Ostriconi

Corbara

ALGAJOLA   D113   D363
⑳

Port de Sant-Ambroggio

PIGNA ⑱

SANT'   Toccone
ANTONINO
⑳

La Revellata   D71   AREGNO ⑳
                            ㉓   Occhiatana   D963

CALVI ②   Lumio   T30   San Colombano

Golfe de
Calvi

Notre Dame
de la Serra   D71
                                           Nessa

D81b   SPELONCATO
                                       ㉔

Calvi Sainte-
Catherine Airport   D451   Muro

                    Moncale   Olmi-
                                                Cappella   D547

Fiume Seccu   Strada di l'Artigiani   Cima di u Cugnolu
                                              1,113 m (3,651 ft)

                    ㉑ CALENZANA   Vallica

AJACCIO AND   San Partéo
THE WEST COAST   1,680 m (5,512 ft)
p104   Mte Grosso
                                        1,937 m (6,355 ft)   Cima di Modica
                                                                1,231 m (4,039 ft)

Barrasca   Tortagine

Giunssani

Algo

CORTE AND
THE INTERIOR
p150

❶ BASTIA

🏛 E2 ✈ Poretta, 25 km (16 miles) 🚌 Place Maréchal Leclerc
🚍 ⛴ From Genoa, Savona, Livorno, La Spezia, Marseille,
Nice, Toulon ℹ Place St-Nicolas; bastia-tourisme.com

Bastia is the second-largest city in Corsica after Ajaccio, and the second-busiest passenger port in France after Marseille. With a rich history dating as far back as Roman times, this city has long been a hotbed of culture, industry and natural beauty, and today it's considered the economic capital of Corsica. Bastia is still protected by its enduring Citadelle, which towers over the city's colourful houses and harbour.

> **Did You Know?**
>
> The city's name stems from the word *bastiglia*, Italian for port.

SHOP

U Muntagnolu

A one-stop shop for Corsica's finest local produce including *figatellu* sausage (made from pork and pork liver), honey, chestnut flour, quail pâté, oils, wine and ewe's cheese.

🏠 15 Rue César Campinchi 🌐 umuntagnolu.com

① Place du Marché

Dominated by the old Mairie (town hall), this square is the heart of Terra Vecchia (Bastia's ancient port area), with streets winding around the Vieux Port, or old harbour. The name *marché* (market) derives from the stalls, which, especially on Sunday mornings, make for a colourful and animated scene. As well as the stands with flowers, fruit, vegetables, cheese and charcuterie, there are those that make a sort of pancake with *brocciu*, the local sheep's milk cheese. The square also has a modern stone fountain designed by French sculptor Pierre Pardon. Shaded by plane trees, the square is a favourite local hangout.

② Église St-Jean-Baptiste

🏠 4 Rue du Cardinal Viale Prela, Place de l'Hôtel-de-Ville 📞 04 95 55 24 60 🕐 Daily; mass: 10:30am Sun

The largest church in Corsica is flanked by two bell towers and has an imposing, austere façade that rises majestically among the roofs of the Terra Vecchia area. Église St-Jean-Baptiste was built between 1636 and 1666, and redecorated in the following century in Baroque style. The façade stands on a narrow alleyway and is one of the most recognizable images of the island.

↑ Twin-towered Église St-Jean-Baptiste rising over Bastia's marina

Inside, the two-aisle nave displays fine marble adornments, gilded stucco work and trompe l'oeil decorations. The high altar pulpit and font are made of polychrome marble and feature a silver tabernacle. Highlights include an 18th-century statue of St John the Baptist and three paintings in the organ gallery that depict the martyr's life.

If you are visiting Bastia during Christmas, don't miss the church's evocative nativity scene and play.

---

③
Chapelle St-Roch

Rue Napoléon 🕿 04 95 32 91 66 ⏰ Mon-Sat

This chapel was dedicated to the saint who protected Bastia's population from the plague. It was built in 1604 for the St Roch Confraternity, founded in 1588. The work of Ligurian architects and artists, the chapel has 18th-century, Genoese-style wooden panelling and a trompe l'oeil roof. It also features a statue of St Roch, which is borne in local processions. The organ was made in 1750 and is housed in an interesting tribune made of sculpted, gilded wood.

④
Palais des Gouverneurs

Place du Donjon

This massive fortified palace was the seat of Genoese power in Corsica from the 14th century until the island was taken over by the French in 1768. Occupied by the Genoese governors, the local bishop and a large staff, it was mainly used to entertain foreign dignitaries. However, when the French transferred Corsica's capital to Ajaccio, it became a prison and military barracks.

The building was damaged by Nelson's bombardment in 1794 and further destroyed by Allied bombings in 1943. Now restored to its former glory, the distinctive peach-coloured palace is the most prominent feature of the Citadelle, though it sits above some particularly grim dungeons.

The palace is home to the **Musée de Bastia**, a state-of-the-art museum with a collection of historical and ethnological items, plus a range of Corsican artworks, including several Renaissance pieces from the Fesch collection. The displays illustrate Bastia's development as a trade and political capital as well as highlight its importance as a cradle of intellectual and artistic movements.

Also worth a visit are the hanging gardens on the edge of the palace ramparts, offering superb views of the city and the old port.

Musée de Bastia
⊛ Palais des Gouverneurs
May-Sep: 10am-6:30pm
Tue-Sun (Jul & Aug: daily);
Oct-Apr: 9am-noon & 2-5pm
Tue-Sat Public hols
musee.bastia.corsica

⑤
St-Charles

 Rue du Général Carbuccia
To the public

Preceded by a stairway, this church, with its impressive façade, was constructed in 1635 for the Jesuits' college and dedicated to St Ignatius Loyola, the founder of the order. When the Jesuits were driven out of Corsica in 1769, the church became the seat of the St Charles Borromeo Confraternity. Inside are several restored paintings, an altarpiece of the miraculous *Virgin of Lavasina* and a statue of the *Virgin Mary and Child*.

⑥
Jardin Romieu

 Escalier Romieu **Daily (gates close at 6pm)**

At the right-hand jetty of the Vieux Port are steps up to the Citadelle along a winding – but not particularly steep – path. The path is lined with elegant statues, vases and a fountain, and crosses over the Jardin Romieu, an oasis of tranquillity. This wooded park was designed in the second half of the 19th century by Bastian architect Paul-Augustin Viale. Palm, pine and laurel trees,

and many succulent plants, thrive here. The views of the harbour from here are superb.

⑦
Vieux Port

Nestled between Terra Nova, the Citadelle and the Terra Vecchia quarter, which frames it with its old buildings, the small cove of the medieval port has retained the atmosphere of an old maritime village. It was once the marina of Cardo and fishers still mend their nets here in the blue-and-white wooden boats, now flanked by luxury yachts.

Lining the quays are cafés, restaurants and boutiques where the locals spend their evenings. In summer, the road is closed to traffic and the old port is transformed into a large and lively pedestrian precinct, excellent for people-watching. The tall façades lining the port have suffered erosion from the sea wind and salty air. Walks along the outer jetties are spectacular: of note are the Môle Génois to the north and the Jetée du Dragon to the south, which ends at the 1861 lighthouse.

 INSIDER TIP
Aziminu

Aziminu is a traditional (and absolutely delicious) Corsican fish soup, usually made with fresh fish caught by local fishers. You can try it at one of the many seafood restaurants on the Quai des Martyrs.

⑧
Quai des Martyrs de la Libération

This quay, enlivened by cafés and restaurants, provides a pleasant walk along the seaside from Place St-Nicolas to the Vieux Port. It is especially known for its lively nightlife during the summer months.

One of the buildings on the quay is the Palais Monti Rossi, a residence of one of Corsica's old families and one of the finest 19th-century constructions in the city. The building miraculously remained intact

↓ Wrought-iron railings flanking a staircase to the Jardin Romieu

→

The impressive
L'Aldilonda walkway
below the Citadelle

after the American bombings
that destroyed 90 per cent of
the Terra Vecchia quarter in the
late summer of 1943. Its façade
features a pediment, arches
and pilasters.

Place St-Nicolas

Facing the new port and
shaded by the old palm and
plane trees, this 300-m (980-ft)
long square occupies the site
of a hospital for the poor that
was destroyed in the early
19th century. In the middle of
the square is a music pavilion
where concerts are held on
summer evenings.

On the south side of the
square stands the white marble statue of Napoleon in the
guise of a Roman emperor. On
the opposite side is a bronze
sculpture group dedicated to
widow Renno, a Corsican lumi-
nary who lost her sons in the
wars of independence, and
to all Corsicans who lost their
lives in war.

On the west side of the
square are bars and cafés
where locals and visitors alike
sit at alfresco tables. It is
worth trying a glass of Cap
Corse, the unique apéritif of
the Maison Mattei concept
store (distilleriemattei.com).
This establishment, listed
as a historic monument, is
located on the square and

offers a range of Corsican
wines, champagnes and local
delicacies. Its façade is decorated with lovely frescoes by
Corsican artist Ivo Borghesi.

Every Sunday morning,
Place St-Nicolas is enlivened
by dozens of market stalls
offering goods of every kind,
and even some interesting
antiques. Behind the charming cafés, there are some fine
19th-century buildings.

L'Aldilonda

Hugging the rocky coast
beneath the Citadelle walls is
L'Aldilonda, a swish seafront
walkway that continues all
the way to Arinella beach. The
word is Corsican for "above
the sea" and, true to its name,
it gives an impression of

floating over the waves, in the
shadow of the defensive wall.
To the south, a spacious tunnel hollowed out beneath a
bulwark leads back into town.

The weatherproof steel
grills and parapets make
L'Aldilonda a popular route
for joggers, cyclists and any-
one out for an evening stroll.

Oratoire de l'Immaculée Conception

📍 Rue Napoléon 🕐 Daily

Constructed in 1611, this is
where sessions of the Anglo-
Corsican Parliament were
hosted between 1794 and
1796, following Pascal Paoli
successfully enlisting the
British to take control of the
island (p49). The chapel's som-
bre façade reveals an ornate
Baroque interior. Wooden
panels, red Genoese velvet
and damask cover the walls.
There is also a beautiful fresco
on the central vault, which
represents the Immaculate
Conception, the Apostles and
the Evangelists. On the small
square outside the building,
black and white pebblestones
are laid out intricately in the
shape of a sun.

THE MAISON MATTEI IN BASTIA

This renowned firm makes tobacconist's products, cork
objects and, above all, delectable liqueurs. These spirits,
including the famous Cap Corse, are distilled from muscat
grapes and flavoured with maquis herbs and quinine.
The Maison was established in Bastia in 1872 by Louis
Napoleon Mattei. The firm's so called "products of nos-
talgia" were exported throughout the world, especially
where there were many Corsican emigrants. While the
original cigarette factory at Toga closed in 1977, the shop
is still in Place St-Nicolas.

(12)

Port de Toga

When the Vieux Port proved unable to take the number of pleasure boats arriving there in the high season, a new port was created between Bastia and Pietranera to cope with all this heavy traffic. The Port de Toga is a long quay that has become a lively, trendy place popular after dark. The restaurant and bar tables almost touch the sea, their multicoloured lights reflecting in the water. Some of the best clubs and bars that are open until late are Le Bounty, Le Café Cézanne and nearby Le Maracana.

(13)

Cardo

Today a chic suburb in the hills above Bastia, Cardo used to be a fishing village. Its marina, Porto Cardo, was the original nucleus of Bastia in the Middle Ages. It became a municipality in its own right in 1844, by order of King Louis Philippe. Cardo offers a spectacular view of the coastline, and there are many paths popular with hikers and cyclists.

The main attraction here is the Neo-Classical church of St-Étienne. It features painted wooden statues from the 17th century and a fine Neo-Gothic organ tribune.

From Cardo, take the scenic Route de la Corniche Supérieure via the D231 and D31. Running at 300 m (980 ft) above sea level, it passes the village of Pietrabugno and proceeds to San Martino di Lota and Miomo. In clear weather, the islands of the Tuscan archipelago can be seen on the horizon.

EAT

Nova

Offering the best local produce, this swanky restaurant offers a range of small plates as well as burgers and risottos. Grab a table in the pretty courtyard.

2-4 Rue Font Neuve
04 95 47 25 22

€€€

(14)

Chapelle de la Scala Santa

Chemin de Monserato
10am-6pm daily

Officially called the Chapelle de Notre-Dame de Monserato, this 16th-century chapel is hidden away in the Bastian countryside. The highlight is the remarkable, red-carpeted Scala Santa (or Holy Staircase). The staircase was gifted by Pope Pius VII in 1816 to thank Bastia's residents for welcoming 424 Christian clergymen (who were exiled here in 1811 under the orders of Napoleon Bonaparte). According to local legend, those who ascend the 33 velvet steps on their knees will be absolved of all their sins. Also of note in the chapel is the marble statue of the *Virgin and Child*, dating from 1647.

The best way to visit the chapel is via a 4-km- (3-mile-) long circular hike from Bastia

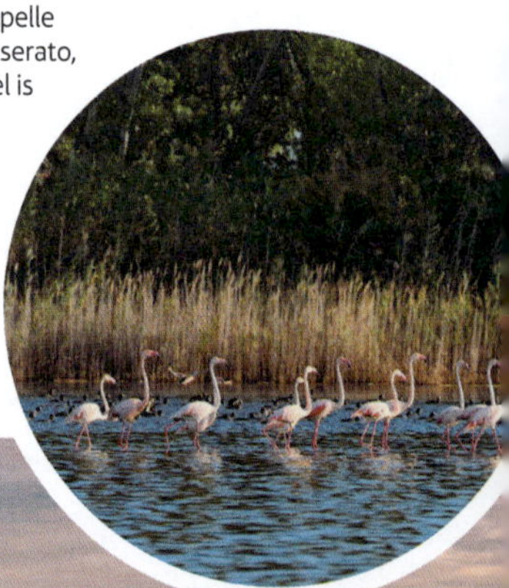

Serene Étang de Biguglia, and *(inset)* a flock of flamingoes at the lagoon ↓

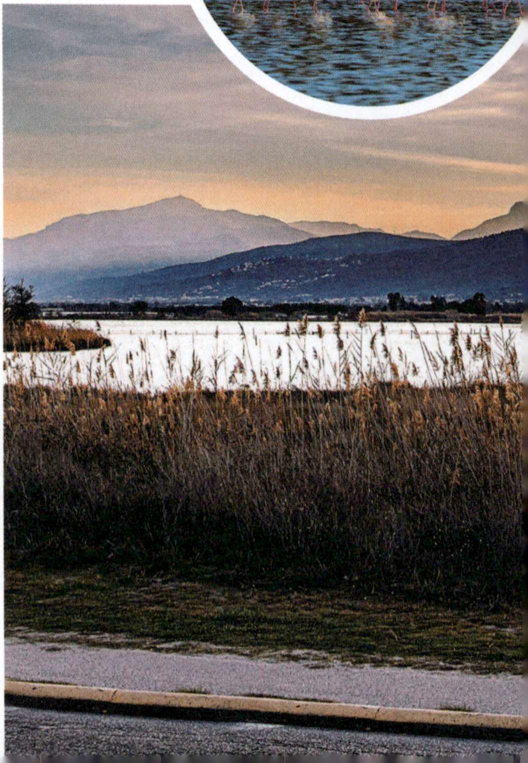

HIDDEN GEM
Mariana

The Roman remains at Mariana, just 25 km (16 miles) south of Bastia, date from the 1st century BCE. You'll find walls and a colonnade, as well as a temple to the god Mithras that was unearthed in 2017.

(follow signs for St-Florent). Some parts of the route are a little overgrown but it's an easy, pleasant walk.

15 Étang de Biguglia

Lido de la Marana, Furiani
04 95 59 51 00

On the southern outskirts of the city, located between the airport, the industrial area and the strip of Marana coastline, is the Étang de Biguglia, a tranquil lagoon designated as a reserve to protect the largest wet zone in Corsica. The lagoon consists of more than 18 sq km (7 sq miles) of pools and rivers, which form a part of the mouth of the Golo river and are connected to the sea in its northern part.

The scourge of malaria, which was an endemic disease around these marshlands for centuries, was eliminated after World War II, when the land was reclaimed and partly used for farming. Now the canebrakes and grassland are the ideal habitat for around 100 species of birds, including the great cormorant, the flamingo and the purple heron. Other inhabitants of the lagoon are marsh tortoises. The reserve is also a stopover for birds migrating from Europe to Africa. The best seasons to observe the 60 or more species of migrators are spring and autumn.

The water, which used to be polluted, has been purified, resulting in the return of the mullet and eel populations. They are caught using traditional methods by a local fishers' cooperative. Since 1994, the *étang* has been a regional reserve, with nature walks, a cycling path and guided tours.

Near the reserve, an old Genoese fort houses the **Eco Museum du Fortin**, dedicated to the history and evolution of the area. Audiovisual exhibits provide an insight into the region's biodiversity, conservation efforts, and the rich culture and traditions of the local inhabitants.

The town of Biguglia, which overlooks the lagoon, was the capital of the island under the Pisans and the residence of the Genoese governors until 1372. The sandy belt that separates the sea from the lagoon is one of the loveliest beaches in Bastia.

Eco Museum du Fortin

Route de Étang
04 95 59 51 00 Jul & Aug: 9am-4pm Tue-Sat; Sep-Jun: 9am-noon & 1-5pm Tue-Sat

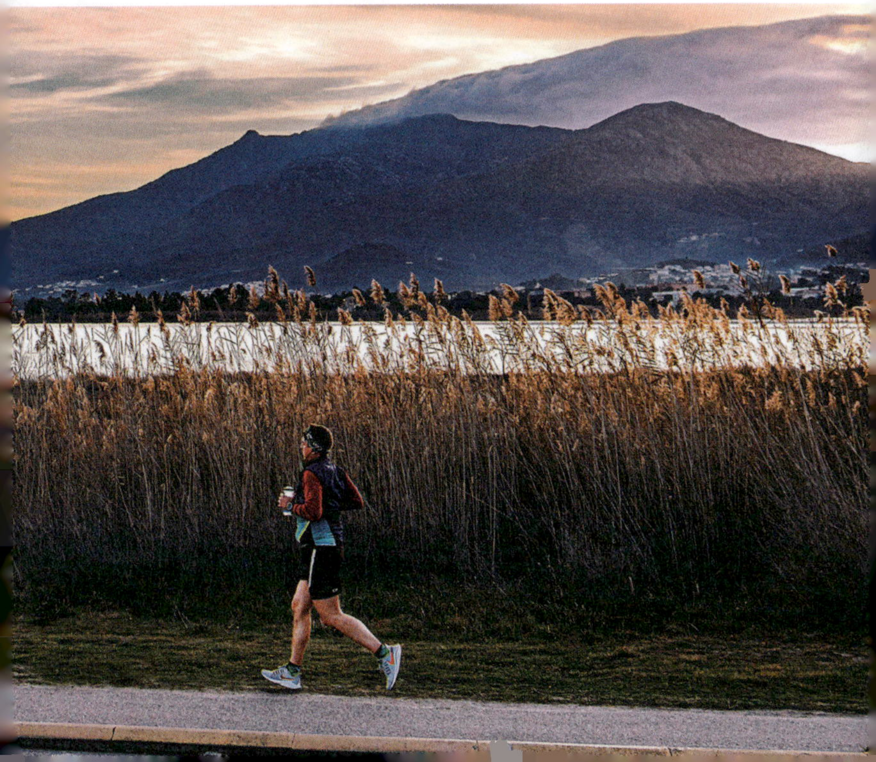

BASTIA: THE CITADELLE

🛈 **Ste-Marie: Rue Notre-Dame de-la-Citadelle, 9am–noon & 2-5:30pm Mon-Sat, mass: 10am Sun; Oratoire Ste-Croix: Rue de l'Évêché, 9am–noon Sun; museudiacorsica.corsica/en/the-citadel**

The old fortified heart of the city, the Citadelle is Bastia's most prominent attraction. It was constructed in 1380, in the heyday of the Genoese empire, by Governor Leonello Lomellini. The cobbled streets of this medieval fortress feature buildings including the Governors' Palace and the Oratoire Ste-Croix.

This impressive structure was built by the Genoese in the 14th and 15th centuries. It's still surrounded by the original ramparts and was once the heart of the historic Terra Nova quarter, which is quite different from modern Terra Vecchia. Unlike the ancient port area, which developed almost at random, the Citadelle was carefully laid out in keeping with rigorous town-planning principles. It is lined with pretty houses and broad squares.

After decades of neglect, a restoration campaign was initiated in the 1980s. The first houses to regain the original pastel colours typical of Ligurian tradition were those on Rue St-Michel, which have a great view of the old quarter.

A gem of Rococo architecture, the Oratoire Ste-Croix houses a statue of the Christ des Miracles, the protector of fishers. The statue is borne in a procession every third year on 3 May.

The Ste-Marie cathedral in Bastia has a majestic yellow façade and a 71-m (233-ft) bell tower. Ste-Marie was consecrated in 1570, when Bastia became a bishopric.

The rampart walls of the Citadelle were built between 1480 and 1521 by the Genoese governor Tomasino de Campofregoso. This section of the walls extends furthest into the sea.

→ Illustration of the Genoese Citadelle in Bastia

↑ The old heart of the Citadelle

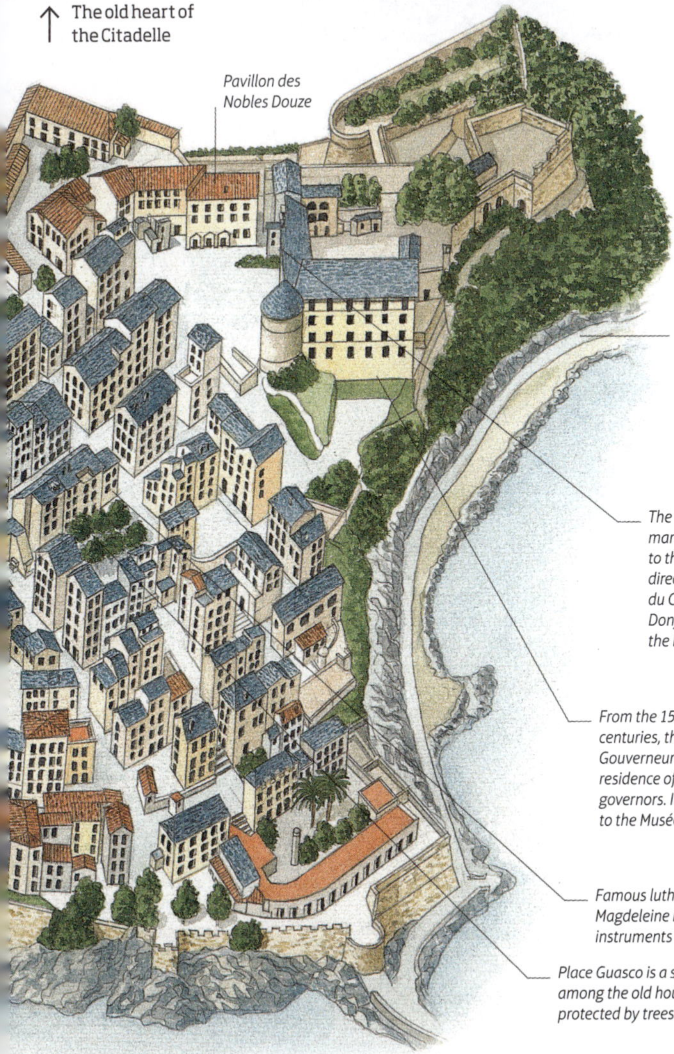

Pavillon des Nobles Douze

The glacis of the Citadelle offers panoramic views of Terra Vecchia and the old port.

The Louis XVI Gate marks the entrance to the Citadelle and directly connects Rue du Colle and Place du Donjon. It was built in the late 18th century.

From the 15th to the 18th centuries, the Palais des Gouverneurs (p77) was the residence of the Genoese governors. It is now home to the Musée de Bastia.

Famous luthier Christian Magdeleine makes stringed instruments at his workshop.

Place Guasco is a square among the old houses, protected by trees.

↑ The town and harbour of Calvi, as seen from the bastions of the Citadelle

2

CALVI

 C2 🚉 Ste-Catherine, 4 km (2 miles) 🚌 Avenue de la République 🚢🚢 From Marseille, Nice, Toulon and Savona ℹ️ 97 Port de Plaisance; ville-calvi.corsica

Calvi, the capital of Balagne, is a lovely seaside resort known for its golden sandy beaches and long bay. It comprises the upper sector, the Citadelle and the picturesque lower town, with houses overlooking the harbour.

Place Christophe Colomb

At the foot of the Citadelle (p86) is a square linking the old and new towns, the ideal start for a walking tour of the city (partly thanks to the large car park). The square is named after Christopher Columbus, who many believe was born in Calvi.

In the middle of the square is a bronze statue commemorating those who died in World War I, while a stone pays homage to the first battalion of the French Liberation Army, which liberated Corsica in 1943. A stairway descends to the Rue Clemenceau, a pedestrian precinct with many restaurants and shops selling beach accessories.

Marina

The marina in Calvi is one of the loveliest in all Corsica, with luxury yachts berthed next to simple fishing craft and other small boats. The marina is the starting point for day-long boat tours of the west coast that go to

the Scandola Nature Reserve and the Calanques de Piana (p116) and continue as far as Ajaccio. Much of this coast, with its fascinating red granite rock formations, can be seen up close only from the sea. The harbour also hosts the boats that belong to nearby diving centres. These take scuba divers to the best spots, such as those around the nearby Pointe Revellata promontory, where short courses for beginners are available.

Quai Landry

This promenade, with its hotels, cafés and restaurants shaded by palm trees and colourful awnings, is one of the liveliest spots in Calvi. Many relaxing hours can be

---

THE HOLY WEEK

Calvi's Holy Week celebrations are among the most fascinating and beautiful in Corsica. They begin on Maundy Thursday in the church of Ste-Marie-Majeure, with the benediction of the *canistrelli* (biscuits made from chestnut flour). Another benediction of *canistrelli* takes place in the Oratoire St-Antoine after a procession of penitence by Calvi's two confraternities, St Erasmus and St Anthony. On Good Friday evening, the Granitula procession starts off from St-Jean-Baptiste and winds through the streets of the lower city and the Citadelle.

> **The marina in Calvi is one of the loveliest in all of Corsica, with luxury yachts berthed next to simple fishing craft and other small boats.**

spent at one of the tables, enjoying a refreshing drink, watching the boats anchoring or setting off, or observing the passersby along the quay. Under the Citadelle at the end of the quay is the Tour du Sel, a medieval lookout post once used as a salt storehouse. Further along is the lighthouse, which dominates the entrance to the harbour.

---

④
Plage de Calvi

Calvi's sandy beach is 4.5 km (3 miles) long, from the marina to the mouth of the Figarella river. It is bordered by a pine grove that was laid out in the 19th century, when the marshland was reclaimed. It has fine white sand and low dunes protected by fencing. The sea is shallow and free from rocks, making it popular with families. A number of campsites, shacks and restaurants offering deckchairs and other beach items can be found among the pines. It is also possible to swim and sunbathe off the rocks at the foot of the Citadelle.

---

⑤
Ste-Marie-Majeure

🏠 Rue Clemenceau 🕐 Daily

This rose-coloured church can be found on a small square next to Rue Clemenceau, in the heart of the lower city. Begun in 1765, with the Neo-Gothic bell tower added in 1838, it is Baroque in style, with a softly rounded dome. The church houses some striking statues, including one of St Erasmus, the patron saint of fishers who is popular here, and a 16th-century *Assumption* that is carried through the city every year in a procession. The chapel in the choir has a wonderful 15th-century oil painting on leather from Cordoba.

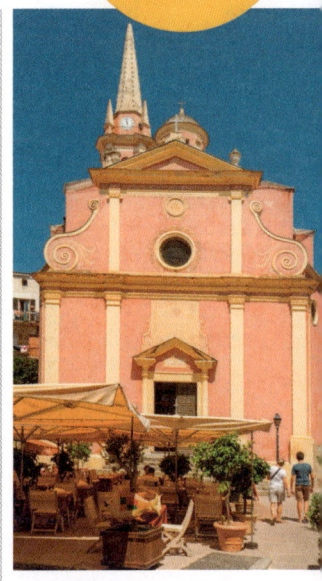

↑ Pretty rose-coloured façade of the church of Ste-Marie-Majeure

---

DRINK

Chez Tao

This legendary piano and jazz bar named after the Calvi-born pianist Tao Khan Kerefoff transforms into a lively club after midnight, with great guest DJs and dancing until dawn.

🏠 Route de la Citadelle 📞 04 95 65 00 73

Ebbrezza

Ebbrezza is one of Haute-Corse's best wine bars, offering a selection of the island's finest vintages. It also hosts tastings and serves a choice selection of tapas and cheese.

🏠 17 Quai Adolphe, Landry 📞 04 95 60 07 14

⑥

CALVI CITADELLE

🛈 Open daily

Situated on a rocky promontory, the Genoese Citadelle dominates the yacht harbour and the promenade of Calvi. It was fortified by the Genoese from the 12th century, with massive bastions protecting it on all four sides, three of which overlook the sea. It offers breath-taking views out from the rocky headland and over the water.

Sitting proudly atop a rocky headland, Calvi's Citadelle was built by Genoese rulers from the 12th century onwards. The Citadelle's five bastions have fended off an array of territory-hungry invaders over the centuries, including Franco-Turks and Anglo-Corsicans.

This grand, fortified section of the city, best explored on foot, stands in stark contrast to the commercial heart of Calvi down below. A particular highlight is the St-Jean-Baptiste cathedral, whose foundations date from the 13th century. Stop in for a peek at the *Christ des Miracles* crucifix; during the 1553 siege, locals paraded this ebony sculpture through the streets, which, according to legend, caused the Turks to flee Calvi.

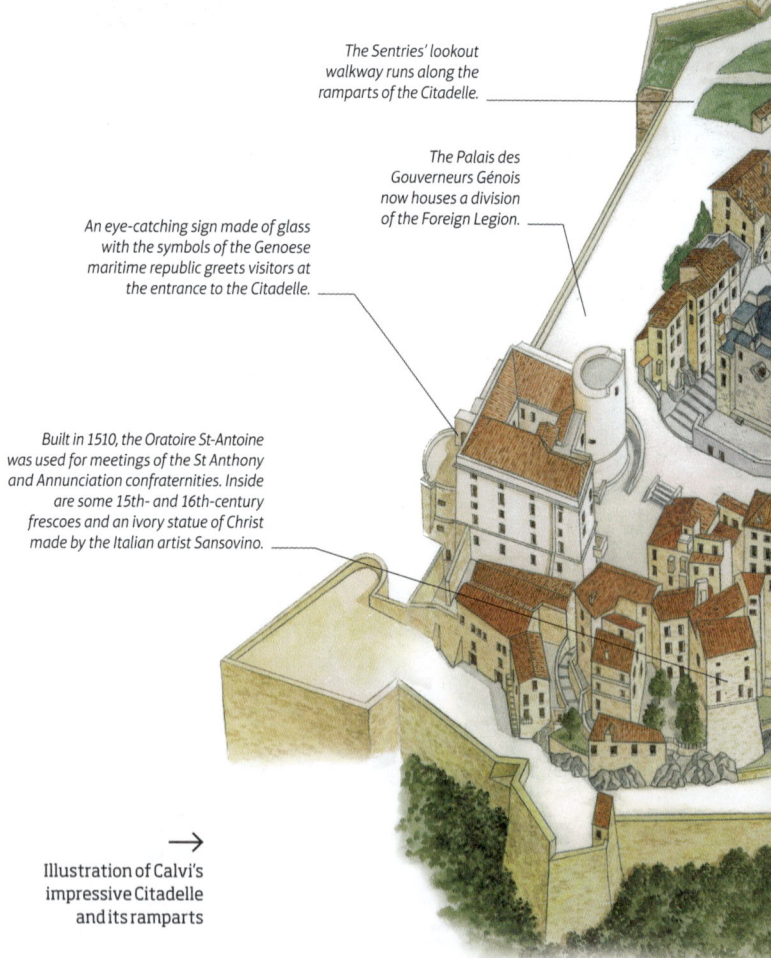

The Sentries' lookout walkway runs along the ramparts of the Citadelle.

The Palais des Gouverneurs Génois now houses a division of the Foreign Legion.

An eye-catching sign made of glass with the symbols of the Genoese maritime republic greets visitors at the entrance to the Citadelle.

Built in 1510, the Oratoire St-Antoine was used for meetings of the St Anthony and Annunciation confraternities. Inside are some 15th- and 16th-century frescoes and an ivory statue of Christ made by the Italian artist Sansovino.

→

Illustration of Calvi's impressive Citadelle and its ramparts

Maison Colombe is where, according to legend, Christopher Columbus was born.

1 The interior of the St-Jean-Baptiste cathedral features a simple nave and a high altar made of polychrome marble.

2 St-Jean-Baptiste opens into the old town of Calvi, which is lined with picturesque, cobbled alleyways and elegant stairs.

3 Marble busts of local saints can be found inside the cathedral, near the altar.

Teghiale Bastion

St-Jean-Baptiste, Calvi's cathedral, is home to two historic artifacts: the Christ des Miracles *crucifix* and the Virgin of the Rosary *statue*.

 GREAT VIEW
View from the Bastions

The monumental walls of the Citadelle and the Tour de St-Antoine overlook the yacht harbour and the lower city. Walk along the ramparts at sunrise or sunset for the best views.

3

SAN MICHELE DE MURATO

16 km (10 miles) from St-Florent 04 95 37 60 10
 May–Oct: pm daily; often closed outside the summer season

Overlooking the fertile Nebbio valley, the church of San Michele de Murato is the most distinctive Romanesque church in Corsica. It features beautiful frescoes and intricate stonework, as well as a tall bell tower, and plays host to a number of local events and celebrations.

This 12th-century church is one of Corsica's best examples of Pisan Romanesque architecture. It lies just north of Murato village, 475 m (1,560 ft) above sea level, and dominates the valley of the Bevincu river and the Nebbio region. San Michele de Murato has a simple structure, with a rectangular nave ending in a small semi-circular apse and a porticoed bell tower set against the middle of the façade. The patterned arrangement of white limestone and green serpentine give the church its striking colouring. The consoles and cornices of the small windows have detailed bas-reliefs with animal and plant motifs, as well as allegorical scenes, such as Eve taking the forbidden fruit and the Lamb attacked by other animals.

TOP 4 **CHURCH FEATURES**

Façade
The striking façade has one main entrance and three blind arches.

Consoles
Blind arches lie on consoles with sculpted motifs and bas-reliefs.

Bell Tower
The square bell tower was enlarged in the 19th century. It forms a colonnaded portico around the entry door.

Carvings
Numerous sculptures of animals and humans cover the church, with Eve in the Garden of Eden on the north wall.

↑ Detailed bas-reliefs adorning the blind arches

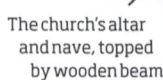

→ The church's altar and nave, topped by wooden beams

Did You Know?

The checkerboard arrangement of coloured blocks is a key feature of the Pisan Romanesque style.

↑ Green-and-white stone exterior of the church of San Michele de Murato

EXPERIENCE MORE

4

Erbalunga

🅰 E2 🏠 10 km (6 miles)
N of Bastia 🚌

Erbalunga, the marina of the district of Brando, was for centuries the port where Pisan ships landed to be loaded with local wine. A 15th-century Genoese tower protects its small harbour, lined today with old stone houses and seafood restaurants.

At the start of the village is the church of St-Erasme, home to the crosses of the Cerca procession: the men's crucifix weighs 60 kg (132 lb); the women's is 30 kg (66 lb). On the evening of Maundy Thursday, the procession winds through the streets to the nearby Benedictine nuns' convent. On Good Friday, it leaves in the morning and proceeds for 7 km (4 miles), through the hamlets of Pozzo, Poretto and Silgaggia.

In Erbalunga, as in many other locations around Cap Corse, there are sumptuous country mansions known as Maisons d'Américains. These were built by Corsicans who had returned home wealthy after emigrating to Latin America. Rich families also had impressive mausoleums built, which can be seen from the D32 all over the cape.

In Castello, 3 km (2 miles) inland, there is a 13th-century fortress. A 15th-century Italian nobleman murdered his wife here, and she is said to haunt Castello. The chapel of **Santa Maria di e Nevi** lies a short walk south towards Silgaggia. It houses the oldest frescoes in Corsica, dating from 1386. Pozzo is the starting point for the six-hour hike to Monte Stello (1,307 m/4,288 ft).

North of Erbalunga, along the D80, is the Sisco Valley.

In Sisco is the Chapelle de St-Martin, housing a precious 13th-century silver mask of St John Chrysostom. From the main road, a path leads to the Romanesque Chapelle de San Michele, built by the Pisans. Closer to the coast is the former Couvent de Santa Catalina, famous for once having housed relics of a fantastic nature, such as a lump of clay from which Adam was made and almonds from Paradise.

Santa Maria di e Nevi

♿ 🚫 🏠 Castello ☎ Chapel:
04 95 33 20 84; tours: 06 86
78 02 38 🕐 For guided tours only, call one day in advance

5

Cap Corse

🅰 E1 🏠 54 km (33 miles) N of Bastia 🛈 Ersa Town Hall;
capcorse-tourisme.corsica

On the northern tip of the peninsula are some villages that have retained the spirit of the past. One of these

←

The small fishing village of Erbalunga, sitting on the edge of the Mediterranean

---

EAT

A Piazzetta
This friendly, Italian-style restaurant is known for its pizzas, pastas and fried seafood, best enjoyed on the shady terrace.

🅰 E2 🏠 Port de Erbalunga, Erbalunga
☎ 04 95 33 28 69

€€€

↑ Hiking the Sentier des Douaniers that runs along the coast of Cap Corse

SENTIER DES DOUANIERS

This coastal footpath (p102) runs along the tip of Cap Corse via Macinaggio, Barcaggio, Tollare and Centuri. The wooded path offers breathtaking views over craggy cliffs and beaches. These sights can also be reached via paved roads. Note that hiking in midsummer is ill advised due to regular bush fires.

is Barcaggio, which is home to a beautiful beach where cows go to graze and a small harbour where time seems to have come to a halt.

The road through Cap Corse, the D80 followed by the D253, is simply spectacular. It descends through dense maquis, holm oak groves and pastures covered in white asphodel, offering a dazzling view of the Île de la Giraglia (p92).

About 2 km (1 mile) west of Barcaggio is Tollare, another small harbour with a tuna fishery near the beautiful trail, the Sentier des Douaniers. From here, a small, scenic

road winds back to the D80 and Ersa, whose church of Ste-Marie has a 17th-century wooden tabernacle. West of here, on Col de Serra is Moulin Mattei, an old, round mill. Once in a poor state of preservation, it was restored in 2004 by the Maison Mattei ,(p79), one of Corsica's most renowned apéritif makers.

6

Pietracorbara

E1 24 km (15 miles) N of Bastia 🚌 ❼Town Hall; **pietracorbara.fr**

A cultivated valley behind a long, sandy beach enclosed by a canebrake protects the village of Pietracorbara. A skeleton found here in 1990 and dating from around 6,000 BCE is proof of the prehistoric origins of this site, which was later used by both the Greeks and Romans as a small military base.

Northwards, along the coast, is the 16th-century Tour de l'Osse (Bone Tower), one of the best preserved in the area, and Porticciolo, a tiny marina with a collection of small houses grouped around a delightful pier.

7

Macinaggio

E1 18 km (11 miles) S of Barcaggio 🚌 ❼Harbour Master's office; **macinaggio rogliano-capcorse.fr**

Arguably the most popular tourist harbour in Cap Corse, Macinaggio has always been a military and commercial port. Controlled by the Genoese for a long time, it was liberated by Pascal Paoli, after years of struggle, in 1761 (p54). Commemorative plaques on the quay mark Napoleon's landing, the empress Eugénie's visit on her return trip from the Suez Canal inauguration in 1869, and that Paoli also stopped here. The port is divided into three basins that can take in more than 500 boats and is surrounded by visitors' facilities.

Inhabited during Roman times, Rogliano was ruled by the influential da Mare family from the 12th to the 16th centuries.

At Bettolacce, the area's main village, a round tower bears witness to its former splendour. The village's highlight is the church of Sant' Agnellu, featuring a beautiful altar of white Carrara marble.

8 Centuri

🅰 E1 🔲 12 km (7 miles)
S of Barcaggio ℹ Town
Hall; 04 95 35 60 06

Located on the western tip of Cap Corse, the small port of Centuri lies on a narrow inlet lined by ochre, grey and white houses with bright green roofs. For centuries Centuri was a loading point for wine, wood, oil and citrus fruits that were then shipped to France and Italy. In fact, there are records of Ptolemy citing a port here in as early as the 1st century BCE. Today, Centuri is the leading fishing centre in Cap Corse.

The docks are covered with fishing nets and lobster pots that are still handmade. The port is full of the typical double-ended fishing boats, which return laden with lobsters (3,000 kg/6,600 lb a year). Fresh catch can be enjoyed in the local seafood restaurants.

The rich sea floor here is a paradise for scuba divers, especially around the islet of Centuri, at the mouth of the bay, which was fortified in the 13th century. There's also a secluded pebble beach, Muté, at the bay, as well as a few hotels and homestays.

From the port, an hour's walk up a path leads through luxuriant vegetation to the village of Cannelle (also accessible by car from the D80 road). There's little to see here apart from a 16th-century fountain, but the hamlet is well worth visiting for its simple charm. Its stone houses are adorned with bougainvillea, and its narrow, cobbled streets and covered passageways offer excellent views of the sea.

On the D80 road, 3 km (2 miles) from Centuri, is the 16th-century Couvent de l'Annonciation dedicated to Our Lady of the Seven Sorrows. The church is considered the largest in Cap Corse. It is not open to the public, except for temporary exhibitions.

Just off the coast of Centuri is the Îlot de Capense. It is now an ornithological reserve with holm oak and arbutus trees, as well as nananthea (*Nananthea perpusilla*) daisies. Keep an eye out for yellow-legged and Audouin's gulls, as well as European shags.

---

9 Île de la Giraglia

🅰 E1 🔲 1 km (half a mile)
N of Barcaggio 🚢 The Moby
Giraglia ferry from Bastia;
mobylines.com

The northernmost part of Corsica, the serpentine rock island of Giraglia is separated from the coast by a stretch of treacherous, fast-flowing sea. A small lighthouse and a crumbling Genoese tower are the only inhabitants of this solitary outpost.

The lighthouse was first constructed on the island in the 16th century. It has since been rebuilt several times (the present building dates from 1848). It was operated by a keeper until 1994 but is now wholly automatic.

Standing just beside it is the historic watchtower. Built from 1582 to 1584 as part of the Genoese defences against Barbary pirates, this grand

> **The rich sea floor here is a paradise for scuba divers, especially around the islet of Centuri at the mouth of the bay, which was fortified in the 13th century.**

↑ Sailboat heading to Giraglia as part of the Loro Piana Giraglia

battlement has an unusual square shape. Its terrace, surrounded by large crenellations, offers superb sea views.

If you're visiting the island in mid-June, don't miss the thrilling annual regatta Loro Piana Giraglia *(loropiana giraglia.com)*. Formerly known as the Giraglia Rolex Cup, this prestigious event is named after the island and was first raced in 1953. The circuit starts in St-Tropez in France, passes Giraglia and finally ends in Genoa in Italy.

 Pino

🏔E1 🚗24 km (15 miles) S of Barcaggio; 🛈 Town Hall; 04 95 35 12 70

This small village at the foot of Col de Ste-Lucie lies in the midst of luxuriant vegetation. Umbrella pines protect the Maisons d'Américains, country mansions built by Corsicans returning from Latin America.

Centuri's harbour, lined with pastel-coloured buildings and boats

Other monumental tombs, surrounded by cypress trees, lie at the junction of the D80 and D180 roads.

Pino is also home to the church of Ste-Marie, featuring a Baroque façade and, inside, two fonts decorated with fish, salamanders and lions. Further down Col de Ste-Lucie, in the picturesque Marina di Scalu, is the 15th-century Couvent St-François. Although it is closed to the public, the Franciscan monastery – and the adjacent Genoese tower – makes an excellent vantage point.

About 5 km (3 miles) from Pino, on the D180 road going up to Col de Ste-Lucie, is the footpath to the remains of the Tour de Sénèque. The tower is at the top of Monte Ventiggiola, 564 m (1,850 ft) above sea level, where the Roman playwright Seneca is said to have been exiled. In reality, the tower is medieval. It can be reached after a steep climb through the maquis that can take over an hour. The view is well worth the climb.

 Canari

🏔E1 🚗40 km (25 miles) S of Barcaggio; 🛈 Town Hall; canarivillage.com

Rather isolated from the D80 highway and divided into various hamlets, the medieval fiefdom of Canari grew significantly from 1932 to 1966 due to a local asbestos mine. Though the mine was closed when this mineral was found to be toxic, it has left its mark on the landscape.

There are a number of sights worth seeing in Canari, particularly its two stately churches. The 12th-century Pisan Romanesque Santa Maria Assunta features a cornice decorated with animal heads and human figures. The church of St-François was originally built in 1506 and then rebuilt in the Baroque style. To explore the interior,

 PICTURE PERFECT
Scala Brocciu

Walk to the beautiful Scala Brocciu viewpoint, past Canari's bell tower, for a quintessential image of the lovely coastline. Look to the east and you can snap the ruins of the old village of Cucolu.

ask for the keys at the Town Hall, as the church is usually locked. Rooms in the church can also be rented for short stays. Other attractions in Canari include an imposing white bell tower, originally built as a lighthouse.

Further south is the Marine d'Albo. This is where, in 1588, Algerian ruler Hassan Pasha's fleet landed and his men sacked the area. The black-pebble beach here is protected by a 16th-century Genoese watchtower. The tiny beach is also a good spot for scuba diving as seabream, comber, wrasse and damselfish inhabit the rocky seabed.

↑ Canari's distinctive white bell tower, a symbol of the village

⑫ Nonza

🅰E2 🏠19 km (12 miles) N of St-Florent ℹ️Town Hall; 04 95 37 82 82

One of the most fascinating villages in Corsica, Nonza clings to a black rock falling steeply down to the sea. Its old stone houses are surrounded by terraces and gardens, and many are reached by steps rather than streets.

Steps also lead up to the 16th-century church of Ste-Julie. Inside is a Baroque altar, a small chapel dedicated to St Erasmus, patron saint of sailors, and a painting of St Julia, one of Corsica's patron saints. Nearby, 54 steps lead down to the Fontaine de Ste-Julie, which is said to have miraculous water.

More steps lead down to the beach, 160 m (525 ft) below the village. Until the early 19th century, the inhabitants left from here in boats to reach the then-fertile Désert des Agriates (p96). Today, the beach offers fine views up to the village and is home to an 18th-century schist tower built by Pascal Paoli (p58). The dark colour of the sand is the result of pollution from an asbestos mine up the coast that was closed in 1966. It is safe to walk here, but bathing is not allowed.

On the outskirts of the town, on the D80 road to Albo, you'll find mausoleums and mortuary chapels owned by affluent Corsican families.

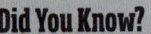

Did You Know?

Corsica has two patron saints, St Julia and St Devota.

⑬ Patrimonio

🅰E2 🏠8 km (5 miles) NE of St-Florent 🚌 ℹ️Town Hall; 04 95 37 08 49

At the foot of the Serra di Pigno and the Col de Teghime, this village in the heart of the Nebbio region is one of the main wine-producing centres on the island. The vineyards, which all belong to small, family-owned wineries, dot the limestone hills that dominate Patrimonio.

While driving along the highway, it is worth stopping at one of the many wineries in the area. Of note are the white Vermentino and a fine red wine made from the Nielucciu grape.

Overlooking the village is the church of St-Martin, built in 1570 and reached by a stairway. At sunset, its façade takes on golden hues. Just down the lane, Next to the church, is a megalithic menhir with a carved face.

⑭ St-Florent

🅰E2 🏠23 km (14 miles) W of Bastia 🚌 ℹ️11 Route de la Citadelle; corsica-saint-florent.com

At the end of a long gulf, the village of St-Florent sits with

← Baroque interior of the church of Ste-Julie in the village of Nonza

its colourful houses along the harbour and a lively promenade with boutiques and cafés. Its old town is centred around a lovely parish church. Although it was an ancient Roman base, the village only really developed in the 15th century around the Genoese fort. However, it was abandoned not long after, between the 17th and 19th centuries, due to an outbreak of malaria. The village only revived in the following century.

The highlight here is the **Santa Maria Assunta**, a striking Romanesque church dating back to 1140. Made of pale limestone, its façade has two tiers of blind arches and a niche with a *Virgin Mary and Child* statue. Inside the church, the remains of St Flor, a Roman soldier mummified in the 3rd century CE, are housed in a glass case.

HIDDEN GEM
Ecology Lessons

While in St-Florent, stop by the Maison du Grand Site de France Conca d'Oru *(grand-site-concadoru.fr)*, an information centre and vineyard with exhibits on the unique ecology of the region.

↑ Idyllic Patrimonio, surrounded by rolling hills and vineyards

Santa Maria Assunta

6 Piani 04 95 37 06 04 Jun-Sep: 9:30am-7:30pm Mon-Sat, 2-7:30pm Sun; Oct-May: by appt only, call ahead

15

Nebbio

E2 11 km (7 miles) S of St-Florent

Nebbio is a small region inland from St-Florent, to the west of Cap Corse, home to the wild Alisu basin. Called Conca d'Oru (the Golden Shell) for its fertile land, the Alisu basin is an area with vineyards and olive and fruit orchards. Via the D38, D82 and D62 roads, a semicircular route passes through the Nebbio region's main towns, from Oletta *(p96)* up to Rapale and Murato (home to the church of San Michele, *p88*). The roads lead to the passes of Col de Teghime (a small road goes up to Serra di Pigno, for an even better view) and Col de San Stefano. From here, the stretch of D62 known as Défilé de Lancone descends all the way down to the coast in steep curves.

DRINK

Patrimonio's and St-Florent's wines are considered Corsica's finest. The best way to try them is by visiting the region's vineyards.

Domaine Montemagni

Family-owned winery open since 1850.

E2 Puccinasca, Patrimonio domaine-montemagni.fr

Domaine Gentile

A vast estate with an organic vineyard where grapes are handpicked.

E2 Olzo, St-Florent domaine-gentile.com

Domaine Orenga de Gaffory

A one-stop destination for tastings, wine-making workshops and walks among the vines.

E2 Lieu-dit Morta Majo, Patrimonio orengade gaffory.com

The charming village of Oletta perched on a densely wooded hillside

alongside olive orchards. It has retained its medieval character, with stepped paths, narrow alleys and vaulted passageways. By the tree-lined central square stands the local church with two bell towers.

Pigna is also steeped in culture; it is a centre for traditional Corsican music and is known for its handicraft workshops. The **Casa Musicale** (Music House) – which also has hotel facilities and a restaurant – studies and promotes Corsican music and other local traditions. In the workshops, ancient instruments, including various types of cittern, are built in traditional style. Scatt'a Musica *(scatt'amusica. fr)* sells musical boxes and, in July, the Estivoce festival celebrates traditional songs.

The Corsican restaurant A Merendella Citadina is also worth a visit.

Casa Musicale

🏠 Fondu di u Paese 🕐 Jan-mid-Feb 🌐 casa-musicale.org

 19

L'Île Rousse

🗺 D2 🚗 24 km (15 miles) NE of Calvi 🚉 Route du Port 🚌 🛳 From Marseille, Genoa, Savona, Toulon, Nice 🛈 Avenue Calizi; ot-ile-rousse.fr

A busy beach with fine sand, a pleasant, Riviera-style promenade, shops and a lively port

> **L'Île Rousse revolves around Place Paoli, where you'll find a mix of cafés and shops, and *pétanque* players in the shade of palm trees.**

 16

Oletta

🗺 E2 🚗 10 km (6 miles) SE of St-Florent 🚌

Immersed in the greenery of the hills of Nebbio is the small village of Oletta. It seems to be clinging to the hillside and is characterized by simple houses of white, ochre and pink. Oletta offers fine views of the Golfe de St-Florent and the Nebbio region. The bell tower of the old Couvent St-François, the only remaining architectural element from the original complex, can also be seen from here. Dominating the view towards the hilltop is the Mausoleum of Count Rivarola, governor of Malta, one of the many monumental family tombs in this region. The 18th-century parish church of St-André has a bas-relief of the Creation on its façade and a wooden triptych inside dating from 1534.

The area around Oletta is renowned for its sheep's-milk cheese and was known for the famous Roquefort variety.

 17

Désert des Agriates

🗺 D2-E2 🚗 21 km (13 miles) E of St-Florent

Situated between St-Florent and the mouth of the small Ostriconi river, this 160-sq-km (60-sq-mile) green desert is virtually uninhabited. Only some shepherds and a few people in the hamlet of Casta live here. Until the mid-19th century, however, this area was the "bread basket" of Bastia and Cap Corse, and it produced wheat, olives and olive oil, wine and fruit. Today, the only remains of this area's fertile past are the barns and stone granaries. The fields are abandoned and the maquis has invaded the terrain.

 18

Pigna

🗺 D2 🚗 23 km (14 miles) E of Calvi

This thriving hamlet in the Balagne is perched on a slope

sum up L'Île Rousse. It was founded in 1758 by Pascal Paoli, who had the port built to counter the presence of the Genoese at Calvi and Algajola. L'Île Rousse revolves around Place Paoli, where you'll find a mix of cafés and shops, and *pétanque* players in the shade of palm and plane trees. In the middle of the square is a fountain with a statue of Paoli.

The square is the starting point for the little train that skirts the bay and goes to L'île de la Pietra. This islet is linked to the mainland by a pier with a tower and a lighthouse built by Paoli in 1857.

At one end of Place Paoli is the covered market, a 19th-century structure similar to a Greek temple, which sells charcuterie, cheese, maquis-flower honey, fish and homemade bread. For shops and restaurants, try the old quarter north of the square, with its well-kept houses and paved streets that descend to the seaside.

Outside the town is the popular but less urban Bodri beach, which can be reached by a dirt track.

L'Île Rousse is the starting point for excursions in the Balagne region; this area is home to the island's best artisans, whose products are exported all over the world. The region is also renowned

MEDITERRANEAN MAQUIS

Known in the Corsican language as *macchia*, maquis is one of the most luxuriant types of vegetation in southern Europe. Cork and holm oak trees, along with shrubs such as rosemary, juniper and myrtle, can be found in maquis ecosystems across the Balagne region, around L'Île Rousse. The maquis is spectacular when it blossoms in spring, flooding hills with white and pink rockrose flowers, yellow broom and strawberry fruit *(above)*. The flowers are used to produce essences, as well as the island's delightfully aromatic honey.

for its many idyllic villages, surrounded by olive groves. Monticello, overlooked by the 13th-century Castel d'Ortica, is a popular attraction. Further inland, the road climbs up to Santa Reparata di Balagna. Here, the 11th-century church of Santa Reparata offers a great view from its terrace.

***

Algajola

C2 **15 km (9 miles) NE of Calvi** **Place de la Gare; 04 95 62 78 32**

Fringed by a beach of golden sand, Algajola is a great base for watersports, especially windsurfing. Founded by the Phoenicians, it later became a Roman army base and was then chosen by the Genoese because of its central position. Sacked repeatedly by the Saracens, Algajola enjoyed a period of splendour in the 1600s, when the bastions were built.

The church of St-Georges is Algajola's main highlight. It houses a 17th-century painting of the Deposition attributed to the Italian artist Guercino. The church is only open for religious services.

Monumental Genoese battlements standing guard over Algajola ↓

INSIDER TIP
Mingle at Le GR20

Walking the GR20? Start or finish at Calenzana's aptly named Le GR20 (le-gr-20-restaurant-calen zana.fr), a bar, restaurant and watering hole for intrepid hikers on Europe's toughest trek.

21

Calenzana

C2 13 km (9 miles) SE of Calvi

Olive oil, wine and honey are still the mainstays of the economy of this town, one of the liveliest in the Balagne region. It is also the starting point of the GR20 long-distance path (p61).

The Baroque collegiate church of St-Blaise, designed by the Milanese architect Domenico Baïna, was built in the late 17th century. The ceiling over the nave has an 18th-century fresco, St Biagio Healing a Child. At the foot of the campanile, a plaque commemorates the battle of Calenzana, fought on 14 January 1732 between Corsican nationalists and the Genoese Republic, in

 Statue of the martyred patron saint in Ste-Restitude, Calenzana

↑ Historic hilltop town of Lama, nestled in Corsica's breathtaking Balagne region

which more than 700 German mercenaries lost their lives.

About 1 km (half a mile) away is Ste-Restitude, a 12th-century church built over a Roman necropolis. It is dedicated to a martyr killed in Calvi in the 3rd century and venerated in the entire region. Her story is told in two 14th-century frescoes, and her sarcophagus is in the crypt.

A short way along the D151 is Montemaggiore. This village, built on a promontory, has a lovely Baroque church and views of the Golfe de Calvi.

22

Lama

D2 50 km (31 miles) E of Calvi

The scenic T30 road winds past the hills halfway between L'Île Rousse and St-Florent towards a number of perched villages, the best known of which is Lama. Here, arcaded houses are built into the rocks and vaulted passageways open into a central square, home to the 16th-century church of San Lorenzu (also known as Notre-Dame-de-la-Visitation).

Lama was once one of the largest producers of olive oil in Corsica but a devastating

fire in 1971 destroyed the village's 350,000 olive trees and all the presses along the valley, causing production to cease. Today, visitors are attracted by the amazing views and easy access to hiking trails up Monte Astu.

Every summer, the village hosts a week-long film festival (festilama.org). Launched in 1994 with a few open-air shows, it has grown over the decades and now presents more than 20 feature-length films, including shorts and documentaries, as well as workshops and cinema-themed activities.

23

Aregno

D2 20 km (12 miles) E of Calvi Town Hall; 04 95 61 70 34

The village of Aregno, surrounded by olive and citrus-fruit trees, should be visited for its two churches: the Baroque parish church of St-Antoine and the Pisan Romanesque church of the

 →
Cycling past scenic Speloncato on the Col de Battaglia

Trinité et San Giovanni. Built in 1177 of green, white and pink granite, the latter has a façade with four blind arches over the portal. It also has a pediment decorated with small arches, in the centre of which is a statue of a man holding his foot while pulling a thorn from it – an allegory for the knowledge of man. The chapel interior features two grand 15th-century frescoes: *St Michael and the Dragon* and *The Four Doctors of the Church*. The interior of the church is only open in July and August; if you're visiting during the rest of the year, ask for the keys at the Town Hall.

 24

Speloncato

A D2 **A** 33 km (20 miles) E of Calvi **i** Town Hall; 04 95 61 59 00

Perched on a spur of Monte Tolo, the small village of Speloncato offers wonderful views of the surrounding

Balagne region. It is named after the *spelunche*, the caves in the vicinity, which include the 8-m- (25-ft-) long Pietra Tafonata. Supposedly, twice a year, on 8 April and 8 September, the setting sun is visible through the tunnel, briefly illuminating the village square with the Baroque church of San Michele.

 25

Sant'Antonino

A D2 **A** 21 km (13 miles) E of Calvi **w** santantonino.fr

An eagle's nest located 447 m (1,467 ft) above sea level, this hamlet overlooks the Regino and Tighiella river valleys. Its unique position affords a magnificent view, from the snow-capped mountains to the sea. Sant'Antonino is laid out in a circle and was one of the fiefdoms of the Savelli family. It was an impregnable fortress that took in the entire valley population when Saracen

pirate ships appeared on the horizon. Today this hamlet still retains its medieval character. The alleys, which are for pedestrians only, are lined with steps and passageways. The dark-granite houses have been restored and now contain shops selling locally made handicrafts.

About 10 km (6 miles) along the D663 road is the village of Feliceto, which has a Baroque church and a mill producing olive oil.

In the opposite direction is the Giussani region, with the villages of Pioggiola and Olmi-Cappella, linked by a number of footpaths. The latter is known for its olive oil.

SHOP

Biscuiterie Artisanale Salvatore
This famous biscuit factory is known for its *canistrelli* biscuits, prepared in a variety of flavours including walnut, lemon and chestnut.

A D2 **A** Place du Canon, L'Île Rousse **C** 04 95 60 01 49

Clos Antonini
This unique shop and bar sells a variety of juices, jams and other produce, with many products made from local lemons.

A D2 **A** Sant'Antonino **C** 04 95 61 76 83

U San Petrone
Corsica's charcuterie delights, including cured meats wrapped in webbing and thick, aged sausages, are sold at this characterful store.

A D2 **A** Place du Canon, L'Île Rousse **C** 04 95 60 01 49

A DRIVING TOUR
STRADA DI L'ARTIGIANI

Length 50 km (30 miles) **Journey Time** 1 day **Stopping-off points** Calenzana, Lumio, Corbara, Pigna, Feliceto, Occhiatana **Terrain** Winding hills; some roads may be steep and have sharp turns

The "Artisans' Road" is a route that leads past some of the finest craft workshops in Balagne, the fertile region behind Calvi and L'Île Rousse. These shops are located in villages perched on hilltops – each one is a popular tourist attraction thanks to fine artisanal wares. The region's olive groves, producing extra-virgin olive oil, are also a big draw. The main centre is Pigna, home to Casa Musicale, an organization dedicated to preserving the island's rich cultural heritage. Road signs indicate different ways to reach Calenzana, Corbara, Santa Reparata, Pigna, Lumio, Feliceto, Monticello, Occiglioni, Lozari, Palasca, Olmi-Capella, Cateri and Occhiatana, all with beautiful architecture and panoramic views.

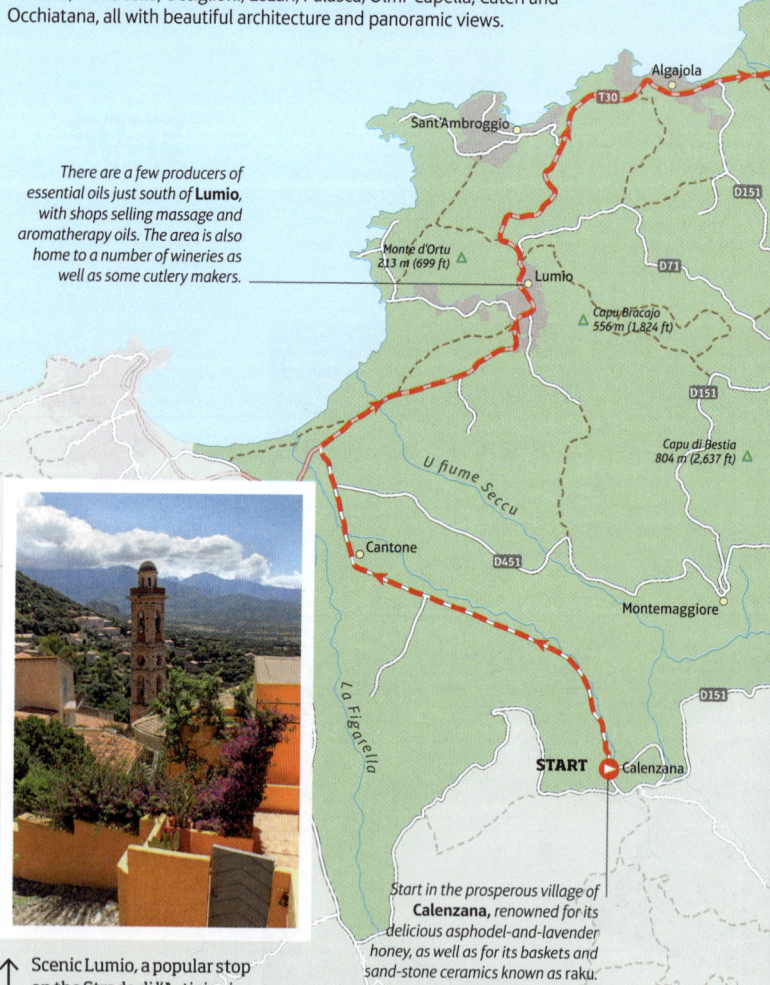

*There are a few producers of essential oils just south of **Lumio**, with shops selling massage and aromatherapy oils. The area is also home to a number of wineries as well as some cutlery makers.*

Algajola

Sant'Ambroggio

T30

D151

Monte d'Ortu
213 m (699 ft) △

Lumio

D71

Capu Brocaju
556 m (1,824 ft) △

D151

Capu di Bestia
804 m (2,637 ft) △

U fiume Seccu

Cantone

D451

Montemaggiore

La Figarella

D151

START ● Calenzana

*Start in the prosperous village of **Calenzana**, renowned for its delicious asphodel-and-lavender honey, as well as for its baskets and sand-stone ceramics known as raku.*

↑ Scenic Lumio, a popular stop on the Strada di l'Artigiani

For those interested in artistic pottery, original tableware and crockery in general, visiting **Corbara** is a must. Here, the craftspeople work mainly with sandstone, a versatile, robust and easily available material.

BASTIA AND NORTH

Strada di l'Artigiani

Locator Map

Musical instruments, music boxes and pottery, along with natural products such as wine, honey, cheese and olive oil can be found in **Pigna**, the region's leading handicraft centre.

The crafts produced in **Occhiatana** include vases, lamps, candlesticks, and other objects and souvenirs of Corsican culture.

L'Île-Rousse

Corbara

Monticello

Santa-Reparata-di-Balagna

Pigna

Lac de Codole

D113

Aregno

Fiume di Regino

D71

Occhiatana

FINISH

Ville-di-Paraso

Avapessa

D71

Nessa

Muro

Feliceto

Zilia

Feliceto is known for blown-glass objects, handmade by two local artisans. The village also has two wineries.

0 kilometres 2

0 miles 2

N

Painting a horse-shaped music box in the Scatt'a Musica workshop in Pigna

A LONG WALK
ALONG CAP CORSE

Distance 26 km (16 miles) **Walking Time** 7 hours, 45 minutes
Terrain Route varies through grassy meadows, steep cliffs, rocky paths and dense maquis **Nearest bus** Macinaggio

Known locally as the "Sentier des Douaniers" (meaning "path of customs officers"), the trail running along the tip of the Cap Corse was once used by customs officers to control smuggling activities. There's now a coastal footpath here, in places offering stunning views. Similar paths run along the entire perimeter of Corsica, but the Sentier des Douaniers, going from Macinaggio to Centuri – among the junipers, mastics and asphodels, and beaches and craggy cliffs – is simply breathtaking. On the way, you'll also discover old lime kilns, windmills and small chapels. This tour can be divided into three stages: Macinaggio–Barcaggio (three hours), Barcaggio–Tollare (45 minutes) and Tollare–Centuri (four hours). It is not particularly difficult and is open all year round, but watch out for bush fires, especially in summer. Drivers can reach the separate sights via inland paved roads.

Tollare, *a tiny port dominated by a Genoese tower, is another stage in the tour that can be accessed by car, from the D153 road.*

Capo Grosso

△ Monte Maggiore
359 m (1,178 ft)

Tollare

D153

Monte Sant'Antuninu
302 m (990 ft)

Poggio

D253

There is a great viewpoint at **Capo Grosso**. *From here, a road leads to the Moulin Mattei.*

Gualdo

Granaggiolo

Those who decide to hike this far along the Cap Corse peninsula will have a challenging but interesting day. At **Centuri**, *delicious seafood makes for an excellent reward.*

☐ Centuri
FINISH

Orche

Monte delle Castelle
603 m (1,978 ft) △

← Boats moored in picturesque Centuri, the last stop on the Cap Corse trail

Locator Map

Sentier des Douaniers

BASTIA AND NORTH

Past the Punta d'Agnello tower and promontory – one of the most panoramic spots in Cap Corse – is the idyllic port town of **Barcaggio**. This is the first stage of the tour that is directly accessible by car, from the D253. The water in the bay, lined by a small beach, is crystal clear.

↑ Taking in the view from the Genoese tower at Punta d'Agnello

Further along the path is the **Chapelle de Santa Maria**, built in the 12th century over an early Christian church. The ruins of a Genoese tower can be found nearby, on the coast along the Santa Maria bay.

The tour begins at **Macinaggio** and leads to the beautiful beach of Tamarone. Just off the beach are the craggy rocks of the Îles Finocchiarola, a nature reserve inhabited by colonies of marine birds.

Barcaggio

Tour Génoise d'Agnello

Cima di a Campana 187 m (614 ft)

L'Acqua Tignese

D253

Acqua Tignese

Chapelle de Santa Maria

D80

Macinaggio
START

Tomino

0 kilometres 1

0 miles 1

N

AJACCIO AND THE WEST COAST

The rugged and undulating west coast of Corsica, home to the gulfs of Porto, Sagone and Ajaccio, is defined by its wild marine landscapes. The red-tinted cliffs make this stretch of coast less accessible to habitation than the land to the east, and there are few signs of prehistoric settlement.

A small town to the north of present-day Ajaccio was established during the Roman Imperial Age, though little is known of its size or origin. After the Genoese took control in the 15th century, they built Ajaccio's grand citadelle and the settlement existed in relative peace for the next two centuries. Even after Pasquale Paoli drove the Genoese from much of the island before declaring the short-lived Corsican Republic in 1755, Ajaccio remained one of the last Genoese strongholds.

The French took control of Corsica in 1768, choosing Ajaccio as the island's capital and instituting a wave of infrastructural development. Just a year later, Napoleon Bonaparte was born in the city. Ajaccio continued to prosper throughout the 19th century, becoming a popular destination for members of the European high society.

Today, the city is Corsica's largest, with modern streets abutting the Genoese citadelle. Beyond the city, the west coast is among Corsica's most favoured destination for outdoor adventures, home to the Scandola Nature Reserve and an array of golden beaches.

AJACCIO AND THE WEST COAST

Must Sees

1 Ajaccio
2 Réserve Naturelle de Scandola

Experience More

3 Îles Sanguinaires
4 Route des Sanguinaires
5 Porticcio
6 Pointe de la Parata
7 Gorges du Prunelli
8 Vallée de la Gravona
9 Tiuccia
10 Forêt de Chiavari
11 Piana
12 Sagone
13 Cargèse
14 Porto
15 Gorges de Spelunca
16 Girolata
17 Galéria
18 Forêt d'Aïtone

Capù di a Conca
725 m (2,379 ft)
D81b
Truccia
Argentella
Punta Ciuttone
Golfe de
Galéria
D81
17 GALÉRIA
Tuarelli
Punta
Piazzo
Île de
Gargali
Forêt
de Fango
Girolata
2 16 GIROLATA
RÉSERVE
NATURELLE
DE SCANDOLA
Cala di
Tuara
The Corniche
D81
Partinello
Plage de Gradelle
Golfe de
Porto
Genoese
Watchtower
Plage de
Bussaglia
14 PORTO
D84
Calanches de Piana
Capo
Rosso
PIANA 11
Capo d'Orto
1,294 m (4,245 ft)
Spelunca
Gorge
Plage d'Arone
D81
Revinda
Sagone
Plage de Chiuni
Lozzi
Plage de Pero
13
CARGÈSE
D70
Coggia
SAGONE 12
Mediterranean
Sea
TIUCCIA
Golfe de
Sagone
9
Torra d'Ancone
Ancône
Lava
Golfe de
Lava
Alata
Capo di Feno
Punta di Pozzo
di Borgo
Les Milelli
Pisinale
AJACCIO 1
POINTE DE
LA PARATA
D111
6
ROUTE DES
SANGUINAIRES
Chemin
des Crêtes
ÎLES
SANGUINAIRES 3
Golfe
d'Ajaccio
Plage de Verghia

BASTIA AND
THE NORTH
p72

S. Parteo
1,680 m (5,512 ft)

Mte Grosso
1,937 m (6,355 ft)

Cima di Modico
1,231 m (4,039 ft)

AJACCIO
AND THE
WEST COAST

D51

Capo di Vegno
1,389 m (4,557 ft)

D251

Monte Corona
2,144 m (7,034 ft)

Asco

Punta Muvrella
2,148 m (7,047 ft)

Haut-Asco

HAUTE-CORSE

Balagne

Taïta

Punta Minuta
2,556 m (8,386 ft)

Manso

Golo

Rusio

D147

Sovéria

Sermano

Paglia Orba
2,525 m (8,284 ft)

Calasima

D84

Casamaccioli

Corte

Lonca

Fango

Casanova

D14

Vallée d'Alesani

T50

D84 **18** FORÊT
D'AÏTONE

Gorges du Tavignano

15 GORGES
DESPELUNCA

Capo Chiostro
2,295 m (7,530 ft)

Marignana

T20

Sagone

Renno

Lac de Creno

D43

Letia

Soccia

CORTE AND
THE INTERIOR
p150

Balogna

D23

Murzo

Guagno

Pietroso

Vico

Forêt de Liblo

Arbori

Pastricciola

Vizzavona

Rosazia

Rezza

Ghisoni

Liamone

Arro

Liamone

Ambiegna

CORSE-DU-SUD

HAUTE-CORSE

D1

Sarl-d'Orcino

T20

Bocognano

D69

Ajola

VALLÉE DE LA GRAVONA

Tavera

L'Iscia

A Cupulatta

Valle-di-
Mezzana

8

Carbuccia

D27

Bastelica

San-Gavino-
di-Fiumorbo

Appietto

T20

Peri

Val d'Ese

Le Prunelli

CORSE-DU-SUD

Tolla

Palneca

Chisa

7

GORGES DU PRUNELLI

GR20

Bastelicaccia

D3

Tasso

Ajaccio Napoleon
Bonaparte Airport

D27

Cauro

Cozzano

Zicavo

Ruisseau de Chiova

D55

Sainte
Marie-Siche

Monte Malo
1,849 m (6,066 ft)

5 PORTICCIO

T40

D83

BONIFACIO AND
THE SOUTH
p128

D302

D2

Agnarello

D55

10 FORÊT DE
CHIAVARI

Guargualé

❶

AJACCIO

🏛 C5 ✈ Ajaccio Napoleon Bonaparte, 7 km (4 miles) E 🚉 Place de la Gare 🚌 🚢 From Porto Torres, Marseille, Nice, Toulon 🛈 3 Boulevard du Roi Jérôme; ajaccio-tourisme.com

The largest city in Corsica, as well as the island's political centre, Ajaccio is best known as the birthplace of Napoleon. It is divided into three sectors: the old Genoese town, with its narrow streets and houses with pastel-coloured façades; the modern city, with tree-lined avenues and outdoor cafés; and the outskirts, which extend up to the hills and offer a marvellous view of the gulf, dominated by the Citadelle.

AJACCIO'S HISTORY

A Roman settlement during the Imperial Age, Ajaccio was annexed by the Genoese in 1492. In 1553, it was invaded by soldier Sampiero Corso for the French but was returned to the Genoese as part of the Cateau-Cambresis treaty (1559). Under Genoa, Ajaccio prospered, thanks to agriculture and coral fishing. By 1723, the city had become the capital of West Corsica and it expanded rapidly under French rule.

①
Citadelle

The construction of Ajaccio's Citadelle, on a rocky spur jutting over the sea, began in 1554 by order of the French Marshal de Thermes, and was completed by the Genoese in 1559. A long-time military zone, the Citadelle is now managed by the city of Ajaccio, which opened it to the public in 2021. The structure faces the innermost part of the gulf and overlooks the Jetée de la Citadelle, a jetty that encloses the Tino Rossi harbour. Its sentry walkways, walls and ramparts still tower over the town's old quarter.

Visitors can walk along the ramparts – here you'll find a café, a viewing station, a for-mer gunpowder room (which hosts art exhibitions), as well as workshops and boutiques in the former casements.

②
Ajaccio Cathedral

🏛 Rue Forcioli-Conti 📞 04 95 21 07 67 🕐 8-11:30am & 2:30-5:45pm Mon-Sat

Dedicated to the Virgin Mary, the cathedral of Ajaccio was built in 1582–93 by Giacomo della Porta in the Venetian Renaissance style, but also has a few Baroque elements.

↑ Striking ochre façade of the city's Cathedral

↑ The town and marina of Ajaccio, Corsica's capital city

The simple façade contrasts with the lavish interior, which features polychrome marble and gilded decoration.

In July 1771, when he was almost two, Napoleon was baptized at the font. According to legend, he remained closely attached to the church and his dying wish was to be buried here; engraved on a marble plaque at the entrance is the following quote from Napoleon: "If they forbid my corpse… a small piece of land in which to be laid, I desire to be buried with my ancestors in Ajaccio cathedral in Corsica". Although Napoleon's remains were interred at the Hôtel des Invalides in Paris, the cathedral briefly served as the Bonaparte family's funeral chapel, before the Chapelle Impériale (p113) was built.

Upon entering, the chapel on the left has a painting by Eugène Delacroix, the *Madonna of the Sacred Heart*. The next chapel, dedicated to Our Lady of Mercy, Ajaccio's patron saint, contains an 18th-century statue of the Virgin Mary.

The high altar, made of white marble with black tortile columns, was donated in 1811 by Elisa Bacciochi, Napoleon's sister and princess of Lucca and Piombino.

③
St-Erasme

 Rue Forcioli-Conti

Founded in 1617 as the chapel of the Jesuit College, St-Erasme later became the chapel of the Royal College. During the French Revolution, the church was closed to the public and turned into a city office. In 1815, it was reconsecrated and dedicated to the sailors' patron saint, Erasmus. Inside, in the true spirit of this maritime chapel, are model ships as well as religious paintings with boats and crafts. There are also three processional crosses and a statue of St Erasmus with angels.

Every year on 2 June, as part of the celebrations for the Feast of St Erasmus, the statue of the saint is carried in a procession down to the seaside. Special mass and prayers are also held at the church.

___

④
Rue Bonaparte

This thoroughfare was the old *carrugio dritto* (straight alley)

 HIDDEN GEM
A Cupulatta

The A Cupulatta tortoise sanctuary *(acupulatta.com)*, just outside the city, has more than 170 species of tortoise and turtle roaming around its huge park. You'll find some giant Galapagos tortoises and the rare snake-necked tortoise.

of the Genoese city, inhabited by merchants and leading citizens. During Genoese rule, Rue Bonaparte divided Ajaccio into two areas: to the north was the Macello, where the poorer working classes lived, and to the south was the larger area occupied by the affluent upper middle classes.

Today, Rue Bonaparte is a pleasant, lively street with unusual antique shops, terraced restaurants, buzzy cafés and a small number of boutiques, including a well-stocked bookshop.

Admiring a portrait of Napoleon in the Maison Bonaparte Museum

⑤ Maison Bonaparte Museum

🅰 Rue St-Charles ⏰ Hours vary, check website 🚫 1 Jan, 25 Dec 🌐 musees-nation aux.malmaison.fr/musee-maisonbonaparte

Built in 1682, this simple villa belonged to the Bonaparte family and is where Napoleon was born on 15 August 1769.

It features an austere façade overlooking the tree-lined Place Letizia, where there is a bust of the emperor's son.

In 1793, Napoleon and his family were forced to flee the house (through a trap door) by supporters of Pascal Paoli (p58), who were seeking revenge because Napoleon, then an officer in the French army, had ordered his troops to fire at a local rally. The house was then impounded by the British (1794–6) and partly used as an arsenal.

In 1797, Napoleon's mother, Letizia, returned to Ajaccio and obtained compensation to refurbish the house. A spacious gallery was built, and the rooms were furnished with chests of drawers from Milan and chairs from Marseilles. Soon after, Napoleon returned here briefly in October 1799 – this was his last visit to his ancestral home.

Maison Bonaparte is now a state-managed museum illustrating the turbulent history of the Bonaparte family. Visitors can explore the rooms used by the family, including the one where Napoleon was born. The second floor features detailed exhibits on life in 18th-century Corsica, and the cellar houses a photography exhibition. Temporary exhibitions are held in an extension to the museum, added in 2004.

A modern-day restoration has revealed Second Empire artworks hidden under layers of wallpaper.

⑥ Salon Napoléonien

🅰 Town Hall (Hôtel de Ville), Place Foch 📞 04 95 51 52 53 ⏰ 9–11:45am & 2–5:45pm Mon–Fri (mid-Sep–mid-Jun: to 4:45pm) 🚫 Mid-Jun–mid-Sep: Mon am, public hols

Housed on the first floor of Ajaccio's town hall, the rooms of the Napoleonic Museum are accessed via a grand staircase. The museum was built between 1824 and 1830, and displays documents, paintings and other memorabilia relating to the life of Napoleon and his family.

In the Grand Salon, under the large Bohemian crystal chandelier donated for the 200th anniversary of the birth of Napoleon, there are fine portraits of the family and several busts, including one of Napoleon's mother, Letizia. A painting by Domenico Frassati celebrates the *Glory of the Emperor* (1840). The portraits of Napoleon III and the empress Eugénie by German artist Franz Winterhalter are also remarkable.

Other interesting items are Napoleon's baptism certificate and a replica of his bronze death mask. The Hall of Medals features a large collection of coins and gold, silver and bronze medals.

⑦ Marina

At the foot of the Citadelle, a long breakwater protects this harbour from the west wind. Next to the passenger terminal of the port, where the large ferries land, are the yacht harbour and the fishers' port, lined with many brightly coloured boats filled with fishing nets. This quay is also the departure point for boats and cruises taking visitors on excursions to the nearby Îles Sanguinaires, the Golfe de Porto and Porticcio.

> **MISS THOMASINA CAMPBELL**
>
> Ajaccio, like the Côte d'Azur, was frequented by English and German holidaymakers and saw the development of an entire district dedicated to tourism. Among visitors to Ajaccio were the English artists Edward Lear and William Cowen, and wealthy Scottish national Thomasina Campbell. Her writings, including the *Notes Sur l'Île de Corse* (*Notes on the Island of Corsica*, 1868), explored the island's rich history and landscape, and popularized Corsica in the English imagination.

⑧

Place Foch

The true heart of Ajaccio, this pretty square was built at the beginning of the 19th century. Formerly called Piazza Porta, it used to be the only gate to the Citadelle. It features a marble statue of Napoleon as First Consul, in the middle of the Four Lions Fountain, which was sculpted by Jérôme Maglioli, a well-known Ajaccio-born artist.

Today Place Foch is lined with lovely cafés, with tables outside in the shade of the palm and plane trees. Every morning from 7am, in the open space in front of the square, there is a lively market offering the day's fresh catch and other local produce.

⑨

Boulevard du Roi Jérôme

Lined with hotels and restaurants, this boulevard is a favourite with locals, who gather here to have a *pastis* or play a game of *pétanque*. Every morning, the area behind the town hall facing the sea becomes a colourful open market offering typical Corsican products: *brocciu* cheese, *lonzu* (smoked fillet of pork), *coppa* (pork neck), *prizuttu* (cured ham), pâtés, honey, fig jam and myrtle liqueur. Vegetables and flowers also fill the market with their scents and colours. The hubbub and gaiety define the adjacent streets, as well as the pedestrianized Rue Cardinal Fesch. Once the main thoroughfare in the Genoese quarter, Rue Cardinal Fesch developed outside the city walls from the 16th century onwards. Halfway down this street is the famous Palais Fesch built by Cardinal Fesch, one of Napoleon's uncles, in 1827–37. It is now a museum containing part of his huge fine art collection.

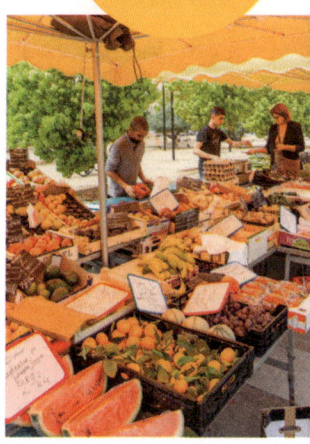

↑ Fruit stalls with fresh produce at Boulevard du Roi Jérôme

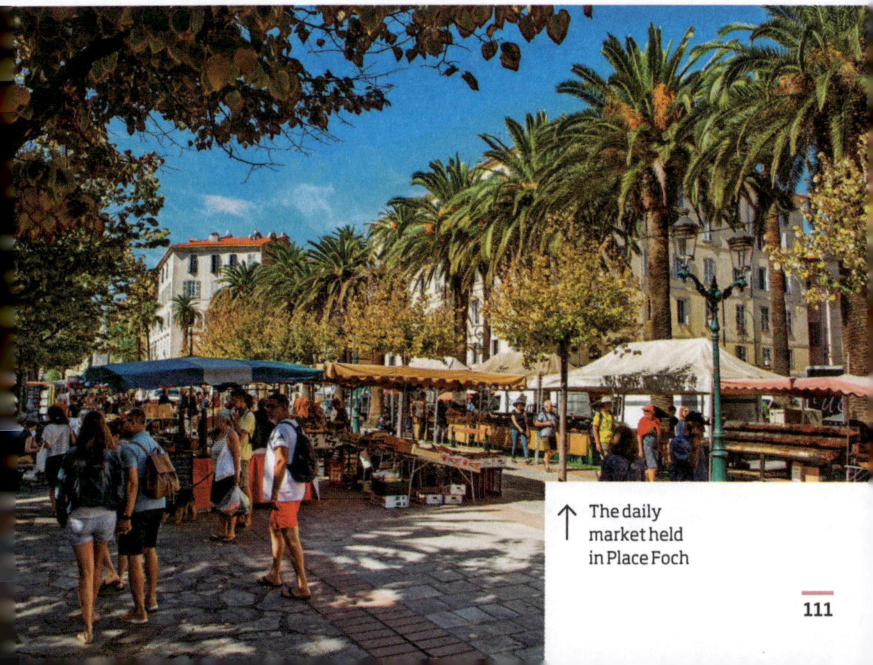

↑ The daily market held in Place Foch

→

Neo-Classical Palais Lantivy and its garden, Cours Napoléon

 ⑩

Musée Marc Petit-Lazaret Ollandini

🏠 Route d'Aspretto
🕐 9am-3pm Mon-Thu (summer: also Sat pm)
🌐 lelazaret-ollandini.fr

Built in the mid-1800s, the Lazaret originally served as the quarantine for the port of Ajaccio. It was classified as a national historic monument in 1977, and opened to the public as a museum in 2008. The museum houses 32 large sculptures by the renowned French sculptor Marc Petit in its permanent collection, as well as other drawings and sculptural works. The building is also a performance venue and hosts cultural events throughout the year.

 ⑪

Place d'Austerlitz

At the western end of Place Foch begins Cours Gandval, a street running parallel to the sea in the direction of the Pointe de la Parata (p119). Cours Grandval ultimately leads to Place d'Austerlitz, a square dominated by an imposing structure, known as U Casone, which features a statue of Napoleon. Preceded by two eagles and a stone that commemorates his victories, this historic monument represents the emperor in a riding coat and wearing his famous two-cornered

 ←

One of the stone eagles of U Casone in Place d'Austerlitz

1769

hat as he looks towards Ajaccio, his native town.

To the left of U Casone is the cave where, according to a local legend, Napoleon pretended he was an emperor when he was a child. Every year, around 15 August, his birthday, Ajaccio commemorates Napoleon's imperial period with impressive parades in period costumes during the lively Journées Napoléoniennes (p51).

 ⑫

Cours Napoléon

The main street in Ajaccio, Cours Napoléon crosses the city from northeast to southwest. It is intersected by many smaller streets that go down to the sea or up to the hills. The thoroughfare is lined with cinemas, shops, banks and cafés, including the famous Café Napoléon, built in 1821. Cours Napoléon is also a great place for leisurely walks, with plenty of seating areas along the seafront. Towards the railway station, the street becomes wider, forming Place Abbatucci, which was once the border between the old town and the countryside.

About halfway down Cours Napoléon is the Chapelle de St-Roch, built in the late 1800s, while towards the southern end of the street is the Palais Lantivy, now home to the prefecture and the General Council. The street ends at Place de Gaulle, a large square with a statue of Napoleon in the guise of a Roman emperor on horseback, surrounded by his four brothers.

 ⑬

Bibliothèque Patrimoniale

🏠 50 Rue Cardinal Fesch
🕐 10am-noon & 2-7pm Tue-Fri, 2-6pm Sat 🌐 biblio theque.ajaccio.fr

The brainchild of Napoleon's younger brother Lucien Bonaparte, this listed library and monument was founded in 1801 and inaugurated in the Palais Fesch in 1868. Alongside its stunning 30-m- (98-ft-) long and 10-m- (32-ft-) high reading room, the library contains more than 40,000 volumes, including 29 incunabula, as well as rare historical,

 INSIDER TIP
City Sands

Cours Napoléon runs down to St-Francois beach, a sandy expanse lapped by calm tides that is perfect for swimming. Close to Ajaccio's centre, the beach is best enjoyed as the sun sets.

medical and theological books. The oldest manuscript is a didactic poem from the Norman poet Gace de la Bigne, dating from c 1379.

The library is currently undergoing a conservation project, which aims to protect more than 18,000 ancient books. Some 100,000 pages of its oldest collections are now digitally available, enabling members of the public to enjoy them without damaging the precious texts.

THE CORSICAN VENDETTA

Vendettas - blood feuds between families - have been a part of Corsican life since Roman times, and a feature of close-knit communities in Ajaccio, where resources have long been scarce. The vendetta could spring from something of seemingly little importance like the disputed ownership of a tree or even a donkey chewing up a neighbour's garden. The brutal acts of vengeance that followed could last for generations and implicate every member of the family. These dramatic feuds inspired many 19th-century writings such as Honoré de Balzac's *La Vendetta* (1830) and Alexandre Dumas's *Les Frères Corses* (1840). Though the last vendetta killing was in 1954, family honour remains a big part of Corsican life.

---

⑭

Chapelle Impériale

🏠 50 Rue du Cardinal Fesch
☎ 04 95 26 26 26 🕒 Hours vary, call ahead

In 1857, Emperor Napoleon III had Cardinal Fesch's palace restored by the French architects Casanova, Paccard and Corona; the project was completed in 1860. Napoleon III decided to use the right-hand wing as a chapel to house the remains of nine members of the Bonaparte family. This included Napoleon I's parents Carlo Bonaparte and Letizia Ramolino (Napoleon's tomb is in Hôtel des Invalides, Paris), and Cardinal Fesch himself.

The sober Renaissance exterior is made of light limestone from St-Florent. Inside, the trompe-l'oeil dome was painted by the Ajaccio-born architect Jérôme Maglioli, and is decorated with the cardinal's insignias, which are also on the stained-glass windows. On the high altar is a gold crucifix that Napoleon gave to his mother when he returned from his campaign in Egypt. The remains of the nine family members are all in the round crypt under the dome.

⑮

Domaine des Milelli

🏠 20090 Ajaccio

Covering an area of 12 ha (30 acres), the Domaine des Milelli comprises a 100-year-old olive grove and the Bonaparte family's former country home. Napoleon spent the last night of his 1799 visit to Ajaccio here.

The house is closed to visitors but the grounds are accessible and make an excellent picnic spot. There's also a small arboretum for children and a vegetable garden.

↑ Intricately carved trompe-l'oeil dome of the Chapelle Impériale

PALAIS FESCH – MUSÉE DES BEAUX-ARTS

🏠 50–52 Rue du Cardinal Fesch ⏰ 9.15am–5.45 pm; May–Sep: Wed–Mon; Oct–Apr: Mon, Wed–Sat; 3rd Sun of month 🚫 Public hols 🌐 muséefesch.com

Housed in a superb 19th-century palace, Ajaccio's art museum holds the largest French collection of Italian paintings outside the Louvre. An array of European masterpieces sit within the permanent collection, with temporary exhibitions showcasing the varied wonders of centuries of European art.

Cardinal Fesch, Napoleon's uncle, had this palace built between 1827 and 1860. He dedicated three wings to housing works of art, which were donated to the city when he died in 1839. The main building has a vast collection of some of the finest French and Italian paintings, as well as works by Spanish, Flemish and Dutch artists. The second floor contains 13th–17th-century Italian paintings, including many depictions of the Virgin Mary and Child and a collection of still lifes. On the first floor are works dating from the 17th and 18th centuries. The ground floor is given over to Napoleon, with statues and paintings, as well as temporary exhibitions. The basement contains modern Corsican art. The left wing houses the City Library, founded by Napoleon's brother Lucien.

Browsing portraits and memorabilia at the Musée des Beaux-Arts ↑

The palace's main entrance, featuring a monument to Cardinal Fesch

Museum Highlights

Jesus and the Samaritan Woman

▷ Created by Étienne Parrocel, an 18th-century French artist, this evocative painting depicts an episode from the Gospel of John where Jesus converses with a Samaritan woman.

Landscapes by Matthijs Bril

Matthijs Bril, a late 16th-century Flemish painter, made surprising and refreshing use of cool colours highlighted by brilliant ochre hues. His works helped to revolutionize landscape painting.

Virgin Mary and Child with Angel

▷ This early masterpiece by the Italian artist Sandro Botticelli (1445-1510) is one of the loveliest works in the museum. It is innovative from an iconographic point of view because the Virgin is standing, and also because of her open display of affection.

The Departure of Rebecca

Francesco Solimena (1657-1747) was one of the most prolific figures of the Baroque period, and his strength lay in the creation of dramatic biblical scenes. This painting depicts Rebecca leaving for her marriage to Isaac, the son of Abraham.

Portrait of a Man with a Glove

◁ This work by legendary Venetian artist Titian (c 1485-1576), depicting an unknown Venetian aristocrat, is the twin of a portrait kept in the Louvre, Paris. Here, Titian limits the colours he uses and darkens the background, drawing attention to the hands and expressions of the subject to create a vivid sense of life and personality.

CARDINAL FESCH

Joseph Fesch (1763-1839) was Napoleon's uncle, but he was only six years older than the emperor. In 1803, he became a cardinal and moved to Rome, where he collected 16,000 works of art; some of these are on display in the museum. It was due to his diplomatic intervention that Pope Pius VII crowned Napoleon emperor. In 1811, Fesch fell into disgrace for siding with the Church against Napoleon.

Réserve Naturelle de Scandola's jagged red cliffs and needles ↑

②

RÉSERVE NATURELLE DE SCANDOLA

⚠ B3 🚢 From Ajaccio, Calvi, Cargèse, Galéria, Porto, Propriano, Sagone (Jul–Aug: six excursions a day; Apr–Jun, Sep & Oct: four excursions a day) 🛈 Quartier La Marine, Porto; 04 95 26 10 55

As you approach the Cape Girolata peninsula by boat, unusual rock formations emerge from the crystal-clear sea and jagged inlets and echoing caves dot the coastline in the distance. This is the Scandola Nature Reserve, part of a UNESCO World Heritage Site and one of Corsica's most distinctive wild landscapes.

Red granite cliffs plunge into the sea at the Scandola Nature Reserve while cormorants perch on the rocks and falcons circle in the sky. Under the water's surface, encrusted with thick (but fragile) algae platforms, is a blaze of colours created by sponges, anemones and corals.

Along with the Calanques de Piana and the Golfe de Girolata, the reserve forms the Golfe de Porto, a UNESCO World Heritage Site. It protects 9.2 sq km (3.5 sq miles) of volcanic land (dating back to the Upper Permian era, some 248 million years ago) and 10 sq km (4 sq miles) of sea between Punta Mucchilina to the south and Punta Palazzo to the north.

The only way into the reserve is by boat, with many providers in Calvi and Porto offering full day excursions, with options to explore the caves and inlets of this remarkable stretch of coast. Visitors also opt to stay at the rugged and remote village of Girolata.

TOP 5 WILDLIFE AT THE RESERVE

Cormorant
These large sea birds make acrobatic manoeuvres above the water.

Osprey
The osprey population here has grown after conservation efforts.

Peregrine
These falcons nest in the taller cliffs.

Grouper
Up to 1.5 m (5 ft) long, these brown fish have distinct spots.

Sea Bream
Sea bream are overfished across the Mediterranean, but the ban on fishing at the reserve means they thrive here.

1

2

1 Ospreys build fragile nests on the reserve's steep cliffs. Eggs are laid during breeding season (January through May).

2 The village of Girolata is located to the south of the reserve. It has good facilities for tourists and is a great base for exploring the area.

3 Dusky grouper, a vulnerable species, roam the reserve's waters in large numbers.

3

EXPERIENCE MORE

❸

Îles Sanguinaires

 B5 12 km (7 miles) W of Ajaccio 🚌 From Ajaccio

The red rock seems to have been the reason behind the name ("sanguinary") of the maquis-covered cliffs that emerge from the sea a short distance from the Pointe de la Parata. However, because the islands mark the southern border of the Golfe de Sagone, some people claim that the name derives from the Latin *Sagonares Insulae*, or Islands of the Gulf of Sagone.

The largest of the islands is the Grande Sanguinaire, also known as Mezzumare. There is a lighthouse, built in 1840, as well as the ruins of a Genoese tower and a leprosy hospital. In spring, this island is clad in white with the Montpellier rockrose in bloom. The Grande Sanguinaire is also home to cormorants, herring gulls and other birds.

In 1863, the French author Alphonse Daudet lived in the lighthouse. He described the Sanguinaires as wild islands populated by Corsican ponies, wild goats and an osprey.

The other three islands are very small; little more than cliffs emerging from the sea.

❹

Route des Sanguinaires

B5 C5 🚗 8 km (5 miles) W of Ajaccio

This panoramic road, the D111, runs along the northern shore of the Golfe d'Ajaccio, passing by the locals' favourite sandy beaches. There are also many cafés and restaurants with terraces from where it is possible to admire cormorants in flight and, with a bit of luck, see pods of dolphins playing.

The best way to enjoy this coastline is by journeying along it, which can done by car or bicycle, as well as by bus or the Petit Train (departure from Place Foch in Ajaccio, *p111*). The coastal route begins at Boulevard Lantivy and continues along Plage St-François, the most central beach in Ajaccio, at the foot of the walls of the Citadelle. It then proceeds along Boulevard Pascal Rossini, where every Sunday from 8am to noon there is a colourful flea market in front of the Fesch Lyceum. The road

---

WALKING THE CHEMIN DES CRÊTES

This stunning 8.7-km (5-mile) walk starts on the Sentier du Bois des Anglais on the northwest edge of Ajaccio and then zigzags up the hill, following signs for the Sentier des Crêtes, with great views of the Îles Sanguinaires and Ajaccio. The path passes through Corsican maquis and is lined by the Tête de Mort rock formation and Monte Salario to the north. The loop takes three hours for a seasoned walker but is also suitable for children and dogs (on leads).

continues through residential quarters, which offer a view of the gulf and are surrounded by Mediterranean gardens.

At the edge of Ajaccio's outer stretches, at Place Emmanuel-Arène, is the Chapelle des Grecs, a Greek Orthodox church built in 1632 and used by the Greek community that had fled from the Peloponnese seeking political asylum. Not far from the main road is a cemetery, with Neo-Classical and Baroque chapels.

Some 5 km (3 miles) further down, the road skirts the beaches of Scudo (with bathing facilities and restaurants), the beautiful Marinella cove, and Vignola beach. The latter also marks the end of the Chemin des Crêtes, a popular, easy-to-follow ridge path with a superb view of the gulf. Waymarked with spots of paint, it starts in the centre of Ajaccio, at Bois des Anglais, behind Place d'Austerlitz (p112), and takes about three hours. The No 5 bus travels back into town.

Dining at a laid-back shack on one of the scenic beaches in Porticcio

---

 5

Porticcio

⚠C5 🚗18 km (11 miles) SE of Ajaccio 🚌🚌From Ajaccio 🛈Les Echappes; 04 95 25 10 09

Just opposite Ajaccio, on the southern coastline of the gulf, is Porticcio. This resort is filled with hotels, residential complexes, and lovely beaches with fine sand and facilities for watersports, from sailing to diving.

The beach with the best facilities is La Viva, while the most spectacular are Agosta and Ruppione, separated by the Isolella peninsula. The Ruppione has coves with turquoise water.

 ←

Grande Sanguinaire's Genoese tower commanding views over the Îles Sanguinaires

On the headland is an old Genoese tower called Tour de l'Isolella. The headland can be reached by taking the D55 road, past the Port de Chiavari and the little Portigliolo cove. From here are fine views of the Golfe d'Ajaccio and of Île Piana, a maquis-covered island.

 6

Pointe de la Parata

⚠B5 🚗12 km (7 miles) W of Ajaccio 🚌From Place de Gaulle, Ajaccio

A black granite headland, the Pointe de la Parata makes for a dramatic end to the D111 road. The cape is dominated by the Tour de la Parata, a tower built by the Genoese in 1608 to defend the island from pirates. A path leads to the end of the cape (about 30 minutes there and back). From here, the view of the red Îles Sanguinaires is grandiose, especially at sunset. Another, longer route starts 500 m (1,600 ft) before the restaurant at the Pointe de la Parata. Further ahead is a 90-minute walk winding through tall maquis to a lovely beach at Anse de Minaccia (the beach is also accessible via the D111-B road from Ajaccio). From here, it is an hour-long trek to wind-swept Capo di Feno, with its Genoese watchtower.

EAT

Brasserie i Sanguinari

This charming seafront restaurant-bar near Pointe de la Parta is a popular haunt for locals and holidaymakers.

⚠C5 🏠Route des Sanguinaires 📞04 95 52 01 70

€€€

La Paillote Le Week-end

Enjoy Mediterranean-style seafood at this local spot a short way inland from the coast.

⚠C5 🏠Route des Sanguinaires 🌐hotel-le-weekend.com

€€€

Le Goeland

The raffia-covered terrace of this beach restaurant is the perfect spot to sip cocktails.

⚠C5 🏠Route des Sanguinaires 📞04 95 52 03 82

€€€

 7

Gorges du Prunelli

C5 **30 km (19 miles) E of Ajaccio**

The Prunelli torrent flows from Monte Renoso, which stands 2,352 m (7,716 ft) high, to the Golfe d'Ajaccio. The torrent has carved a deep canyon, or gorge, partly irrigated by the water from an artificial lake created by a dam.

From Ajaccio, the D3 twists along the north bank of the torrent. At the tiny village of Eccica-Suarella, a stone commemorates the site where the conquering soldier Sampiero Corso was killed in the 16th century.

A little further along the D3, at the pass of Col de Mercuju, 716 m (2,349 ft) above sea level, a path begins. It leads to a belvedere with great views. Around 10 km (6 miles) north

---

**INSIDER TIP
Preserving Pozzines**

Small pools of water called *pozzines* are scattered across Corsica's wetlands, including near the Gorges du Prunelli. Stick to trails when passing as they house delicate habitats.

---

is the pristine Tolla lake, flanked by a small village and nestled between dense orchards. From here, the road joins the D27 leading up to Bastelica. This peaceful hamlet on the slopes of Monte Renoso is known for its wild-pig charcuterie and for being the birthplace of Sampiero Corso. The soldier is portrayed in a bronze statue in front of the parish church. The house he was born in is in Dominacci, a nearby hamlet.

If driving back towards Ajaccio, it is possible to follow the D27 along the south side of the gorge. Here, between Col de Marcuggio and Col de Cricheto, is the Forêt de Pineta, with pine, beech and chestnut trees. A footpath descends from the road towards the Èse torrent and the Genoese bridge of Zipitoli.

Continuing north from Bastelica, the D27 initially ascends to Col de Scalella, then descends to Tavera, a village in the Vallée de la Gravona.

 8

Vallée de la Gravona

C5 **30 km (19 miles) E of Ajaccio**

This wide valley is traversed by the N193 highway, one of

Did You Know?

The area around the Liscia river was once home to bandits such as the infamous Spada, "the Tiger of Cinarca".

Corsica's main roads, which leads to Corte and Bastia. Parallel to the N193, but further up on the slopes, are the winding roads leading to the villages of Peri, Carbuccia, Ucciani, Tavera and Bocognano.

Peri can be approached via the D229. Here you'll find a small bridge with beautiful natural pools on both sides – the perfect spot for a swim.

At the hamlet of Carbuccia is A Cupulatta, a reserve for 166 species of tortoise and the largest of its kind in Europe.

Bocognano, the main village in the valley, lies at the foot of Monte d'Oro and is surrounded by chestnut trees. The village marks the start of many paths. The most popular begins 4 km (2 miles) southwest of the village, down the D27, and leads to the Cascade du Voile de la Mariée ("Bride's Veil Falls"). Another, more demanding route leads up Punta dell'Oriente, which offers views over the valley.

Solitary remains of the
Capraja Castle
in Tiuccia

villages with splendid views of
the coast, such as Sari d'Orcino
and Calcatoggio.

 Forêt de Chiavari

C5 **35 km (22 miles) S
of Ajaccio** **Parc Naturel
Régional de la Corse,
2 Rue Major Lambroschini,
Ajaccio; pnr.corsica**

The large Forêt de Chiavari
extends for 18 sq km (7 sq
miles), from the coast to
an altitude of about 600 m
(1,970 ft) on top of the hills
separating the Golfe d'Ajaccio
from the Golfe de Valinco. The
forest consists mainly of holm
oaks, eucalyptus (imported
from Australia in the 19th century to reclaim the land and
help eliminate malaria), maritime pine and shrubs such as
strawberry trees, ruscus and
thyme. It also has a number of

footpaths and mountain-bike
paths of all levels of difficulty
and for all tastes. One of the
most pleasant is the Sentier
de Myrte ("Myrtle Path"),
which starts and ends at Plage
de Verghia, a beach with a café.

At 485 m (1,600 ft), perched
on a hill at the edge of the
forest, is the hamlet of Côti-
Chiavari, with a tree-lined
terrace offering a splendid
panoramic view of the gulf.
Destroyed in the 16th century
by Barbary pirates, this village
was repopulated in 1713,
when the Genoese govern-
ment decided to transfer here
the inhabitants of Chiavari, a
locality in the Gulf of Tigullio.

Not far from Côti-Chiavari,
there are interesting viewpoints that take in both sides
of the surrounding hills and
the two large gulfs on the
west coast, Golfe d'Ajaccio
and Golfe de Valinco.

On the narrow D55 road
that leads up to Côti-Chiavari
from Verghia is the old agricultural penal colony that
was constructed in 1855.
The prison was abandoned
in 1906 and the inmates were
transferred to Cayenne.

 Tiuccia

C4 **8 km (5 miles) S
of Sagone**

Situated on the Golfe de Liscia,
between the Genoese towers
of Capigliolo and Ancone, is
the seaside resort of Tiuccia.
It is dominated by the ruins
of the Capraja Castle, which
once belonged to the Counts
de la Cinarca. In the 13th–16th
centuries, this family resisted
Genoese rule and established
its hold over southern Corsica.

The mouths of the Liscia
river and, further north along
the coast, of the Liamone river
have created long, sandy
beaches surrounded by hills
covered in maquis. These
secluded beaches and coves
can be reached via the Ancone
footpath along the coast.

Tiuccia is also the starting
point for excursions to Capo
Rosso, Girolata (p124) and the
Calanques de Piana (p116).

The valley of the Liscia river
forms La Cinarca, a fertile area
covered with woods, olive and
orange trees and vineyards.
Livestock raising is the main
activity here. At an altitude of
400–600 m (1,300–2,000 ft) are

→
Swimming in the waters
of the Plage de Verghia,
Forêt de Chiavari

STAY

Hôtel Le Scandola
A popular base for hikers, this hotel offer fine views.

C4 Route des Cargèse, Piana
hotelscandola.com

€€€

Hôtel Capo Rosso
Unwind in the large pool and enjoy the sundeck of this four-star hotel.

C4 Route des Calanques, Piana
caporosso.com

€€€

Hôtel Les Roches Rouges
The highlight of this hotel, open since 1912, is the large lounge bar.

C4 Route des Porto, Piana lesroches rouges.com

€€€

→ Taking in the impressive view from the busy marina in Porto

Piana

C4 11 km (7 miles) NE of Porto Place de la Mairie; otpiana.com

With its white houses, large Baroque church and the granite formations of the Calanques in the background, Piana occupies a panoramic position overlooking the Golfe de Porto. One of the "Plus beaux villages de France", the village is the ideal base for excursions along this stretch of coastline.

Among the beaches here is the Anse de Ficajola, situated among red rocks at the end of a winding road descending to the sea. The D824 road leads to Plage d'Arone, a pretty beach surrounded by verdant maquis.

A difficult hike (four hours return trip) from the roadside 2 km (1 mile) above the beach leads to Capo Rosso and the Tour de Turghiu, which, from its position 300 m (1,000 ft) above sea level, offers a great view of the area.

Sagone

C4 36 km (22 miles) N of Ajaccio

The wide Golfe de Sagone, between Punta di Cargèse to the north and Capo di Feno to the south, has long, sandy beaches formed by the silt carried by the Sagone, Liscia and Liamone rivers.

The small village of Sagone was once a major Roman city and owed its prosperity to timber from the nearby Forêt d'Aïtone. In the 6th century CE, it became a bishopric, and, in the 11th century, the cathedral of Sant'Appiano was built near the port. Its ruins can still be seen there. In the Middle Ages, however, the town declined because of malaria outbreaks from the stagnant river water.

Thanks to land reclamation, Sagone is now a pleasant seaside resort. Among the many activities on offer are sailing, scuba diving and boat trips to Scandola and Girolata.

A scenic 15-km (9-mile) road goes up the Liamone river valley to Vico, a hilly village with narrow houses packed around two squares. Until the 18th century, Vico was the residence of the bishops of Sagone. Here, the church of the Couvent St-François is notable for housing a wooden crucifix; sculpted in the 15th century, it is one of Corsica's oldest crucifixes.

The road continues through lush vegetation to Guagno Les Bains, a small spa with two springs: the Occhiu (37°C/ 98.6°F), which is used to cure eye and throat ailments, and the Venturini spring (52°C/ 125.6°F), frequented by those afflicted by rheumatism and sciatica. Among the illustrious guests at this spa were Pascal Paoli and Napoleon's mother, Letizia. Further along the road is the small village of Soccia, the starting point for a gentle, flat footpath to the Lac de Creno, a lake surrounded by the island's native Laricio pines (the route is a two hours return trip).

 13

Cargèse

B4 **13 km (8 miles) NW of Sagone** **Rue Dr Dragacci; 04 95 26 41 31**

In the mid-17th century, a group of Greek families that had fled from the Peloponnese following the Turkish invasion asked the Genoese for political asylum. First they settled at Paomia, 50 km (31 miles) from Ajaccio, and then moved to Cargèse. To this day, this village, which is about 100 m (330 ft) above sea level, reflects its Greek history. Two 19th-century churches stand opposite each other: a Greek-Orthodox church, with a 13th-century panel of the *Deposition of Christ*, and a Latin church, with a Neo-Classical interior. The terraces of both offer fine views of the gulf.

 14

Porto

C3 **43 km (26 miles) N of Sagone** **Quartier La Marine; 04 95 26 10 55**

A modern seaside resort with facilities for watersports of every kind, Porto is also an ideal base for making inland excursions. Its favourable geographic position was providential for Porto, which, during the Genoese period, was the only outlet to the sea in the agricultural zone of Ota.

On either side of the village are towering cliffs that conceal enchanting beaches. Overlooking the village's harbour is the massive Genoese tower that defended the valley. This quadrangular construction was built in 1549 on levelled red-granite cliffs and offers magnificent views of the gulf.

Next to Porto is the marina, which has a wide beach. The marina can be reached via a wooden footbridge leading over the estuary of the little river where fishing boats and yachts are anchored. This port is the departure point for boat excursions along the coastline. The Golfe de Porto, part of the Parc Naturel Régional (*p44*), can be seen in all its splendour from the sea – the boats go as far as the Calanques de Piana nd the Scandola Nature Reserve (*p116*).

South of Porto loom the imposing Calanques, which reach an altitude of 1,294 m (4,245 ft) at Capo d'Orto. North of Porto, among the coast's granite cliffs, are some lovely beaches, the Gradelle, Caspiu and Bussaglia among them. They can be reached either by car (by taking turn-offs from the D81 road) or by boat.

The stretch of the D81 road to Galéria is arguably the most spectacular in all Corsica. Small lay-bys along the road make for good viewpoints, as does the Col de la Croix, from which a path leads to the beaches of Tuara and Girolata (three hours return; also accessible by boat).

GENOESE BRIDGES

Built from 1284 onwards, many of the bridges erected by the Genoese are intact and still in use today. They are made of dry-stone, have a single arch and are never more than 20 m (65 ft) long; they often have openings on the sides of the arch to let water pass through in case of a flood. Examples are found across the island, with a strking example, Pont de Pianella, found near Porto.

GENOESE TOWERS

In the 16th century, the Genoese built 67 towers along the perimeter of the island. Designed to spot pirates and afford refuge for the populations of seaside villages, these towers are either square or round and differ in size. Some, such as the towers of Girolata or Campomoro (p146), were the centres of forts, while others were merely outposts. They also contained storehouses and a cistern to collect rainwater.

 15

Gorges de Spelunca

🅐 C3 🅗 7 km (4 miles) E of Porto

Behind Porto is a splendid valley from where it is possible to admire this gorge, formed by the Aïtone and Tavulella torrents. Fine views of the Gorges de Spelunca (also known as Evisa-Ota) can be had from the D84 road that goes up to Evisa on the south side of the valley.

On the north side of the valley, at an altitude of 310 m (1,017 ft), is Ota, a delightful mountain village with simple stone houses that was once famous for its citrons, which were exported to Europe. Today, the orchards are partly overrun by scrub. Ota is one of the stops on the *Mare e Monti* path (p66) in the Parc Naturel Régional (p44).

Interesting sights in this area are the Genoese bridges, about 2 km (1 mile) along the road to Evisa. The first of these, at Pianella, is a perfect arch. The nearby bridge of Ota lies where the Aïtone and Tavulella torrents meet and passes over both of them. This point also marks the start of the old mule track that once linked Ota and Evisa through the gorges, passing over the Vecchio and Zaglia bridges (90 minutes return). The latter, built in 1745, is one of the gems of Genoese architecture.

The entire area around the Gorges de Spelunca is reminiscent of American canyons. There's also a ravine that can be followed along the path hewn out of the rock.

 16

Girolata

🅐 C3 🅗 24 km (15 miles) NW of Porto 🆆 port-girolata.com

A tiny fishers' hamlet facing a splendid cove sheltered from the wind, Girolata can be reached only on foot (90 minutes from Col de la Croix) or by one of the boats that offer excursions from Porto in the summer. On the headland is the majestic square Genoese fort, which is protected by a defensive wall. It was in the sea in front of Girolata, that, in 1540, the Genoese led by Andrea Doria captured the infamous Turkish pirate Dragut Rais.

In the summer, the bay area becomes crowded with yachts and loses much of its charm, even though the sea beds and red cliffs are still beautiful.

 17

Galéria

🅐 C3 🅗 50 km (31 miles) N of Porto 🚌

The only residential area of any importance between Calvi (p84) and Porto, this isolated village is an excellent base for visits to the Scandola Nature Reserve (p116), dives and watersports in general. Galéria is also the departure point for numerous excursions along the coast; the coastline has a panoramic path that penetrates the maquis and skirts the Golfe de Galéria and Punta Ciuttone to the north, and Punta Stollu to the south.

Just behind Galéria is the Vallée du Fango, created by the river Fango, the mouth of which forms a vast pebbled beach. The valley was a transhumance route along which flocks of sheep from the mountains above the Vallée de Niolo were moved to the sea for winter. They stayed

→ The village of Evisa overlooking the Forêt d'Aïtone, and *(inset)* a chestnut tree bearing fruit

there until spring, when they made the return trip.

The D351 road penetrates the valley for about 10 km (6 miles), traversing the Forêt du Fango. Here, the Fango river flows between low rock faces, creating transparent water holes ideal for a swim. Shortly before the village of Barghiana is the spectacular meeting point of the Fango and the Taita torrent.

Forêt d'Aïtone

A C3 **A** 28 km (17 miles) E of Porto **i** Parc Naturel Régional de Corse, Ajaccio; pnr.corsica

With the atmosphere of an enchanted forest, the Forêt d'Aïtone can be explored through its easy, enjoyable and well-marked footpaths.

An ancient forest, its name seems to have derived from the Latin word *abies*, meaning fir tree. The forest covers an area of 24 sq km (9 sq miles) at an altitude of 800–2,000 m (2,600–6,500 ft). The Genoese used the wood to make their ships and, in the 16th century, built a road to transport the trunks to Sagone *(p122)*. The forest is made up mostly of Laricio pines, a sweet-scented variety of *Pinus nigra* that can grow to more than 45 m (150 ft) high and live for 200 years. In addition, there are also a plethora of maritime pines, beeches, larches and firs that protect the rich undergrowth and its wild fruit and mushrooms. The forest is inhabited by foxes, mouflons and wild boars.

Just west of the forest, at 830 m (2,723 ft) above sea level, is Evisa. Surrounded by chestnut groves that yield high-quality fruit, this village plays host to a famous chestnut festival in November. Evisa is situated at the junction of the *Mare a Mare* and *Mare e Monti* footpaths *(p66)* and is therefore a great starting point for excursions.

About 4 km (2 miles) from Evisa, on the road to Col de Verghio *(p169)*, is the starting point of the scenic path that leads to the Cascades d'Aïtone (30 minutes return), a series of cascading waterfalls formed by the Aïtone torrent, at the foot of which are limpid pools perfect for a midday swim.

The Sentier de la Sittelle (the French word for the nuthatch, a local bird) is a path beginning by the park information centre of Paesolu d'Aïtone and going through the forest along the Sentier des Condamnés (two and a half hours), a circular path named after convicts who, in the 19th century, felled the trees for firewood.

Did You Know?

The Corsican mouflon, a wild sheep, can be found grazing in the Forêt d'Aïtone.

A LONG WALK
ALONG THE CALANQUES DE PIANA

Distance 3 km (2 miles) **Walking time** 4 hours
Stopping-off points Café les Roches Bleues
Terrain Mostly paved hill roads; there are some
long, steep ascents **Nearest Bus** Piana

The granitic rock formations known as the
Calanques de Piana feature sensational
colour changes from gold to pink to bright
red depending on the time of day. The
wind and water have sculpted the granitic rock, creating awesome cavities,
known as *tafoni*, and intriguing formations. Although it is possible to cover the
route in half a day, or a full day with a
lunch break, it might be more relaxing to
explore the Calanques in two separate
walks, especially during summer. For those
who are driving, this stretch of the D81 road
is at its most beautiful and impressive at sunset.

Château Fort ○•

*A worthwhile detour leads to a block of granite
resembling a fortress. The* **Château Fort** *forms a
terrace overlooking the gulfs of Porto and Girolata
and Capo Rosso. It can be reached in 30 minutes
from the Tête du Chien through a maze of rocks.*

Capu di Ghineparu
515 m (1,690 ft) △

Ruisseau de Dardo

D81

Once back on the **D81**, *walk
500 m (500 yards) towards
Piana (p122). This stretch of
road offers great views of the
Calanques. Turn back and
follow the D81 to the parking
area, 45–60 minutes away.*

Ruisseau de Mezzanu

D81

D81

The D81 Road
FINISH

← Cycling on the winding
D81 highway, one of
Corsica's most beautiful roads

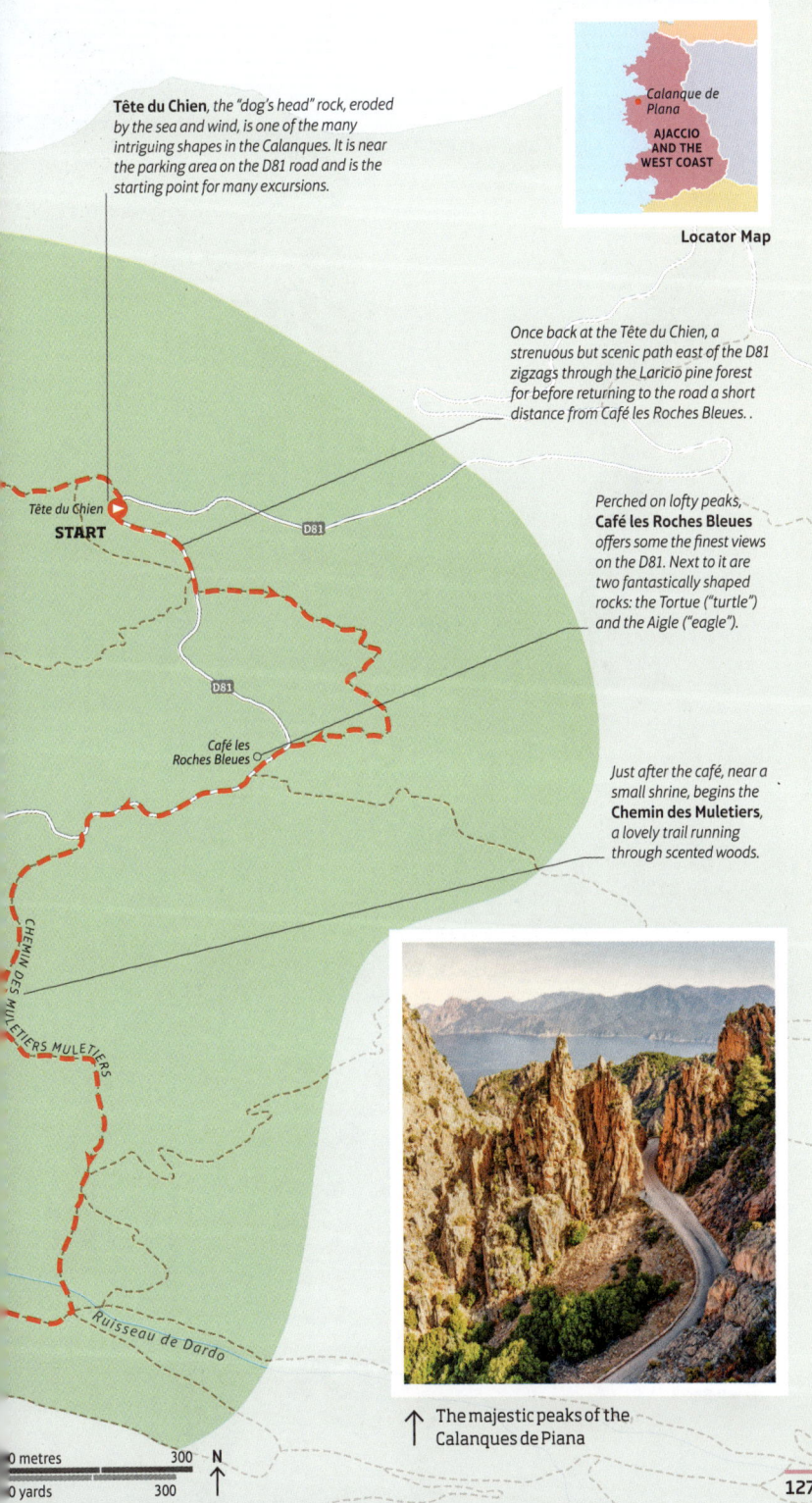

Tête du Chien, the "dog's head" rock, eroded by the sea and wind, is one of the many intriguing shapes in the Calanques. It is near the parking area on the D81 road and is the starting point for many excursions.

Locator Map

Calanque de Piana

AJACCIO AND THE WEST COAST

Once back at the Tête du Chien, a strenuous but scenic path east of the D81 zigzags through the Lariciò pine forest for before returning to the road a short distance from Café les Roches Bleues. .

Perched on lofty peaks, **Café les Roches Bleues** offers some the finest views on the D81. Next to it are two fantastically shaped rocks: the Tortue ("turtle") and the Aigle ("eagle").

Just after the café, near a small shrine, begins the **Chemin des Muletiers**, a lovely trail running through scented woods.

Tête du Chien
START

D81

D81

Café les Roches Bleues

CHEMIN DES MULETIERS MULETIERS

Ruisseau de Dardo

The majestic peaks of the Calanques de Piana

0 metres 300
0 yards 300

N

BONIFACIO AND THE SOUTH

The human history of southern Corsica stretches back over 8,000 years, with many of the island's most remarkable prehistoric discoveries found in this region. Long before the Pisans, Genoese and Spanish fought for control here, southern Corsica was the centre of an indigenous population that left traces of its presence in the alignments of menhirs at sites like Filitosa, Palaggiu, Stantari and Renaggiu.

The fortified city of Bonifacio is one of the most ancient on the island, built around 828 CE. In 1195, the city became a Genoese colony. Shortly after, it became a republic unto itself, was granted the right to mint its own money and began construction of its defensive walls. The city was conquered in 1553 by the French before being recaptured by the Genoese, and, in the 17th century, it was fortified with modern military structures. Although the town fell under French rule in the 18th century, it has retained its Italian influence and is now a charming medley of styles and periods.

Away from Bonifacio, the south of the island is home to a number of historic towns which now rub shoulders with 20th-century tourist resorts. Some of Corsica's most popular attractions, such as Propriano, Solenzara and the beach town of Porto-Vecchio, are located here, while the island's striking geology is on full display with the jagged needles of the Aiguilles de Bavella.

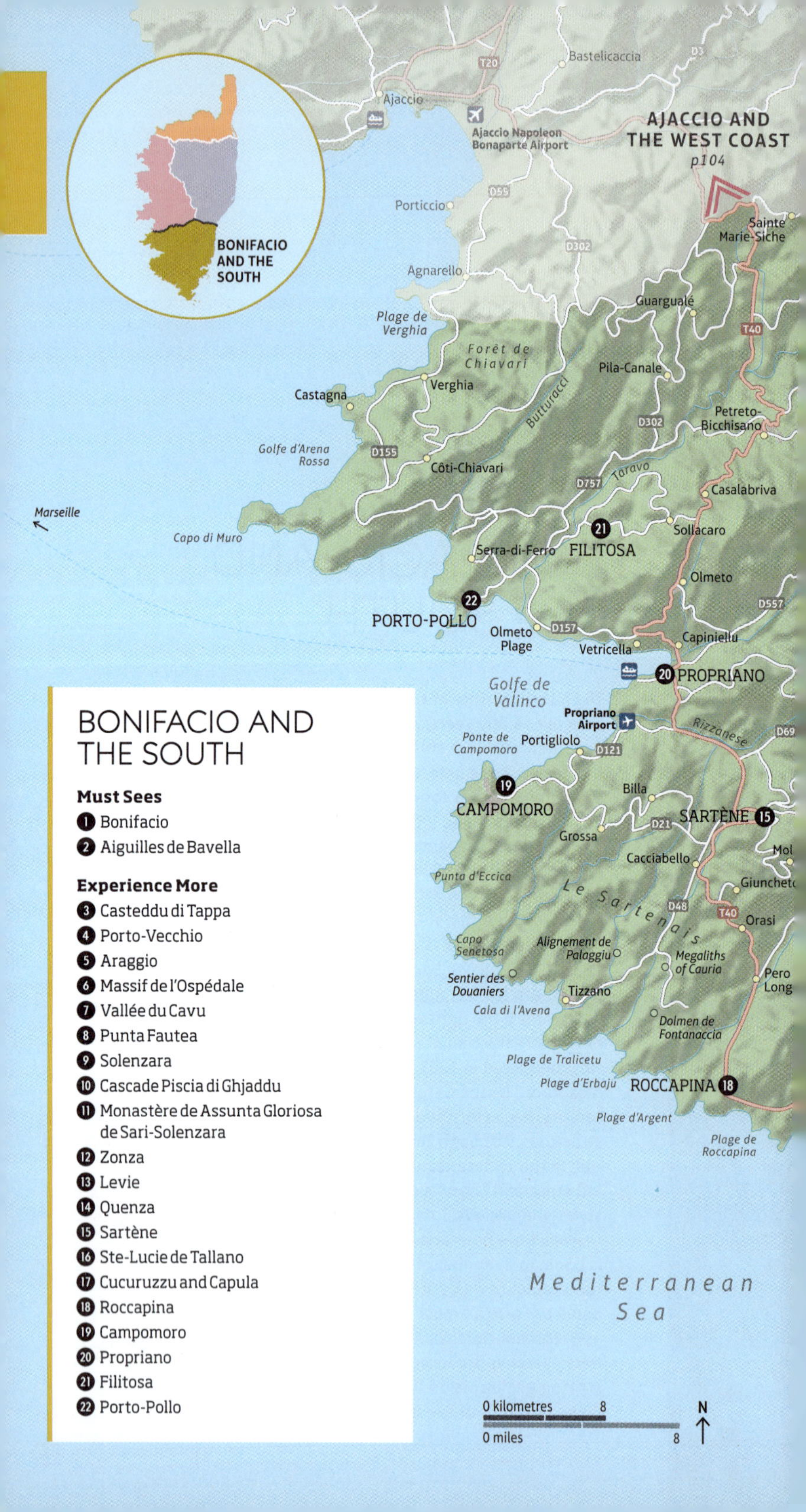

BONIFACIO AND THE SOUTH

Marseille

Ajaccio

Ajaccio Napoleon
Bonaparte Airport

Sainte
Marie-Siché

Porticcio

Agnarello

Guargualé

Plage de
Verghia

Forêt de
Chiavari

Pila-Canale

Petreto-
Bicchisano

Castagna

Verghia

Golfe d'Arena
Rossa

Côti-Chiavari

Casalabriva

Capo di Muro

Serra-di-Ferro

Sollacaro

FILITOSA 21

Olmeto

22 **PORTO-POLLO**

Olmeto
Plage

Vetricella

Capiniellu

Golfe de
Valinco

20 **PROPRIANO**

Propriano
Airport

Rizzanese

Ponte de
Campomoro

Portigliolo

Billa

19

CAMPOMORO

Grossa

SARTÈNE 15

Mol

Punta d'Eccica

Cacciabello

Giunchet

Capo
Senetosa

Alignement de
Palaggiu

Le Sartenais

Orasi

Sentier des
Douaniers

Megaliths
of Cauria

Pero
Long

Cala di l'Avena

Tizzano

Dolmen de
Fontanaccia

Plage de Tralicetu

Plage d'Erbaju

ROCCAPINA 18

Plage d'Argent

Plage de
Roccapina

Mediterranean
Sea

BONIFACIO AND THE SOUTH

Must Sees

1 Bonifacio
2 Aiguilles de Bavella

Experience More

3 Casteddu di Tappa
4 Porto-Vecchio
5 Araggio
6 Massif de l'Ospédale
7 Vallée du Cavu
8 Punta Fautea
9 Solenzara
10 Cascade Piscia di Ghjaddu
11 Monastère de Assunta Gloriosa
de Sari-Solenzara
12 Zonza
13 Levie
14 Quenza
15 Sartène
16 Ste-Lucie de Tallano
17 Cucuruzzu and Capula
18 Roccapina
19 Campomoro
20 Propriano
21 Filitosa
22 Porto-Pollo

0 kilometres   8
0 miles   8

N

Tasso

D45

Ventiseri

Cozzano

D757

D28

Zicavo

Ruisseau de Luvana

GR20

le Travo

Travo

Solaro

Marine de Solaro

D69

D83

Tavaro

Mvonte Malo
1,849 m (6,066 ft)

Punta Mozza
1,656 m (5, 433 ft)

9 SOLENZARA

Olivese

Monte Incudine
2,134 m (7,001 ft)

Plateau de
Coscione

11

Argiusta-
Moriccio

Fozzaninco

AIGUILLES DE
BAVELLA

2

D268

Solenzara

MONASTÈRE DE
ASSUNTA GLORIOSA
DE SARI SOLENZARA

D420

CORSE-DU-SUD

Bavella

T10

Favone

Aullène

QUENZA

14

Trou de la
Bombe

Tarcu

Alta
Rocca

ZONZA **12**

GR20

Cavu

Conca

Barracci

D69

Bocca di Pelza

Col de Siu

D19

D268

CUCURUZZU
AND CAPULA

17

VALLÉE
DU CAVU **7**

PUNTA
FAUTEA

8

D368

Ste-Lucie de
Porto-Vecchio

Olmucciu

STE-LUCIE
DE TALLANO **16**

13 LEVIE

T10

Pinarellu

Lecci

Île de
Pinarellu

Carbini

CASCADE PISCIA
DI GHJADDU

10

Tirolo

Bains de
Caldane

A Vacca Morta
1,315 m (4,314 ft)

MASSIF L'OSPÉDALE **6**

San Ciprianu

Civitavecchia

D148

Force

Bilzese

5 ARAGGIO

Cala Rossa

Barrage
de l'Ortolo

Vallée de l'Ortolo

Golfe de Porto-Vecchio

Pavellone

Ortolo

Montagne de
Cagna

D59

PORTO-VECCHIO **4**

Punta di
a Chiappa

Giannuccio

Caccia

Piccovaggia

Îles
Cerbicale

Sotta

3 CASTEDDU
DI TAPPA

Plage de
Palombaggia

Monacia-
d'Aullène

D22

D859

Stagiacco

T10

Figari-South
Corsica Airport

Chera

D59

Pietra-Longa-
Salvini

Santa Giulia

Tyrrhenian
Sea

Pianotolli-
Caldarello

Figari

L'Oriu di Canni

Suartone

Lac de
Talza

Plage de Rondinara

T40

Punta di Curugnola
250 m (820 ft)

T10

Golfe de
St Manza

Golfe de Ventilegne

Plage de Balistra

Ermitage de la Trinité

Gurgazu

Plage de Piantarella

1 BONIFACIO

Bouches de Bonifacio Marine Reserve

Capo Pertusato

Plage de
Petit Sperone

Île Cavallo

Îles Lavezzi

The town of Bonifacio perched atop white limestone cliffs ↑

 3

BONIFACIO

▲ D2 ✈ **Figari-Sud-Corse, 21 km (13 miles) NW** 🚌 🚢 **from Sardinia** 🛈 **Rue Fred Scamaroni; bonifacio.fr**

Commanding superb coastal views from its narrow cliff-top promontory, Bonifacio is as remarkable for its natural setting as it is for its long history. The ancient town is home to a fortified harbour, a marina and the striking medieval upper town. Just beyond the town's borders, some of Corsica's most biodiverse marine landscapes await, with dramatic cliffs and secluded islets.

This medieval town perched on a limestone promontory was developed by Bonifacio, Marquis of Tuscany, who passed by upon his return from an expedition to Africa in 828 CE. For three centuries, the harbour was partly under the rule of Pisa. In 1195, the town became a Genoese colony and took in a number of immigrants from Liguria. At around the same time, Bonifacio became a republic and was granted the right to mint its own money, before it began construction of the massive walls, fortified with new military structures. Although the town fell under French rule in the 18th century, it has kept an Italian flavour and a certain sense of isolation from the rest of the island.

The heart of Bonifacio is the upper town, which perches on the promontory high above the fjord-like inlet that forms the harbour. Bordered by Avenue Charles de Gaulle and the massive ramparts, this is the oldest section of the city. Around the cathedral, tall, narrow houses line the streets, the outer rows balancing dangerously on the cliff's edge. Further out on the promontory, west of the city walls, the wind-battered Bosco area stretches out towards the sea, offering panoramic views from the Esplanade St-François.

 ①

Marina

Bonifacio's historic port has been the town's lifeline and its greatest curse. A key location for trade and fishing, it also meant the town was long vulnerable to attack from the sea. The port was the site of fierce battles between Pisa and Genoa in the 12th and 13th centuries, before the Genoese built the vast battlements that surround the Marina. It wasn't until the 15th century that the area around the port became the bustling maritime quarter that we see today.

The quays of the old port of Bonifacio are now home to a popular promenade filled with cafés and restaurants. In the summer, this area remains lively until late at night, with

---

 GREAT VIEW
Marina From Above

For a bird's-eye view of Bonifacio's Marina, head up the steep Montée Rastello. The hill leads to a Genoese gate, offering a sublime outlook over the port and medieval centre.

an array of bars serving food and drink throughout the evening. This is also the departure point for cruises to the Grotte du Sdragonatu and the Îles Lavezzi. Further along, towards the mouth of the inlet, is the commercial port with the Gare Maritime (passenger terminal). In the Middle Ages, the port was entrusted to the benevolence of St Erasmus, the patron saint of sailors and fishers who is honoured by a church named after him in the heart of the Marina.

Bonifacio's Marina is also the starting point for a number of water sports and activities. Sailing is renowned in the town, with a host of prestigious events including the Tour of Corsica making use of the port. While exploring, you'll likely see a number of expensive boats and yachts moored up.

Did You Know?

In 1420, the King of Aragón laid siege to Bonifacio for five months, prompting new defences.

②

Bastion de l'Étendard

🕐 10am–4:30pm daily (Jun & Jul: 9am–6:30pm)

The sight of this massive bastion – the tallest in France – towering over the quays of the Marina and the port is one of the most famous iconic views of the town. The bastion was built in the 16th century by modifying the existing fortifications, and its function was to house the powerful heavy artillery that at that time was bringing about a drastic change in military architecture. Along with the Porte de Gênes, it was the strong point of the walls of the heavily defended Bonifacio. The upper platforms of the bastion afford a magnificent view of the narrow inlet of Bonifacio and the Marina below. Four halls in the interior now house a small museum featuring reconstructions of moments in Bonifacio's history.

Admittance to the bastion also includes entry to the underground rooms. Here, an array of installations can be found, including a film interweaving contemporary views of Bonifacio with 3D images of the medieval city.

STAY

Cala di Greco
Overlooking Bonifacio's medieval centre, this luxury hotel has a truly enviable location.

📍 D7 🏠 Bancarello
Ⓦ hotel-caladigreco.com

€€€

Hotel Santa Teresa
Housed in a converted mansion, Hotel Santa Teresa offers both simple rooms and luxurious suites.

📍 D7
🏠 Qur Saint-François
Ⓦ hotel-santateresa.com

€€€

Hôtel Version Maquis Citadelle
This chic hotel has a large pool and an excellent spa.

📍 D7
🏠 Lieu-dit Brancuccio

€€€

③ Porte de Gênes

During Genoese rule, the Porte de Gênes was the only entrance to Bonifacio's upper town. Surrounded by tall ramparts, the gate gave access to the Place d'Armes, beyond the walls. These walls were so thick that, to get to the square, one had to pass through eight successive barriers reinforced with iron. In 1588, a drawbridge was added at the end of these barriers. The drawbridge was raised and lowered by a complex system of counter-weights that can still be seen.

④ Ste-Marie-Majeure

 Rue de la Loggia and Rue du St-Sacrement ⏱ Daily

Bonifacio's cathedral was the heart of the city's religious and cultural life for centuries. At the front of the building is a vast loggia with porticoes, which, in the past, was the meeting point for the town notables and the seat for administering justice. The structure was built over a large cistern that is now used as a conference room.

Construction of Ste-Marie-Majeure was begun in the 12th century, before the Genoese conquered the city, by Pisan artisans, and was completed a century later. This extremely long delay has led to a mixture of styles that does not, however, diminish the beauty of the whole. The first floor of the bell tower, for example, is Romanesque, while the upper three are Gothic with some Aragonese relief decoration. The three-aisle interior is partly Baroque. Inside, to the left of the entrance, is a 3rd- or 4th-century Roman sarcophagus and a magnificently wrought tabernacle executed by Genoese masters in the mid-1400s. The high altar dates from 1624 and is clearly Baroque in style. In the sacristy is a relic of the True Cross. In the past, during particularly dangerous times and when there were heavy storms, the curate and mayor carried the Cross in a procession through the streets of Bonifacio.

⑤ Porte de France

In addition to the Porte de Gênes, a second entrance to the *haute ville* (upper town) was created in 1854, when the French Army Engineers' Corps built a road to the St-Nicolas fort. This new gate also featured a drawbridge. Within

the city walls around the Porte de France, traces of the oldest quarters of Genoese Bonifacio can still be seen. These include the Fondaco, or staple (commercial warehouse), that once stood proudly in the Place Montepagano area.

⑥ St-Dominique Haute Ville

⏱ Jul-Aug

Outside the city walls, but inside the fortifications that once protected the Pisan quarter, is this church dating from 1343. It stands on the site of an earlier Romanesque church, which was begun by the Pisans and finished by the Knights Templars. The present church was built by the Dominicans and, until the French Revolution, was part of a monastery complex. The

←

Bonifacio's small marine cemetery with its pale mortuary chapels

↑ Descending the
Escalier du Roi
d'Aragon

Gothic bell tower is unusual: its square base is surmounted by an octagonal section topped with battlements, and the white limestone façade is decorated with an ogival portal. Inside are groups of statues depicting Mary and the other holy women at the foot of the Cross and an image of St Bartholomew.

Opposite the church doorway are the Montlaur barracks, which were built by the Genoese. Later this building became the home of the Foreign Legion troops. Next to the church is the Mairie (Town Hall), which is linked to St-Dominique by an arch that was once part of the old Dominican monastery.

Bosco

At the tip of Bonifacio's promontory is the Bosco area. Here, there is a cemetery with many small, pale-coloured mortuary chapels. At the cemetery, commanding a great view across the waves, hundreds of small crosses are arranged in orderly rows. The best time to visit is at sunset,

when the golden light glints off the pale stone.

Near the edge of the promontory, the structure of the St-Antoine battery was constructed in the period between the two World Wars. The position of the battery allowed complete control of the maritime traffic in the Straits of Bonifacio. It was once equipped with a powerful torch bright enough to illuminate the surrounding seascape at night. Today, it offers a great view of the Bouches de Bonifacio *(p41)*.

Escalier du Roi d'Aragon

⏱10am–5.30pm daily
On the west side of the headland, where the craggy cliff is at its most precipitous, this steep rock-cut stairway descends to sea level. According to legend, its 187

steps were hewn in just one night, during the Aragonese siege of 1420. It is, in fact, more likely that the stairway was built in a much earlier period and served as access to a well with good drinking water. The Escalier could be clearly monitored from above and was never used by any of the foreign troops that tried to storm Bonifacio.

Generally open all year round (though access to the steps may close in wet or windy conditions), this legendary staircase reveals a 180-degree panorama as you climb or descend: the white of the cliffs blends with the turquoise waters as various seabirds dive into the waves close at hand. Entry tickets to the steps can be purchased near the start of the descent; sturdy walking shoes or trainers are mandatory, and a decent level of fitness is highly recommended to reach the top.

> **On the west side of the headland, where the craggy cliff is at its most precipitous, a steep rock-cut stairway descends to sea level.**

Grotte du Sdragonatu ⑨
COSTA
CARTARANA
Le Grain ⑬
de sable
Craggy Cliffs ⑩
Punta di San Mulari
110 m (361 ft)
Pic de Rognouse
107 m (351 ft)
PIANTARELLA
FALATTE
CIAPPILI
Capo Pertusato ⑪ ⑫ Fanale di Pertusatu
Île Cavallo ⑭

Mediterranean Sea

Îles Lavezzi

0 km   1   N
0 mile   1

Île Lavezzi ⑮

EXPLORING THE COAST AND CLIFFS OF BONIFACIO

The coast around Bonifacio is made up of a rugged chalk outcrop furrowed by the region's distinctive cliffs. Extending as far south as Capo Pertusato and towards Pointe de Sperone, these cliffs are formed of sedimentary rocks that have been sculpted over time by the wind and sea to create this craggy coastline. Beyond the main island, small islets home to glorious nature reserves are strung like jewels across the water. The cliffs and outlying islands are best admired from the sea; ferries and chartered boats to Lavezzi and Cavallo run from Bonifacio.

⑨ Grotte du Sdragonatu

Created by natural erosion, this sea cave is illuminated by sunlight, which penetrates through a large crack in the vault. The local tourist guides claim that this long, narrow opening uncannily resembles the shape of Corsica.

⑩ Craggy Cliffs

The white limestone cliffs in the area are perhaps one of the most famous sights in Corsica. They are also geologically interesting, since limestone is an unusual presence in this mostly granitic island. The uniquely undulating, rocky coastline has many fine belvederes from which the beauty of this splendid shore can be fully enjoyed. Among the many seabirds that nest in this wild stretch are shags, herring gulls and the rare Audouin's gull.

⑪ Capo Pertusato

Viewed from the sea, the southernmost point of Corsica appears rugged and shaped by the waves. A view from the land highlights a colossal cave carved out of the limestone. Capo Pertusato was named after this natural opening – in Genoese dialect, the language of the former rulers of Bonifacio, the word *pertusato* means "perforated". Most boat trips in the region travel close to this cave to reveal its huge expanse.

← A small dinghy on the water near Bonifacio

→ The undulating limestone cliffs of Bonifacio

Capo Pertusato Lighthouse

Sitting proudly at the end of the headland is the Capo Pertusato Lighthouse, first activated in 1844. Clearly visible at night from the nearby coast of Sardinia and the surrounding hills, the lighthouse was built to guide sailors through the rocky passages on the approach to the island.

It was Napoleon himself who initiated the programme of building lighthouses around the coast of France, one of many vast engineering projects he pioneered. Compared to other European nations, France's coast was poorly lit in the early 19th century, leading to a huge number of shipwrecks, particularly around the Straits of Bonifacio. One of the most famous was that of the *Sémillante*, a French frigate that set sail from Toulon in February 1855 with a crew of 301 to take 392 French soldiers to Crimea. On the night of 15 February, a storm caused the ship, which was full of gunpowder, to explode on the rocks of Île Lavezzi. The *Sémillante* sank quickly and there were no survivors.

Grain de Sable

This solitary stack – which now has the curious nicknames "grain of sand" or *"U Diu Grossu"* (the big finger) – broke off from the main cliff around 800 years ago. It is one of the most recognizable cliff features around Bonifacio, and is best admired from the sea, so as to appreciate the curious form and the seabirds that nest on its shelves.

Île Cavallo

This beautiful island is private property, with a number of luxury hotels and villas hidden among its rocks and low vegetation. There is even a small airport catering to the island's few residents and hotel guests. Mooring is forbidden along the island's entire coastline.

Île Lavezzi

Like the rest of the marine archipelago around Bonifacio, this island is a nature reserve, full of fascinating stone formations and a varied range of flora and fauna. It is the largest and most accessible of a clutch of tiny protected islets in the area. The wider archipelago is made up of granitic-rock islands.

Inland on Île Lavezzi, although the scenery appears to be extremely barren, there are plenty of endemic plant species. The Îles Lavezzi lie in the middle of a large marine reserve and mooring is strictly regulated. In summer, a number of operators based at Bonifacio's marina (and also in nearby Porto-Vecchio) offer boat trips. Many visitors choose to bring a picnic lunch to enjoy as they explore the small island.

TOP 4 THINGS TO SPOT ON ÎLE LAVEZZI

Seabirds
Large shearwaters, crested cormorants and Audouin's gulls call the island home, so keep your eyes to the skies.

***Semillante* memorial**
A small plaque on the island commemorates those who lost their lives in the *Semillante* shipwreck in 1855.

Neolithic shelters
Eerie rock structures dating back to the Neolithic period indicate that the island was once inhabited.

Shepherd huts
Abandoned shepherd huts are relics of a time when sheep grazed.

②

AIGUILLES DE BAVELLA

⚠ D6   ℹ Office du Tourisme de l'Alta Rocca, Zonza; 04 95 78 56 33; open May–Oct

The jagged pinnacles of the Aiguilles de Bavella make for one of the most thrilling mountain landscapes in Corsica. This group of needle-shaped peaks lies at the foot of the Monte Incudine massif, which, at 2,134 m (7,001 ft), is the highest mountain range in south Corsica.

Winding through extraordinary mountain landscapes, the route through the Aiguilles de Bavella is among the most popular attractions in Corsica. This unforgettable 75-km (45-mile) route, which can be driven or cycled, passes dramatic rock formations, dense forests and deep gorges carved by rushing torrents – all crowned by the lofty red granite pinnacles that form Corsica's archetypal landmark.

The area has a number of footpaths and treks, including the southernmost stretch of the GR20 long distance hiking route (p188). A more demanding alpine route cuts through the Aiguilles themselves.

TROU DE LA BOMBE

One of the geological highlights of the Aiguilles de Bavella is the Trou de la Bombe, found near the Punta Tafonata peak. This huge, circular hole through the centre of a giant rock was created over thousands of years by natural erosion. It can be reached by a beautiful hike through the heart of the mountains, with the main trailhead found near the Col de Bavella.

↑ Natural pool formed by the area's main river, the Solenzara

PICTURE PERFECT
Calamint in Bloom

When spring arrives, the meadows lining the road and the footpaths of the Aiguilles de Bavella are covered in the pink of calamint flowers. You can snap a shot from the side of the road.

Taking in the dramatic landscape from a lofty massif ↑

Did You Know?

The region's Laricio pines live for a considerable time; many are three or four centuries old.

↑ Rocky spikes of the Aiguilles de Bavella towering over pine forests

EXPERIENCE MORE

 3

Casteddu di Tappa

D6 **Ceccia, 8 km (5 miles) E of Porto-Vecchio**

This impressive Neolithic site is found in the village of Ceccia, just ten minutes from Porto-Vecchio. Consisting of fortified dwellings built around two gigantic structures, it has been through some difficult times, having been treated as an open-air quarry. Tappa was saved from a worse fate by a private citizen who bought the land to protect it.

Archaeological excavations in the area have revealed that Tappa was already inhabited by the Torréens (p36), so called because of their distinctive tower structures dating from the 2nd millennium BCE. This makes the Casteddu di Tappa one of the most ancient settlements in Corsica.

On the southwestern side of the settlement is a round, non-fortified monument dating from 1350 BCE. Access was gained via a steep rock-cut stairway. A round cell in the interior was likely used to preserve foodstuffs and other valuables. Besides serving as a storehouse, this monument was likely also used as a place of worship and as a watchtower.

_____

 4

Porto-Vecchio

D6 **28 km (17 miles) E of Bonifacio** **From Marseille (04 95 70 06 03)** **Rue Général Leclerc; ot-portovecchio.com**

It was the Genoese governors of the Bank of St George who decided, in the early 16th century, to found the port town of Porto-Vecchio. Its function was to fill a long gap in the series of strongholds on the coastline between Bastia and Bonifacio. Porto-Vecchio was then known as the "City of Salt" after its most precious resource. However, due to its proximity to the marshes created by the Stabiacciu and Osu rivers, the town was plagued by malaria for centuries.

Around 1553, the period of the revolt headed by Sampiero Corso (p108), Porto-Vecchio became a refuge for pirates; then, until the mid-1900s, the town lived off the cork industry and the local salt works.

At the end of World War II, land reclamation stemmed the danger of malaria and paved the way for future development. Porto-Vecchio is now an important town, famous above all for its lovely beaches. Traces of old Genoese fortifications survive in the upper part of the town. In summer tourists flock to the many outdoor cafés and restaurants here.

Did You Know?

The port of Porto-Vecchio is thought to have existed since Roman times.

TOP 4 BEACHES NEAR PORTO-VECCHIO

Plage de Palombiagga
D6

One of the world's most beautiful beaches, usually busy in summer.

Plage de Pinarello
D6

Lovely bay lined with pine trees, offering crystal-clear waters.

Plage d'Acciaghju
D6

A lovely beach near the last cove on the Palombaggia peninsula.

Plage de Santa-Giulia
D6

This beautiful spot is known for its for sailing, kayaking and diving.

Along the southern coast of the Golfe de Porto-Vecchio, there is a series of popular tourist resorts. Past the water-shed that ends at Punta di a Chiappa are the famous white sand beaches of Palombaggia and Santa Giulia, which face the Îles Cerbicale reserve.

Araggio

D6 10 km (6 miles) N of Porto-Vecchio

On the way towards the island's hilly interior, the hamlet of Araggio (or Araghju) is the departure point for a steep walkway leading to the nearby *casteddu*. This mule track is quite narrow and hard to climb, ascending without a break along a stony ridge. Then, suddenly, the loose

Exploring a narrow, cobblestoned street in Porto-Vecchio

stones and sheepfolds are interrupted by the light-coloured walls of a massive fortress standing on a rocky spur. The walls of the *casteddu* of Araggio are about 4 m (13 ft) high and 2 m (6 ft) thick. The megalithic complex inside these fortifications consists of rooms that in prehistoric times (16th–12th centuries BCE) served as living quarters, kitchens and storehouses. From the *casteddu*, there is a view of the gulf and the countryside around Porto-Vecchio.

Massif de l'Ospédale

D6 19 km (12 miles) NW of Porto-Vecchio

Behind the town of Porto-Vecchio is a large wooded and rocky region that offers panoramic views of the sea and many fine trails frequented by hikers in the region. The village of Ospédale lies 800 m (2,600 ft) above sea level, halfway up the mountain of the same name. It may owe its name (meaning "hospital") to the fact that, in the past, affluent Porto-Vecchio families used to come here to spend the hot season away from the unhealthy marshes.

One of the best hikes in the area starts from the hamlet of Cartalavonu, 4 km (2 miles)

↑ Massif de l'Ospédale, as seen from the Ospédale lake

further up the hill, and leads to the 1,315-m (4,300-ft) high A Vacca Morta peak, which offers marvellous views.

Beyond Ospédale, a dense maritime pine forest spreads out, covering the entire massif and surrounding the artificial lake of Ospédale. The whole area is part of the Parc Naturel Régional (p44).

Vallée du Cavu

D6 21 km (13 miles) N of Porto-Vecchio

A 30-minute drive north of Porto-Vecchio, the spectacular Vallée du Cavu features a series of natural swimming pools with smooth, sloping sides and crystal-clear water. The pools near the car parks can become crowded on hot summer afternoons, but it's worth walking a little upstream into the wilds of the pine forest surrounding the Cavu river for a serene place for a dip and a picnic lunch.

Within the forest is the A Tyroliana water park (atyro liana.com), offering opportunities for treetop walks, zip lining and canyoning.

↑ Beachgoers at the Plage de Pinarellu, and *(inset)* the ruins of the Genoese tower at Punta Fautea

8 Punta Fautea

 E6 ⏺ 30 km (19 miles) S of Solenzara 🚌 From Porto-Vecchio (in summer) ℹ alta-rocca-tourisme.com

North of the low coastline of the gulf of Porto-Vecchio is the Cala Rossa promontory, which marks the beginning of a rocky stretch interspersed with a few beaches, including the pretty Plage de Pinarellu. About 20 km (12 miles) from Porto-Vecchio, towards Solenzara, is the turn-off for Punta Fautea. Here, not very far from the main road, is a restored Genoese watchtower built in the late 16th century and partly destroyed by fire in 1650.

From here to Solenzara is the Côte des Nacres, a rocky coast with many coves, crystal-clear waters and fascinating sea floors. The name of this coast derives from the large triangular shells that can be found locally. They are as much as 50 cm (20 in) long and the inside is covered by a thin layer similar to mother-of-pearl (*nacre* in French).

9 Solenzara

 E5 ⏺ 38 km (23 miles) N of Porto-Vecchio 🚌 From Porto-Vecchio ℹ Vechja Scola, Sari-Solenzara; 04 95 57 43 75

What was once a tiny hamlet at the mouth of the Solenzara torrent has become one of southeast Corsica's most lively tourist resorts. Solenzara has a port that can take in about 450 boats and a sandy beach bounded by eucalyptus trees. Sari-Solenzara, a hamlet above Solenzara, overlooks the port and is worth visiting for the splendid views of the Bavella.

10 Cascade Piscia di Ghjaddu

 D6 ⏺ 15 km (9 miles) S of Zonza

Although this river can only be reached on foot, it is possible to park in the vicinity, near the top of the D368 road leading to the pass of the Massif de l'Ospédale.

After some streams is a larger watercourse with wide, round pools, known as Marmitte dei Giganti. Further along the path, the river rushes through a rock crevice, creating a waterfall that is about 46 m (150 ft) high. The best viewpoint for the Cascade Piscia di Ghjaddu can be reached by following the path that goes around the rocks and then descends to the right. The whole walk will take about 90 minutes to the viewpoint and back, and for a long stretch consists of rocky terrain, so hiking boots or robust shoes should be worn.

11 Monastère de Assunta Gloriosa de Sari-Solenzara

 E5 ⏺ 3 km (2 miles) S of Sari-Solenzara ⏰ 11:30–4:30pm Tue-Fri & Sun, 12:30–5pm Sat

Constructed in 1988 within a pine forest just above the hilltop village of Sari, this modernistic monastery is inhabited by nuns from the order of Bethlehem, the Assumption of the Virgin and St Bruno. Mondays are days of absolute silence in the monastery, but on other days visitors are welcome to see the starched white property,

which offers wonderful views of the red granite Aiguilles de Bavella and, southeastwards, to the Tyrrhenian Sea. The nuns wear white habits with cowls and will happily offer a tour of the chapel, cloisters and their workshops, where they produce pottery and striking religious carvings.

Zonza

🅐 D6 🚗 40 km (25 miles) SW of Sari-Solenzara
ℹ️ Town Hall, Sainte-Lucie village; 04 95 71 48 99

In the middle of the Alta Rocca region, among pine and oak forests and high along the course of the Asinao river, is Zonza. During summer, this small town, with the bulk of the Aiguilles de Bavella in the background, is a magnet for those who love outdoor activities: hiking, climbing and even paragliding are the main attractions here. Along the main street are shops selling guides with climbing, rafting, trout fishing and hiking itineraries. There are also many associations of tourist guides who can offer advice.

In 1953, sultan Mohammed V of Morocco lived in Zonza in exile, but the climate proved too harsh for him, and he moved to L'Île Rousse (p96), on the north coast.

STAY

Les Hauts de Cavanello
Relax in the tranquil pool of this hotel, located at the foot of the Aiguilles de Bavella.

🅐 D6 🏠 Hameau de Cavanello, Zonza
🌐 locationzonza.com

€€€

Hotel Le Tourisme
A five-minute walk from Zonza, this three-star hotel has a spa, sun terrace and a play area for children.

🅐 D6 🏠 Route de Quenza, Zonza
🌐 hoteldutourisme.fr

€€€

Résidence Chiar' di Luna
The villa apartments here surround a heated pool. There's an on-site wellness centre, too.

🅐 D6 🏠 Ferrulaghjolu, Zonza 🌐 chiar-diluna.com

€€€

↑ Minimalist interior of the Monastère de Assunta Gloriosa de Sari-Solenzara

SHOP

La Cave Sartenaise
Run by the Gambini family since 1955, this gourmet deli serves the finest local produce, including cheeses and charcuterie.

 C6 Place Porta 20100, Sartène lacave sartenaise.com

13

Sartène

C6 40 km (25 miles) SW of Zonza Cours Soeur Amélie; 04 95 77 15 40

Prosper Merimée, who in the 1800s was the Inspector of Antiquities in Corsica, called Sartène "the most Corsican of Corsican towns". Located in the middle of an area rich in prehistoric ruins, this town with a history of vendettas (p113) lies halfway up the hill in the valley of the Rizzanese river.

The old town has a maze of streets lined with mansions. Most alleys are surmounted by arches and vaults. On Good Friday evening, the Baroque church of Ste-Marie, in Place de la Libération, is where the Catenacciu Procession begins. One of the most ancient religious ceremonies in Corsica, the procession re-enacts the crucifixion walk to the Golgotha. The *Catenacciu* ("chained one") represents the Great Penitent. After spending two fasting days in isolation, he dons the traditional red tunic and a hood covering his face while bearing the Cross and heavy chains through the streets. The White Penitent, who represents Simon of Cyrene, helps him carry the Cross, while behind them eight black-clad figures bear a statue of Christ. A traditional chant, "*Perdonu miu Diu*" (Forgive me, Lord), accompanies the slowly moving procession, which comes to a halt back in front of the church where it started.

Sartène is also worth a visit for the **Musée Départemental de Préhistoire Corse et d'Archéologie**, which is similar to the one in Levie and chronicles the long, ancient history of the island. Among the many items on display, the cardial ware (Neolithic pottery) is worth a look, as are the small obsidian arrowheads from nearby Sardinia and the large collection of funerary vases, many of which date from the second and first millennia BCE.

Musée Départemental de Préhistoire Corse et d'Archéologie
 Boulevard Jacques Nicolai 04 95 77 01 09 Hours vary, call ahead

---

14

Levie

D6 10 km (9 miles) S of Zonza Town Hall, Rue Sorba; 04 95 78 00 00

The area around Levie, a short distance from the Aiguilles de Bavella, is one of the most interesting prehistoric zones in Corsica, with many important sites unearthed by digs.

Levie also houses one of the main archaeological museums in Corsica. The engaging **Musée Départemental d'Alta Rocca** has information on the flora, fauna and geology of the island and also houses the famous *Dame de Bonifacio*, the skeleton of an old woman who was buried in 6570 BCE. It is the most ancient relic of the island's past.

About 8 km (5 miles) from Levie, across the Fiumicicoli river valley, is Carbini. It was in this village that the religious sect of the Giovannali was founded (1352) and thrived. The meeting place of the followers was the 14th-century Pisan Romanesque church of St-Jean-Baptiste. As a result

↑ Dining at a café in one of Sartène's arched alleyways

of the 1362 crusade ordered by Pope Urban V against the "satanic heretics", the members of this sect were burned at the stake at the foot of the Monte Kyrie Eleison, the name of which (Greek for "Lord, have mercy") has a particularly poignant ring in this context.

Musée Départemental d'Alta Rocca

 🏠 Quartier Pratu 📞 04 95 78 00 73 🕐 10am–5pm Tue–Sat (Jun–Sep: Mon also)

Quenza

🅰 D6 🏠 8 km (5 miles) N of Zonza 🚌

This village at the foot of the ascent leading to the Col de Bavella is surrounded by a thick oak and chestnut forest. Quenza has two churches. St-Georges, in the village, has a pulpit carved in the form of a Moor's Head supported by sea monsters. The second church, the Romanesque Chapelle de Ste-Marie, was founded around the year 1000 and stands on the road to Aullène.

16

Ste-Lucie de Tallano

🅰 D6 🏠 18 km (11 miles) SW of Zonza

On the road descending west from the Alta Rocca plateau towards the Golfe de Valinco is the village of Ste-Lucie de Tallano, famous for its Couvent St-François, a monastery founded in 1492 by the local lord, Rinuccio della Rocca.

On the village square is the church of Ste-Lucie, which contains a beautiful Catalan-style altarpiece with Christ, St Peter and St Paul in the middle, and three small figures of saints below them. The altarpiece is attributed to the Master of Castelsardo, an artist from the late 15th to the early 16th centuries

↑ Monumental ruins in Cucuruzzu dating from the 2nd millennium BCE

who probably came from the large Franciscan monastery of Castelsardo, in Sardinia. The church of Ste-Lucie also has a *Crucifixion*, which some art historians have attributed to the same artist.

17

Cucuruzzu and Capula

🅰 D6 🏠 17 km (11 miles) SW of Zonza 🕐 Apr–Oct: daily; Nov–Mar: by appt with town hall

A visit to the archaeological site of Cucuruzzu and the medieval castle of Capula involves a pleasant walk through an oak and chestnut forest on the Levie plateau.

Right next to the ticket office, where audio-guides are handed out, is the start of a winding mule track. Cucuruzzu's ruins appear after a 15-minute walk. This *casteddu*, with its wall, huge fireplaces and inner stairway leading to the upper levels, dates from the 2nd millennium BCE. Digs carried out in the 1960s brought to light an entire ancient citadel covering a surface area of 1,200 sq m (12,900 sq ft). Some of the enormous blocks that make up the citadel's walls weigh more than one tonne.

Once back on the trail, a short walk leads to the Chapelle San Lorenzo, which was built using stone blocks from an earlier church, the ruins of which can also be seen here.

A short distance above these are the ruins of the medieval castle of Capula, a Roman fort that was destroyed in 1259 by Giudice della Rocca, who had been made count of Corsica by the Pisans. This site of Capula had already been inhabited in prehistoric times, as confirmed by the nearby menhir-statue of an armed prehistoric warrior (Capula I), which was unearthed during the archaeological digs.

> ### ARCHAEOLOGY IN CORSICA
>
> Archaeologists have unearthed some of Corsica's oldest Bronze Age treasures in the area around Cucuruzzu, and the island's prehistoric riches show no sign of abating. Though excavations on the island began in earnest in the 1950s, new finds keep coming. In 2024, the first Etruscan home was excavated near Ghisonaccia, yielding insights into pre-Roman civilization on the island.

EAT

Chez Pierre Paul U Spuntinu

Enjoy classic French dishes on the terrace of this seafront restaurant.

C6 🚗Entrée du Belvédère-Campomoro 🌐u-spuntinu.fr

€€€

La Mouette

This simple, no-frills restaurant celebrates locally caught seafood.

C6 🚗Place de l'église, Belvédère-Campomoro 📞04 95 74 22 26

€€€

Le Ressac

Le Ressac is known for its fresh, organically produced ingredients.

C6 🚗5A Vignaredda, Belvédère-Campomoro 🌐hotelressac.corsica

€€€

18

Roccapina

C7 🚗22 km (14 miles) S of Sartène

On the N196 road towards Bonifacio, a terrace on a hilltop affords a fine panoramic view of the Golfe de Roccapina and the Pointe de Roccapina promontory; its characteristic pink granite rocks were inhabited in prehistoric times. One of these rocks, which is flanked by a massive Genoese tower, looks like a colossal crouching lion, hence the name Le Lion de Roccapina, or Lion's Rock.

19

Campomoro

C6 🚗17 km (11 miles) W of Proprianos 🛈Town Hall, Belvedere-Campomoro; 04 95 74 20 27

Situated on the south coast of the Golfe de Valinco, the small village of Campomoro is a peaceful place to relax.

A ten-minute walk along a well-marked path dotted with informative signs leads to the 16th-century Genoese Tour de Campomoro. This fortress, the largest in Corsica, allows visitors to explore the interior of a typical defensive tower and offers magnificent views of the gulf. It can be visited from mid-April to September.

Experienced hikers can also explore another splendid coastal path that runs south from Campomoro to Tizzano.

20

Propriano

C6 🚗14 km (9 miles) NW of Sartène 🛈Quai St-Erasme; 04 95 76 01 49

The town of Propriano lies at the innermost point of the Golfe de Valinco. It is a popular yacht harbour and seaside resort thanks to the beaches and coves dotting the gulf.

Propriano developed as a trade centre for Etruscans, Carthaginians, Greeks and Romans in the 2nd century BCE. During the Middle Ages, the area was governed first by the Pisans and then by the Genoese. After Sampiero Corso's anti-Genoa revolts in the 16th century, the town was virtually destroyed by pirate raids. The same period

Pink granite rocks flanking the lovely beach at Roccapina

also saw the demise of the beautiful Santa Giulia di Tavaria abbey, now in ruins.

Propriano came to life again in the 19th and 20th centuries. Now the village is one of the leading resorts on the island, with beautiful beaches and well-developed facilities.

About 9 km (6 miles) from Propriano is Olmeto, a large hamlet housing the ruins of the Castello della Rocca. This is the fortress that Arrigo della Rocca used as a base when he began his rebellion against the Genoese rulers.

21 Filitosa

C6 22 km (14 miles) N of Propriano Apr-Oct: daily; Nov-Mar: by appointment Station Préhistorique de Filitosa, Sollacaro ilitosa.fr

The ancient site of Filitosa offers almost 5,000 years of history. Populated in very

Remarkable anthropomorphic menhir in Filitosa

ancient times because it was both fertile and easy to defend, the area was filled with large constructions and menhirs from 1800 BCE to 1100 BCE. The fortified town dominated the valley of the small Taravo river. It was here, among the stones of one of the structure's walls, that one of the most significant alignments of anthropomorphic menhirs was found. Details of the faces, weapons and helmets of ancient warriors are still clearly visible on the surface of these rocks.

Most of the ruins of Filitosa date from between the late second millennium BCE and 700 BCE. With the rise of Christianity, the menhirs were considered pagan and therefore destroyed. Their remains were heaped together in piles, like mere stones, and had to wait many centuries to be rediscovered.

The tour of Filitosa begins with a fine statue (Filitosa V) standing on the track that leads to the fortified settlement, also known as *oppidum*. Here are the ruins of a village and three monuments, the middle one of which is preserved. Downhill, in a valley,

is the quarry where the stone for the sculpture was extracted. Statues found in the surroundings have been placed around the quarry.

Next to the entrance to the site is a small museum that displays fragments of three menhir statues, the most famous of which is the Scalsa Murta menhir (1400 BCE). Armour and weapons can be seen on these menhirs, as well as holes on the upper part of the head, probably where ornamental ox horns were placed.

22 Porto-Pollo

C6 21 km (13 miles) NW of Propriano Town Hall; 04 95 74 02 12

At the mouth of the Taravo river, Porto-Pollo is a small seaside resort. During the summer, it is popular with people who are attracted by the tranquillity of the place and its delightful beach along the Golfe de Valinco.

Not far from the village, on top of the Pointe de Porto-Pollo, is the Genoese Tour de Capriona. The sea and seabed along its promontory are popular with scuba divers, who love diving down to the so-called *cathédrales*, rocky pinnacles at a depth of 10 m (32 ft).

A DRIVING TOUR
THE MEGALITHS OF CAURIA

Length 20 km (12 miles) **Stopping-off points** Sartène, Tizzano **Terrain** Winding hills; some roads may be steep and have sharp turns

Corsica is a treasure trove of mysterious prehistoric sites. In the region of Sartène alone, after almost two centuries of archaeological research, no fewer than 500 prehistoric sites have been explored. A tour of the barren plateau of Cauria, south of Sartène, offers the chance to visit some of the island's most important megalithic sites. Although Palaggiu is rather remote, it's worth starting your journey into Corsica's prehistory here: the site is home to some of the most important menhir alignments on the island.

BONIFACIO AND THE SOUTH

Megaliths of Cauria

Locator Map

Start at the ancient site of **Palaggiu,** home to 258 menhirs. Just 5 km (three miles) after the Cauria turn-off on the D48 is a mule track to the "stone forest".

Your next detour leads to the smooth **Stantari** menhirs. Each one has a carved stone face and appears to be holding a weapon.

Discovered in 1840 by Prosper Merimée, the dolmen (tomb) at **Fontanaccia** is about 100 m (320 ft) from the parking area.

Palaggiu
START

D48A

Ruisseau de Navara

Ruisseau de Navara

D48

D48A

Ruisseau d'Acquella

Fontanaccia ○*Stantari*
FINISH
Renaghju

0 klometres   1
0 miles   1

N

Finish your tour at **Renaghju**, the most ancient Neolithic settlement in Corsica. The oldest menhirs here date from 4000 BCE.

↑ Megaliths in Palaggiu, prehistoric
structures likely used for astronomical
observations and ceremonial events

CORTE AND THE INTERIOR

There is evidence of a small Bronze Age settlement at Corte, which sits at the island's rugged centre. The ancient Romans, who conquered Corsica in 259 BCE, were aware of the strategic importance of this settlement, given its central location. Though they fortified the town, Corte's most effective defence has long been the landscape itself: the city is skirted by a jagged spine of tall mountains that made it difficult for conquering armies to reach.

Following the departure of the Romans, Corte was further fortified in 1419 by the Viceroy of Aragón – with the construction of the militarized Citadelle – before it was ruled intermittently by the Genoese and the French. It wasn't until the 18th century that the town played its momentous role in the island's politics. In 1735 it became the cradle of patriotism when the constitution for an independent state was drafted here. Just 20 years later, when Corsica was liberated by Pascal Paoli, Corte briefly became the island's capital, and Paoli founded the island's first university here.

No longer the island's capital, Corte retains immense pride in its past, with the Citadelle now home to one of the island's foremost museums, the Musée de la Corse. The island's interior attracts visitors both for Corte's remarkable history and for the superb valleys and mountains, the highest of which is the towering Monte Cinto.

CORTE AND THE INTERIOR

Must See

1 Corte

Experience More

2 Bozio
3 Gorges de la Restonica
4 Col de Vizzavona
5 Forêt de Vizzavona
6 Cascade des Anglais
7 Prunelli-di-Fiumorbo
8 Vallée du Tavignano
9 Aléria
10 Vallée d'Alesani
11 Sovéria
12 La Porta
13 Gorges du Tavignano
14 Cervione
15 La Canonica
16 Vescovato
17 Vallée de l'Asco
18 Ponte-Novo
19 Penta-di-Casinca
20 St-François de Caccia
21 Scala di Santa Regina
22 Calacuccia
23 Casamaccioli
24 Col de Verghio
25 Forêt de Valdu Niellu

D71

Nessa

D547

Montemaggiore

Olmi-
Cappella

Cima di ı Cugnolı
1,113 m (3,651 ft)

Mte Grosso
1,937 m (6,355 ft)

Tortagine

Giunssani

Cima di Modico
1,231 m (4,039 ft)

Monte Corona
2,144 m (7,034 ft)

Monte Padro
2,391 m (7,844 ft)

VALLÉE DE L'ASCO

D147

Balagne

Punta Muvrella
2,148 m (7,047 ft)

17

Pont Génois

D147

Forêt de
Carozzica

Tavlo

Haut-Asco

HAUTE-CORSE

Monte Cinto
2,706 m (8,878 ft)

D84

Paglia Orba
2,525 m
(8,284 ft)

SCALA DI
SANTA REGINA 21

Calasima

22 CALACUCCIA

Cascade
de Radule

23 CASAMACCIOLI

24 COL DE VERGHIO

25 FORÊT DE
VALDU NIELLU

Tavignano

13 GORGES DU
TAVIGNANO

3

GORGES DE LA
RESTONICA

D84

Liamone

Capo Chiostro
2,295 m (7,529 ft)

Lac de Crena

AJACCIO AND
THE WEST COAST
p104

D23

Guagno-
les-Bains

Pastricciola

Monte d'Oro
2,389 m (7,838 ft)

Rosazia

Vallée de la Gravona

Gravona

Bocognano

T20

Sarl-d'Orcino

D1

Tavera

D27

Carbuccia

Peri

CORSE-DU-SUD

T20

Tolla

CORTE AND
THE INTERIOR

D3

D27

0 kilometres   10

0 miles   10

N

CORTE

⚐ D3 🚊🚌 ℹ Station Touristique de l'Intérieur, La Citadelle; tourisme-centrecorse.corsica

Located in the rugged heart of Corsica, Corte was formerly the capital of the island during the short reign of Pascal Paoli (p58). The small town has long been the cradle of the Corsican independence movement, and its grand buildings the setting for many of the island's most important political meetings. The city's mountainous location and excellent museums make it a great place to visit.

① Place Paoli

At the foot of the *haute ville* (upper city) is a large and lively square named after Pascal Paoli. The focal point of Corte, Place Paoli was laid out in the late 19th century by sculptor Victor Huguenin. The centre of the square features a monument to the renowned patriot and instigator of Corsican independence. The statue is surrounded by many bars and cafés, some of which feature traditional Corsican architecture and stone façades, contributing to the square's historic atmosphere.

② Place Gaffori

West of Place Paoli are the ramps of Rue Scoliscia, which lead to the heart of the city and Place Gaffori. Walls still pock-marked by musket fire from the 1740s are among the square's historic features. In the middle is a large bronze statue commemorating General Jean-Pierre Gaffori (p156). On the statue's pedestal are two bas-reliefs depicting the feats of this Corsican leader and those of his wife Faustina. Also on Place Gaffori are the Église de l'Annonciation and the house where Gaffori was born.

From the square, narrow winding streets lead to the carefully preserved medieval districts of Chiostra, Calanche and Mascari.

③ Église de l'Annonciation

⚐ Place Gaffori 📞 04 95 46 26 70 🕐 Hours vary, call ahead

Founded around the mid-15th century, this church is one of the oldest buildings in Corte. However, the façade as it stands today dates from the 18th century. Commissioned

↑ Shops and historic buildings surrounding Place Paoli

> **The Église de l'Annonciation is the church where Joseph Bonaparte, Napoleon's elder brother, was christened in 1811.**

by Alexandre Sauli, who later became bishop of Aléria, it has five pilasters with Corinthian capitals. The tall, slender bell tower that dominates the entire quarter is Baroque.

Inside the church is an altar made of the local grey marble, a carved wooden chair and a 17th-century organ. A wax statue of St Theophilus (the town's patron saint) and a series of Baroque statues – including a white-marble *Virgin* dating from 1613 – are the other highlights here.

The Église de l'Annonciation is best known as the church where Joseph Bonaparte, Napoleon's elder brother, was christened in 1811. The historic Rue Feracci runs in front of the church.

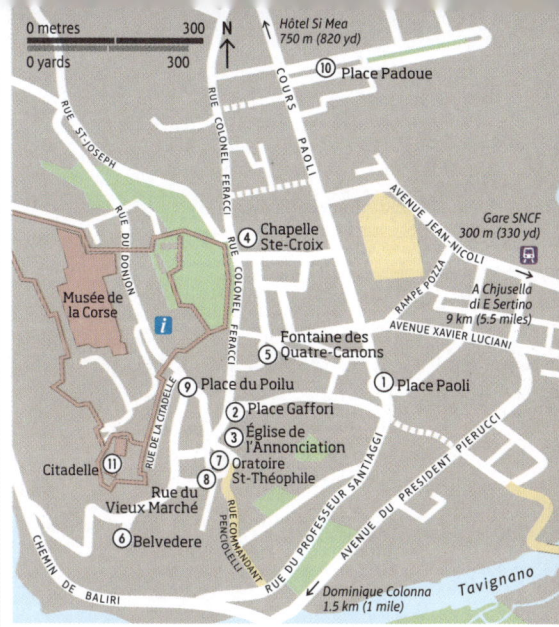

0 metres 300
0 yards 300

N

Hôtel Si Mea 750 m (820 yd)

🔟 Place Padoue

RUE ST-JOSEPH

RUE COLONEL FERACCI

RUE DU DONJON

COURS PAOLI

AVENUE JEAN-NICOLI

Gare SNCF 300 m (330 yd)

RAMPE POZZA

RUE COLONEL FERACCI

4️⃣ Chapelle Ste-Croix

Musée de la Corse

ℹ️

AVENUE XAVIER LUCIANI

A Chjusella di E Sertino 9 km (5.5 miles)

Fontaine des Quatre-Canons

5️⃣

9️⃣ Place du Poilu

2️⃣ Place Gaffori

3️⃣ Église de l'Annonciation

7️⃣ Oratoire St-Théophile

8️⃣

1️⃣ Place Paoli

RUE DE LA CITADELLE

AVENUE DU PRÉSIDENT PIERUCCI

Citadelle

11️⃣

Rue du Vieux Marché

6️⃣ Belvedere

CHEMIN DE BALIRI

RUE COMMANDANT L'HERMINIER

RUE DU PROFESSEUR SANTIAGGI

Dominique Colonna 1.5 km (1 mile)

Tavignano

A short, steep descent along this road leads to a pretty Baroque mansion known as Maison Palazzi.

4️⃣
Chapelle Ste-Croix

🏠 Rampe Ste-Croix
🕐 Mon-Sat

Near Place Paoli is the austere Mannerist façade and small bell tower of the 17th-century church of Ste-Croix. Its pillarless nave, featuring a barrel vault and an aisle paved in grey marble, has trompe-l'oeil effects. By the altar is a colourful Baroque retable and a large medallion with a relief of the *Madonna of the Apocalypse*.

This church is also the home of the Ste-Croix Confraternity, which has always played a leading role in the religious life of the city. During the Holy Week, the Chapelle Ste-Croix marks the starting point of Corte's religious procession.

A short descent along a ramp in front of the church, leads to a square, which is dominated by the Fontaine des Quatre-Canons (*p156*).

STAY

Corte's towering Citadelle, as seen from the Belvedere

⑤ Fontaine des Quatre-Canons

The 8-m- (26-ft-) high conical frame of the Fontaine des Quatre-Canons ("fountain of the four cannons") is one of Corte's most iconic symbols. Commissioned by Louis XVI in 1769, this fountain was only completed in 1778 after its construction was interrupted due to a lack of funds. Its original purpose was to channel water from the Orta torrent to the city to furnish the local garrison with a sorely needed supply of water. Today it is accessible to the public and is a popular local haunt.

From the fountain square, ramps go up to the massive walls of the Citadelle (p158).

⑥ Belvedere

Before visiting the Citadelle, it is worth making time for a walk along the uphill road that skirts its walls. This road leads to a platform known as the Belvedere, which offers a magnificent view of the castle, the Nid d'Aigle ("eagle's nest") tower and, below this, the city and the confluence of the Tavignano and Restonica rivers.

From the Belvedere, a steep 2-km (1-mile) path, the Sentier du Patrimoine, winds past the city's oldest bridge and leads to the banks of the Tavignano river. The short trek is enjoyable by itself though, and rewards visitors with impressive panoramic views over Corte and the rocky cliffs of the Citadelle.

INSIDER TIP
Explore Corte on a Treasure Hunt

Discover Corte's history and architecture on a self-guided "treasure hunt" organized by the Altipiani agency (alti piani-corse.com), who also detail Corte hikes on their website.

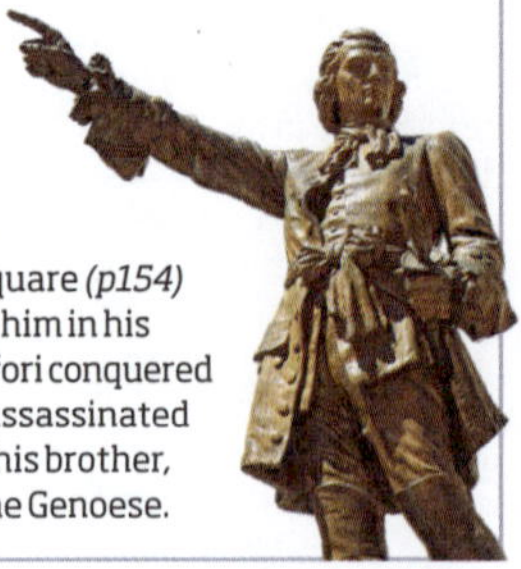

⑦ Oratoire St-Théophile

 Place St-Théophile

The renowned Franciscan monk and freedom fighter Blaise de Signori, better known as St Theophilus, was the first and only Corsican to be canonized. Corte's patron saint, he is honoured with

---

JEAN-PIERRE GAFFORI

A leader of the Corsican independence movement along with Pascal Paoli, Jean-Pierre Gaffori was born in 1704 in Corte. One of his exploits was the taking of Corte in 1746 - a square (p154) in the city was named after him in his honour. Made a general, Gaffori conquered most of the island but was assassinated in an ambush organized by his brother, who was in the service of the Genoese.

this open-air, arcaded chapel sited close to his birthplace.

The interior features a modest altar, along with a few religious paintings and statues (including one of St Theophilus). The chapel's historical significance and quaint charm make it a lovely stop for visitors to Corte.

Rue du Vieux Marché

The name "Vieux Marché" translates to "Old Market", reflecting this avenue's history as a major commercial centre in Corte. Located right next to Corte's Citadelle and university (*p158*), this bustling street is still lined with a number of boutiques and restaurants, as well as coffee houses and bars that cater to the growing student population in the city. A stroll along Rue du Vieux Marché provides visitors a glimpse into the everyday life of Corte's residents.

The avenue is also home to one of Europe's oldest grocery stores, the **Épicerie**

Ghionga Jean Marie, which dates from the 18th century. Easily identified by its bright-orange façade, the store offers a range of local specialities, including cheeses, honey, cured meats and wines.

Épicerie Ghionga Jean Marie

 9 Rue du Vieux Marché
🕒 8am–1pm & 3–7pm Mon–Sat

Place du Poilu

In front of the entrance to the bastions of the Citadelle is Place du Poilu. One of the main attractions in the square

Did You Know?

Napoleon Bonaparte made his brother, Joseph, King of Naples in 1806.

is the historic Maison Arrighi de Casanova. This manor was the ancestral home and birthplace of Jean-Toussaint Arrighi de Casanova, one of Napoleon Bonaparte's generals and, later, the Duke of Padua. Napoleon's parents, Charles and Letizia, lived in this mansion for a few years; it was here that his elder brother Joseph, who went on to become king of Spain, was born in 1768.

Another highlight in Place du Poilu is the 17th-century Palais National. Once the residence of the Genoese governors and then of Pascal Paoli, this is the site where Corsican independence was declared. For 14 years (1755–69) following independence, this palace was the home of the new Corsican parliament. It was then converted into a prison in the 19th century, and later, in the 20th century, to a museum.

Today the Palais National is home to the University Institute of Corsican Studies, a separate branch of the University of Corte, which is based in the Citadelle. The branch is dedicated to studying the rich historical and cultural heritage of Corsica, as well as the island's environment and strategies for sustainable development.

Place Padoue

This small, secluded square is named after General Arrighi de Casanova. The square is dominated by a few shops and restaurants and a statue of Napoleon's general. Just behind it is a war memorial honouring residents who fought in the World Wars.

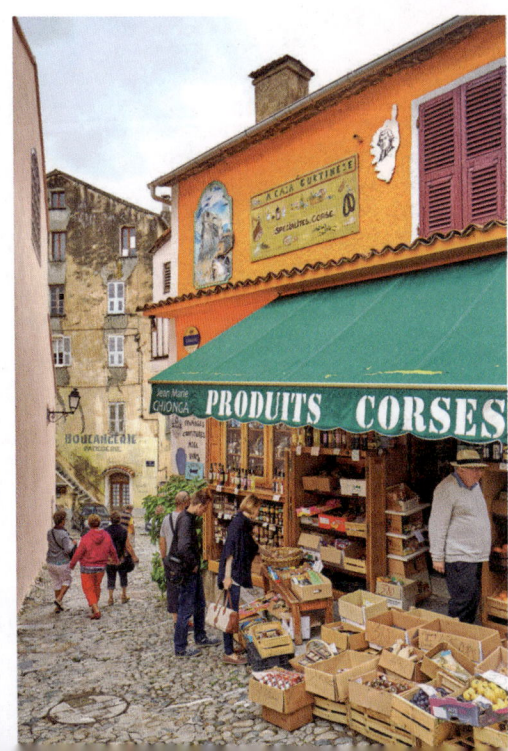

←

The famous Épicerie Ghionga Jean Marie on Rue du Vieux Marché

THE CITADELLE

ℹ Musée de la Corse and La Citadelle: May–Oct: 10am–7pm daily;
Nov–Dec & mid-Jan–Apr: 10am–5pm Tue–Sat; museudiacorsica.corsica

Perched atop a near-vertical crag and built around a lofty castle, the Citadelle is the historical and cultural heart of Corte. Today, it is home to the University of Corsica and the Musée de la Corse.

Already fortified before the Genoese conquest in the 13th century, the Citadelle was transformed into a true fortress in 1419. After many years of foreign rule, the Citadelle became the symbol of the islanders' struggle for independence, especially when Pascal Paoli established Corsica's first university in Corte. When the French took control of Corsica in 1769, the Citadelle became a military zone. The historic site now houses a tourist office, a museum, an art institute and many historic archives, located on the lower level.

Built in 1419 on the southern tip of the rocky spur by Vincentello d'Istria, the castle is the oldest part of the Citadelle.

On top of the bastions, the Nid d'Aigle (eagle's nest) tower offers an impressive view of the precipitous walls of the Citadelle.

The Fond régional d'Art Contemporain is an institute that organizes exhibitions of the region's modern art.

Austere and fortified, as befits a military structure, the entrance portal to the Citadelle is a simple arch surmounted by a tympanum.

Did You Know?

From 1962–1983, the Citadelle was a base of the French Foreign Legion.

Illustration of Corte's Citadelle spreading out from its rocky crag ↑

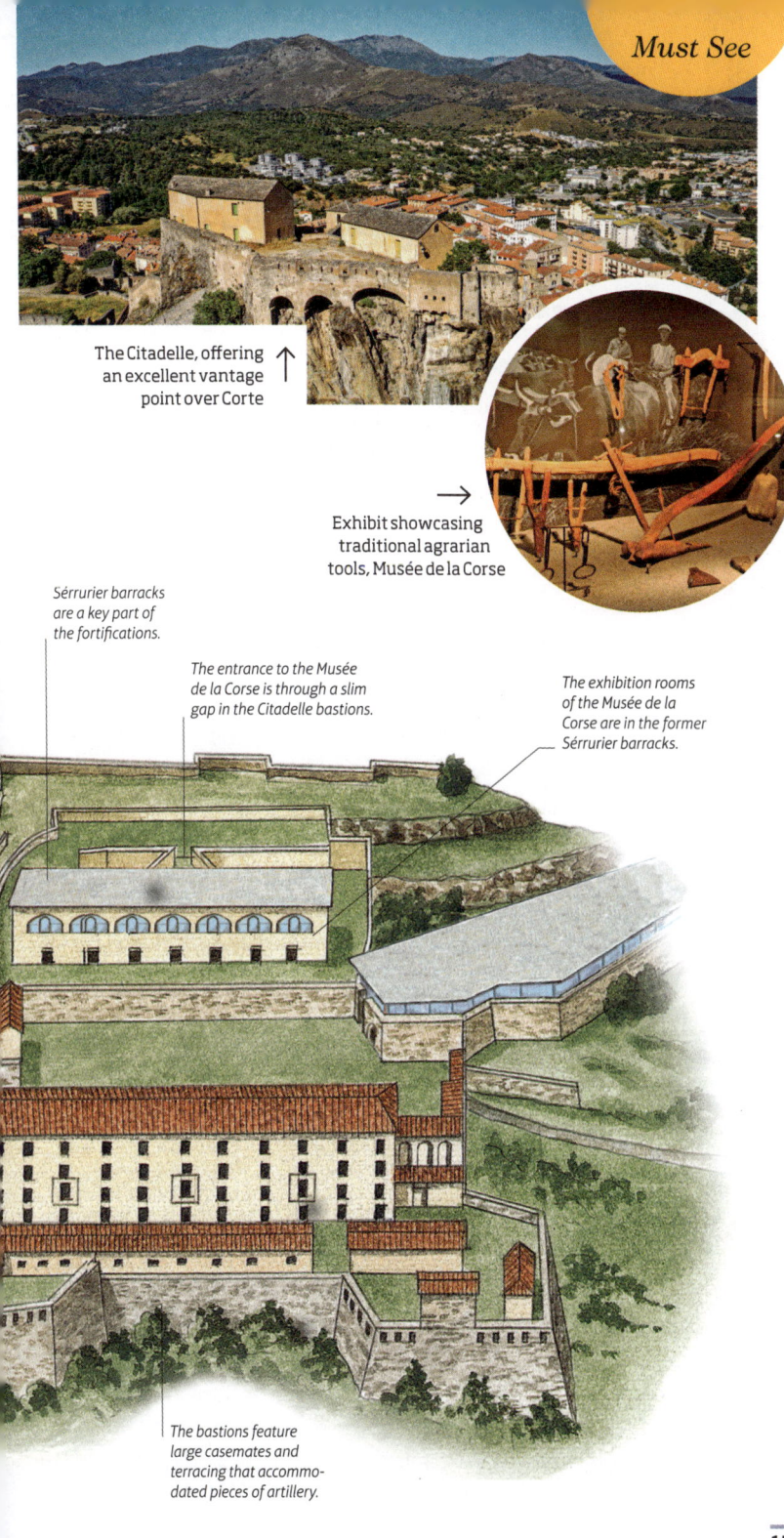

The Citadelle, offering an excellent vantage point over Corte ↑

→ Exhibit showcasing traditional agrarian tools, Musée de la Corse

Sérrurier barracks are a key part of the fortifications.

The entrance to the Musée de la Corse is through a slim gap in the Citadelle bastions.

The exhibition rooms of the Musée de la Corse are in the former Sérrurier barracks.

The bastions feature large casemates and terracing that accommodated pieces of artillery.

EXPERIENCE MORE

Bozio

A E3 **O** 20 km (12 miles) E of Corte

The hilly regions of Bozio and Castagniccia, respectively east and northeast of the town of Corte, comprise a dozen or so hamlets that were once dominated by agricultural production. The region has seen heavy depopulation in recent decades, but a corner seems to have been turned over the past few years, with the creation of holiday cottages, guesthouses and hostels. Many of the region's small hamlets are also now home to various artisans, shepherds and producers, who display their works in small workshops or chapels. Journey through the charming hamlets of Sermano, Favalello, Castirla and Omessa to find chapels with some of the finest frescoes in the entire region.

The regions east of Corte are worth exploring for their natural landscape, which features hills, gorges and winding valleys. The constant curves and hairpin turns make the average speed on these roads extremely low. However, they do offer beautiful views.

Gorges de la Restonica

A D3 **O** 16 km (10 miles) E of Corte **B** Jul & Aug: bus across the length of the valley (the last stretch of the D623 might be closed to private cars at this time)

The scenic, narrow valley that descends from the seven lakes of Monte Rotondo (p43) towards Corte lies between steep slopes, creating a series of awesome gorges. Despite the terrible fires that, in 2000, damaged the centuries-old forest covering its slopes, this

fascinating valley is still very popular among hikers who, from spring onwards, look for relief from the heat along the pebbled shores of the torrent.

After leaving Corte, the Restonica road (D623) goes past the Hotel Dominique Colonna (p155) and up the hills. For some stretches, the gorge becomes deep and seems to be hewn out of rock.

After about 14 km (9 miles) are the Bergeries de Grottelle, which lie 1,375 m (4,511 ft) above sea level. These typical stone-hut complexes house shepherds and sheep in the summer. This is where the motorable road ends and there are some kiosks open in spring and summer.

From the Bergeries de Grottelle, a steep path goes over a rocky crest. Here, the hardest stretches have metal ladders; should it rain, be careful of the slippery rocks. After about an hour's walk is the first of the small lakes in this area, the Lac de Mélo, at an altitude of 1,711 m (5,613 ft). From the shore of the lake, the views encompass the surrounding mountains and the Vallée de la Restonica. Further along the path, at 1,930 m (6,331 ft), is the Lac

> **Many of the region's small hamlets are also now home to various artisans, shepherds and producers, who display their works in small workshops.**

←
Jagged peaks looming over the Melu lake in Gorges de la Restonica

du Capitellu, a glacial lake surrounded by steep cliffs. At an altitude of about 2,000 m (6,500 ft), the landscape is open and impressive: to the left is the 2,622-m (8,602-ft) high Monte Rotondo, and to the right is the crest of Capo Chiostro, which reaches a height of 2,295 m (7,529 ft).

The two sides of the valley have many paths leading to

lakes and *bergeries*. In summer, it is possible to stay at the Tuani campsite, known for its delicious pizzas, midway along the D623.

4

Col de Vizzavona

 D4 35 km (22 miles) S of Corte Vizzavona

The road linking Bastia and Ajaccio (the N193, one of the main roads on the island) crosses Corsica's inland mountain ranges at the pass of Col de Vizzavona. This mountain, at an altitude of 1,161 m (3,809 ft), marks the border between Haute-Corse and Corse-du-Sud. The pass has tables and benches for a stopoff and picnic and is populated by wild pigs that are not disturbed by visitors.

From Col de Vizzavona, which is often quite windy, there is a fine view of the 2,389-m (7,838-ft) high Monte d'Oro. An easy, uphill path leading north off the N193

CLIMBING MONTE RENOSO

A tough 9-km (6-mile) hike begins northwest of Ghisoni, not far from Col de Vizzavona, in a signposted carpark before heading to the Source de Pizzolo. From here, it's an easy stretch to the clear Lac de Bastani (swimming is not permitted), before a steep incline to the panoramic summit of Monte Renoso. The peak offers remarkable views over the wider Monte Renose massif.

road to Bastia stretches for about 400 m (1,300 ft) to the ruins of a Genoese fortification. Many other footpaths cross this area, including the GR20 long-distance path *(p61)*.

5

Forêt de Vizzavona

 D4 38 km (23 miles) S of Corte Vizzavona

Of all the forests in the large, green heart of the island, the Forêt de Vizzavona is one of the most famous and popular. Dotted with hazelnut and chestnut trees as well as tall Corsican pines and other conifers, the forest stretches for around 1600 ha (3950 acres).

The area is traversed by the GR20 long-distance path *(p61)*, and in spring and summer, many groups of hikers disembark at the small railway station of Vizzavona, 3 km (2 miles) away.

The Forêt de Vizzavona is also crossed by the N193 road linking Ajaccio and Bastia and by the railway line inaugurated in 1894.

←
The L'Agnone river flowing under a bridge in Col de Vizzavona

The Cascade des Anglais gushing into a crystal-clear pool

the last in Corsica to agree to abide by French law, and tales of the battles between the French army and the locals are today the stuff of legend.

The region is a little way from the usual Corsican tourist trail, and its small villages, rolling hills and lush gorges make for great rural adventures. Of note are the hamlets Pietrapola, with its hot springs, and Ghisoni, which crosses the Defilé de l'Inzecca gorge.

Vallée du Tavignano

E4 **25 km (16 miles) SE of Corte**

The Vallée du Tavignano is traversed by one of the oldest roads on the island, the N200, connecting Aléria and Corte.

Travelling from Aléria along the course of the Tavignano river, which begins at Lac de Nino, in the middle of Corsica, there are many narrow gorges.

On the north side of the valley, the narrow D14 road leads to villages typical of the region, perched halfway up the hills in panoramic positions. One of these, Piedicorte di Gaggio, offers views towards the coast and has an ancient Roman architrave in the wall of its parish-church bell tower.

A Genoese bridge still stands at Altiani, as promised by its engineers, who guaranteed the bridge would remain standing in all circumstances "save a deluge".

The village of Erbajolo, towering over the canyon carved by the Tavignano river, offers a breathtaking view of the profiles of Monte Renoso and Monte d'Oro. On the belvedere square is a plaque indicating interesting natural and historic attractions.

Cascade des Anglais

D4 **35 km (22 miles) S of Corte** **Vizzavona**

One of the most popular walks in this area is the hike along the GR20 long-distance path (p61). The leg runs from the road near the hamlet of La Foce to the Cascade des Anglais (meaning "waterfall of the English"), a beauty spot much admired by early English visitors to this area. This trip, which is on an easy and well-marked path, takes less than two hours up and back, and follows the course of the Agnone torrent.

Beyond the Cascade des Anglais, which stands 1,100 m (3,600 ft) above sea level, the water has carved a series of deep potholes that are ideal for a swim.

In fair weather, and with adequate equipment, it is possible to continue up to the head of the valley towards the summit of Monte d'Oro. However, this is a strenuous hike of around seven to eight hours from Vizzavona and is only recommended for fit and experienced hill walkers.

The summit of Monte d'Oro overlooks all the main Corsican peaks and from there it is even possible to see the Italian coast.

Prunelli-di-Fiumorbo

E5 **30 km (12 miles) SW of Aléria**

The main village in the Fiumorbo region, vibrant Prunelli-di-Fiumorbo is home to a fortified church that offers excellent views over the lush surrounding countryside.

The village is named after the Fium'orbu ("blind river" in Corsican), which flows from the slopes of the nearby Monte Renoso and winds its way down through the deep Strette and Inzecca gorges. This wild region was one of

⑨

Aléria

△E4 **△48 km (30 miles) SE of Corte** **ℹ80 Avenue St-Alexandre Sauli; oriente-corsica.com**

The history of the ancient settlement of Aléria, on the marshy east coast of Corsica, began when Greek colonists set up a commercial outpost here in the 6th century BCE. The outpost, then known as Alalia, served as a base for trade with the Italian and southern French coasts.

Following a period of Carthaginian domination, in 259 BCE Alalia was invaded by the Romans, who renamed the settlement Aléria. Aléria was the capital of Corsica in the Imperial Age, and Augustus Diocletian and Hadrian beautified it with large public works. In the 5th century CE, the increase of malaria and invasion by the Vandals led to the abandonment of the city.

Visits to the archaeological site begin at a Genoese fort, Fort Matra. Built in 1484, this site is now the home of the **Musée d'Archéologie Jérôme Carcopino**, named after the great scholar of Corsican origin. The items on display here include Greek, Phoenician, Roman, Apulian and Etruscan ceramics that were found on the hill where the city rose up. Among the most interesting works are two *rhytons* (wine vessels) that were made in Attica, Greece, one in the shape of a mule's head, the other representing a dog.

Outside the museum are the ruins of the Roman city. To the left of the Forum is a temple flanked by two porticoes and, to the right, the Praetorium – the official residence of the governor of the island – and the Capitol. In addition, traces of past civilizations dating as far back as the 6th century BCE have been found throughout the area.

Musée d'Archéologie Jérôme Carcopino and site of Aléria

⊗ **△**Fort Matra **☎**04 95 57 00 92 **◷**Daily **✕**Nov–Mar: Sun & public hols

Aléria's Ancient Sites

1. Forum
2. Temple
3. *Domus cum Domus* (townhouse)
4. *Domus cum Impluvium* (water storage)
5. Shops
6. South portico
7. North portico
8. *Thermae* (warm baths)
9. *Balneum* (baths)
10. *Calidarium* (steam rooms)
11. Chambers
12. Industrial edifices
13. Pools
14. *Praetorium* (governor's residence)
15. Capitol
16. North arch
17. South arch
18. *Decumanus* (street)
19. Bastions

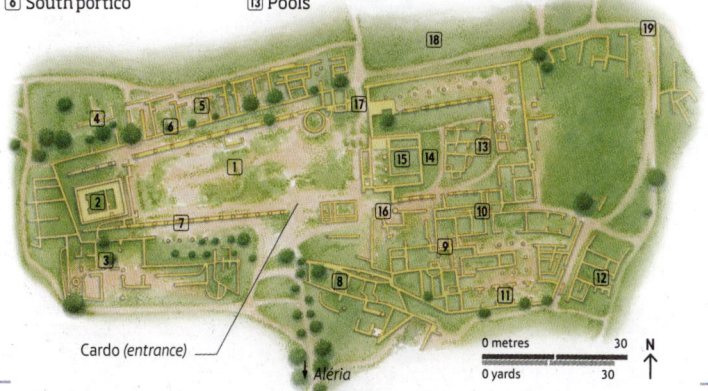

Cardo (entrance)

Aléria

0 metres   30
0 yards   30

N ↑

⑩ Vallée d'Alesani

Ⓐ E3 **Ⓗ 35 km (22 miles) SE of La Porta**

This area consists of a group of hamlets scattered on the upper course of the Alesani river. The region is linked to Theodor von Neuhoff, the first and only king of Corsica; he was crowned in the Couvent St-François in the nearby village of Piazzali in 1736. The monastery, dating from 1716, houses the *Virgin of the Cherry* (1450), a painting attributed to Sienese artist Sano di Pietro.

The neighbouring village of Perelli is known for being the home of the legendary Grosso-Minuto, a popular comic character in Corsican folklore.

---

⑪ Sovéria

Ⓐ D3 **Ⓗ 8 km (5 miles) N of Corte** **Ⓡ Sovéria**

Not far from Corte is the pretty village of Sovéria, located over the Vallée du Golo, a stone's throw away from the Vallée de l'Asco and the regions of Bozio and Castagniccia. Sovéria is appreciated for the harmonious architecture of its houses.

In antiquity, the countryside around Sovéria was given over to vineyards and winemaking. The landscape has changed, however, and today the soft hills are covered with oak and chestnut groves; the area is renowned for its production of excellent nougat.

Outside town, along the D18 road, is the 10th-century church of Santa Mariona. The only remaining original parts of this church are the apses made up of grey stone from the local schist mountains.

---

⑫ La Porta

Ⓐ E3 **Ⓗ 45 km (28 miles) SE of Corte** **ⓘ La Porta Town Hall; 04 95 39 21 48**

Situated in a fertile area covered in woods, the village of La Porta ("the door") owes its name and prosperity to its location – in the past, this village was the only access route to the region of Castagniccia.

Today, La Porta is famous because of the beautiful church of St-Jean-Baptiste, which stands out among the slate roofs of the village. It is considered to be the most complete work of Baroque architecture in Corsica.

DOROTHY CARRINGTON

Bohemian aristocrat, academic and explorer, British-born Dorothy Carrington moved to Corsica in 1948 and spent over 50 years exploring the island's wild landscapes. She lived in the rugged mountainous terrain east of Corte, where she wrote her book *Granite Island: A Portrait of Corsica* (1971), a populat study of Corsica's ethnography and ecology.

Construction of the church began in 1648 and continued for nearly half a century under the Italian architect Domenico Baina. The façade was completed in 1707, although it had later alterations. It has been restored to its original ochre colour, which, combined with the vertical pilasters, gives a spectacular impression.

The lower part of the façade is rather austere, with tall pilasters forming a strict pattern. This is broken up by the upper level's elaborate Baroque elements with hints of Rococo, in the shape of pilaster strips, swirly volutes and cartouches. The excesses of the Italian Baroque style have been avoided through this juxtaposition of the plain base

> **Today, La Porta is famous because of the church of St-Jean-Baptiste, which stands out among the slate roofs of the village.**

← Mountain village of Sovéria, nestled in oak and chestnut groves

with detailing on the higher parts, while the overall harmony of the building has been maintained. The 45-m (147-ft) bell tower next to it shares the same pattern of design.

The interior has a single nave flanked by side chapels separated from one another by columns with Corinthian capitals. The walls and ceiling are decorated with late 19th-century stucco work and fine trompe-l'oeil art by the artist Girolamo da Porta. Above the entrance is a monumental organ used in concerts. Other interesting works here include the high altar, made of white Carrara marble, with the altarpiece framed by two small columns, and the pulpit.

The interior contains many beautiful works of art. Among these are *Decapitation of St John the Baptist* to the right of the choir, and two 17th-century wooden sculptures representing Christ and the Virgin Mary.

13

Gorges du Tavignano

 D3   9 km (6 miles) W of Corte

East of Corte, the lower course of the Tavignano river extends to Aléria and the sea, its upper course consists of a narrow valley. Here are gorges that can be reached only by walking along easy paths paved for much of their length in original medieval cobbles and steeped in nature.

One of these paths starts from below Corte's Citadelle and leads to the Arche de Corte (also known as the Arche de Padule), a rocky crest surrounded by *bergeries* lying at an altitude of around 1,500 m (4,921 ft). The path passes through chestnut groves in the hilly zone and then, above 1,000 m (3,300 ft), through conifer woods. Strenuous rather than difficult, it entails a walk of over five hours each way. Looking back from the

↑ Hiking a medieval cobbled trail in the Gorges du Tavignano

gorges, the impressive rock of the Citadelle can be seen, still seeming to have control over the entire region.

14

Cervione

 D3   40 km (25 miles) SE of La Porta

At the foot of Monte Castello and in the easternmost part of Castagniccia, Cervione is surrounded by vineyards, olive orchards and chestnut groves. After the destruction of Aléria, Cervione became a bishopric and, to mark the occasion, the cathedral of St-Erasme was built.

In 1714, the original church was replaced by a new complex, Ste-Marie-et-St-Erasme, the present-day cathedral. The Bishop's Palace and the seminary – now the home of an ethnographic museum – were also built during this same period.

Cervione is the starting point of the panoramic D330 road, also called Corniche de la Castagniccia. About 2 km (1 mile) from the town, along this route, is the 9th-century Chapelle Ste-Christine, with twin apses and some frescoes.

 The 12th-century Romanesque cathedral of La Canonica

15 La Canonica

⚠ E3 📍 Lucciana, 36 km (22 miles) N of La Porta 🕐 Cathedral: summer: daily; winter: Mon–Fri (ask for the key at Lucciana Town Hall)

During the period of the Roman conquest (c 259 BCE), many colonies were founded in Corsica. While the main colonial city was Aléria (p163), another one, Mariana, lay nearer to present-day Bastia. It was named after the Roman general Marius, who in 100 BCE founded a colony for the veterans of his army near the Étang de Biguglia. Destroyed by the Vandals in the 5th century CE, Mariana was dealt its final blow by the malaria epidemics that struck the inhabitants of the coastal plains.

The Pisans built one of their finest cathedrals nearby, **La Canonica**, which was consecrated by the archbishop of Pisa in 1119. He resided in the nearby bishop's palace, of which only traces of the foundations remain. Known by its original name, even though it was dedicated to Santa Maria Assunta, La Canonica was abandoned for reasons of health and security two centuries later, when the bishop moved to nearby Vescovato.

The church is considered the prototype of all the Pisan churches in Corsica. The nave is divided into three sections and ends in a semicircular apse; its elegance is created by the colours of the stone (from the Cap Corse quarries) and by few architectural decorative elements. Above the main portal are friezes representing griffons, a lamb, a wolf and a deer being chased by a dog. The series of holes on the outer walls of the church have been said to have originally contained multicoloured stone inlays, but they are in fact damage caused by scaffolding.

16 Vescovato

⚠ E3 📍 Lucciana, 28 km (17 miles) N of La Porta ℹ Town Hall, Place Luce de Casabianca; 04 95 36 70 19

Located on a mountainside at the northern end of the Castagniccia region, the town of Vescovato was founded by refugees who had abandoned the city of Mariana, which had proved too vulnerable to invasions and malaria.

For centuries, Vescovato was the capital of the small hilly region of Casinca, which lies between the Golo river and the Vallée du Fium'Alto and which, thanks to its fertile soil, for a long period had the largest population on the island. Formerly known as Belfiorito, it was renamed Vescovato ("bishopric") because it was the bishop's seat from 1269 to 1570, when it was replaced by Bastia. To make the most of a visit here, it is advisable to park at the only tree-lined square and walk through the alleys.

In the middle of the village is the Baroque church of San Martino, with a 16th-century tabernacle sculpted by the Italian Antonello Gagini. Next to the church, a vaulted passageway leads to the main square, which has a handsome fountain guarded by an eagle.

There are also three other churches in town: the church of the Capuchin monastery, the Romanesque Chapelle San Michele and the chapel of the Ste-Croix Confraternity.

The coast east of Vescovato is lined by increasingly popular sandy beaches and swish tourist resorts.

---

17 Vallée de l'Asco

⚠ D3 📍 Lucciana, 40 km (25 miles) W of La Porta

The long, diagonal Vallée de l'Asco – which runs for 30 km (18 miles) southwest of Ponte Leccia – is one of the most isolated areas in Corsica. The road that traverses it follows the winding course of the river Asco up to Corsica's most striking range of mountains, dominated by the dark profile of Monte Cinto, the highest peak on the island at 2,706 m (8,878 ft). Along the road is the Cirque de Trimbolocciu, a

 🔍 HIDDEN GEM Natural Pools

From the village of Asco, you can take a 15-minute hike to the secluded Pont Génois. Near the bridge, a number of small natural pools provide the perfect place for a restorative swim.

Monte Cinto towering over a
Genoese bridge near Ponte
Leccia, Vallée de l'Asco

spectacular natural "amphithe-atre" surrounded by cliffs.

In an open area of the valley is the village of Asco, which was one of the centres of the Corsican resistance against the Genoese. An unsurfaced road full of hairpin bends drops down from Asco towards the banks of the river and then to a marvellous Genoese bridge with the typical arched span.

As the valley rises, the vegetation changes, and the shrubs give way to the pines and larches of the Forêt de Carozzica. After this forest, the road ends at the ski resort at Haut-Asco. At an altitude of 1,450 m (4,757 ft), this resort is a favourite starting point for hikers on their way towards Monte Cinto (eight hours up and back) or for those on the GR20 long-distance path (p61), which crosses the Haut-Asco area. The route passes near the 2,556 m (8,385ft) high Punta Minuta and arrives at the Tighjiettu refuge.

 18

Ponte-Novo

Ⓐ E3 **Ⓐ Along the N193 road, 8 km (5 miles) NE of Ponte Leccia**

This locality was named after a bridge built by the Genoese, but its fame throughout the island is due to the battle fought on the banks of the Golo river between the French troops commanded by Count de Vaux and the Corsican pat-riots led by Pascal Paoli (p58).

On 8 May 1769, the invading French troops, who had been defeated the year before at Borgo, were attempting to find an entry point to the interior of Corsica, which was under the control of the independence fighters. The 2,000 Corsican patriots were driven back by the French and retreated along the bridge, where they were quickly overcome. After this defeat, Paoli was forced to abandon the struggle against the French and, in June 1769, left the island for England. Thus ended the Corsicans' dream of independence and freedom.

Today, the original bridge is in ruins because of bom-bardments during World War II. A bridge was built over the river, but the battle is com-memorated by a monument and a plaque, accompanied by flags with a Moor's head, the symbol of the Corsican nation. A visit here offers a great insight into the independent spirit of the island's people.

→

Enjoying the view
from a high archway
in Penta-di-Casinca

19

Penta-di-Casinca

Ⓐ E3 **Ⓐ 23 km (14 miles) E of La Porta**

Penta is one of the Casinca region's most captivating vil-lages, dominated by a 16th-century Genoese tower.. Tall, grey-stone buildings with roofs tiled with green schist slate give Penta a character-ful, almost forbidding look.

The village's Romanesque chapel has been superseded by a grander Baroque church, but the former is worth visit-ing to see the archway to its cemetery. It reads, *"Oghje a me"* (today me) at the entrance and *"Dumane a te"* (tomorrow you) at the exit.

St-François de Caccia

D3 Castifao, 21 km (13 miles) W of Ponte-Novo

At the beginning of the Vallée de l'Asco, leaving the D47 road in the direction of Moltifao, a detour of about 4 km (2 miles) leads to the ruins of the monastery of St-François de Caccia, located near the picturesque village of Castifao.

Founded in the early 16th century and destroyed by the Genoese in 1553, the monastery and its church were reconstructed thanks to the efforts of friar Augustinu da Populasca. The complex was then entrusted to a group of Franciscan monks. The church, built in 1569 and rebuilt in 1750, collapsed in 1782. Here, in 1755, Pascal Paoli *(p58)* took part in the assembly of Corsican deputies who drew up the island's constitution.

 Scala di Santa Regina

D3 6 km (4 miles) N of Calacuccia

The Vallée du Golo has always been an important communication link between the interior and the west coast of Corsica. If you follow the course of the Golo river, it leads to the highest motorable pass on the island, the Col de Verghio, at 1,464 m (4,803 ft) above sea level. From here, one can descend towards Porto and Ajaccio.

Along the valley, on the right-hand side of the road, is the Scala di Santa Regina gorge, which, according to popular tradition, was created thanks to the intervention of the Virgin Mary at the end of a fierce battle between St Martin and Satan. With the reddish hues of the local granite, this narrow gorge is an impressive sight from the road, stretches of which are often cut from the steep rock.

Parts of a narrow mule track, along which commercial traffic travelled in the past, are still visible from the paved road on the opposite slope of the valley.

 Calacuccia

D3 27 km (17 miles) W of Corte Route de Cuccia; 04 95 47 12 62

The main town in the Niolo mountain region and in the pass that leads to the Col de Verghio, Calacuccia stands 1,000 m (3,300 ft) above sea level. It is known for its stunning position on the banks of the lake created by a dam that blocks the flow of the Golo river. Small hotels and restaurants which are crowded in summer provide relaxation and magnificent views of Monte Cinto *(p166)* to the northwest and Capo Tafonato, which rises up next to Col de Verghio.

From Albertacce, around 5 km (3 miles) southwest of Calacuccia, orange waymarks lead from opposite a large white crucifix on the western edge of the village to the Pont de Muricciolu; the latter is an old Genoese footbridge overlooking natural pools that are popular bathing spots.

On the south bank of the artificial lake is the hamlet of Casamaccioli and going up towards the 1,592-m- (5,223-ft-) high Bocca di l'Arinella pass, an unpaved road offers breathtaking views.

> According to tradition, the Scala di Santa Regina was created thanks to the intervention of the Virgin Mary at the end of a fierce battle between St Martin and Satan.

EAT

Auberge U Fucaghjolu
With stunning views of nearby Monte Cinto, this local favourite serves up hearty classics, including excellent pizzas and fresh burgers.

D3 Pianotoli, Calacuccia
+33 4 95 59 82 18

€€€

A Casa Niulinca
An excellent choice for those on the way back from Monte Cinto or the Aïtone forest, this friendly spot serves an excellent charcuterie board.

D3 Calacuccia
+33 6 03 35 60 03

€€€

Hiking through the verdant forest near Calacuccia ↑

Casamaccioli

🗺 D3 🚗 4 km (2 miles) S
of Calacuccia

Opposite Calacuccia, across the artificial lake and at an altitude of 850 m (2,800 ft), is Casamaccioli, a hamlet with fewer than 100 permanent inhabitants. Besides offering a marvellous view of the lake, the Monte Cinto massif and the surrounding chestnut forests, this village has an interesting tradition that attracts visitors. In the Nativité parish church, beside a wooden statue of St Roch, there is a sculpture of the Virgin Mary, or "La Santa". On 7–10 September, it is carried in the Nativity of the Virgin procession during the festivities in her honour.

_____

Col de Verghio

🗺 C3 🚗 17 km (11 miles)
SE of Calacuccia

The road towards Porto (D84) passes over the Col de Verghio, the highest point in the island's road network.

Just east of the Col de Verghio pass, along this route is the small winter-sports resort of Verghio, which is a favourite with hikers in the summer. Here, it is possible to make the ascent to the small Lac de Nino (p64), the grassy basin of which is grazing land for small herds of wild horses during the summer. Another popular hike in the area leads to the Cascate di Radule, located north of the Verghio pass.

Beaten by the wind and extremely wild, Col de Verghio is part of the itinerary of the GR20 long-distance path (p61), which, heading north, passes by the Cascades de Radule and then heads up to the Ciuttulu di i Mori refuge at the foot of the majestic Capo Tafonato mountain and the nearby peak of Paglia Orba.

_____

Forêt de Valdu Niellu

🗺 D3 🚗 13 km (8 miles) S
of Calacuccia

Southwest of Casamaccioli, on the left-hand side of the road is this vast forest, the largest

in Corsica. Although severely damaged by fires in the height of summer, the Forêt de Valdu Niellu covers a surface area of more than 46 sq km (18 sq miles) in a mountain zone at an altitude of about 1,000–1,600 m (3,300–5,250 ft). It is dominated by birch and beech trees as well as Laricio pines, trees found only on the island of Elba, in parts of the Italian region of Calabria and here in Corsica. At Valdu Niellu, there are Laricio pines as much as 500 years old.

The forest offers many activities, including hiking paths of several levels of difficulty. There is one that takes an hour, going from the Popaja rangers' house to the heart of the forest and then to the Bergeries de Colga. A harder path goes to the 1,743-m- (5,718-ft-) high glacial Lac de Nino (a walk of three-and-a-half hours), the source of the Tavignano river. The descent to the Cascades de Radule takes a further 90 minutes. The forest also offers some great picnic spots as well as ample opportunities for photographers and bird-watchers alike.

A DRIVING TOUR
CASTAGNICCIA

Length 120 km (75 miles) **Journey time** 2–3 days, depending on your pace **Stopping-off points** San Tommaso di Pastoreccia, Morosaglia, San Pantaleo, San Quilico, La Porta, Piedicroce, Couvent d'Orezza **Terrain** Winding hills; some roads may be steep and have sharp turns

Named after its numerous chestnut (*castagna*) groves, Castagniccia was one of the first areas on the island to be inhabited. The highlights of a journey through this region include numerous 12th–16th-century Baroque chapels with impressive frescoes – many of which were restored between 2005 and 2010 – and the complex 17th- and 18th-century architecture of the churches of Piedicroce and La Porta. Castagniccia also played a key role in the history of Corsica – Morosaglia was the birthplace of independence leader Pascal Paoli, and the region became the centre of a thriving arms industry during the Corsican revolution.

*The church of **San Pantaleo**, featuring a beautifully frescoed apse, is on the D639 road going down from Morosaglia in the direction of the village of Saliceto. Ask for the keys at the only house in Pieditermini.*

*On the D639 road is the Pisan chapel of **San Quilico**, the lovely tympanum of which is sculpted with Adam and Eve being tempted by the serpent, and with a bas-relief of a man fighting a dragon.*

Valle-di-Rostino

San Pantaleo

Saliceto

San-Lorenzo

San Quilico

Cambia

Carticasi

↑ Quaint buildings near the D71 and D506 roads in Castagniccia

San Tommaso di Pastoreccia has survived excessive restoration that, in the 1930s, destroyed half of its original structure. In the apse is an Annunciation; on the walls are the remains of a Last Judgment.

The ruins of Couvent d'Orezza, near Piedicroce

START
San Tommaso di Pastoreccia

Morosaglia

D515

La Porta

Ficaja

Croce

D515

D71

△ Monte San Petrone
1,767 m (5,797 ft)

Verdèse

D46

*Couvent
d'Orezza*

Piedicroce   **FINISH**

Pie-d'Orezza

D71

△ Monte Calleruccio
1,484 m (4,868 ft)

Corsicans attach special importance to **Morosaglia**, the hamlet where Pascal Paoli was born. His ashes are interred here. A short walk from Paoli's house-museum is the small church of Santa Reparata.

In 1751, an assembly met in **Couvent d'Orezza**, a monastery in the outskirts of Piedicroce, to confer military and executive power on Jean-Pierre Gaffori. The monastery was reduced to ruins during World War II.

At **Piedicroce**, the Baroque church of Sts-Pierre-et-Paul dominates a soft landscape of rolling green hills. Built between 1684 and 1696, its façade is decorated with white pilasters and friezes. Inside are frescoes and Rococo decorations.

| 0 kilometres | 2 |
| 0 miles | 2 |

N
↑

NEED TO KNOW

The red rocks of the Calanques de Piana

Before You Go...174

Getting Around...176

Practical Information...............................180

BEFORE
YOU GO

Things change, so plan ahead to make the most of your trip. Be prepared for all eventualities by considering the following points before you travel.

AT A GLANCE

CURRENCY
Euro

AVERAGE DAILY SPEND

ON A BUDGET
€65

MODERATE SPENDER
€165

SPLASH OUT
€300

BOTTLED WATER
€2

COFFEE
€3.50

BEER
€7

DINNER FOR TWO
€60

ESSENTIAL PHRASES

Hello	Bonjour
Thank you	Au revoir
Please	S'il vous plaît
Thank you	Merci
Do you speak English?	Parlez-vous anglais?
I don't understand	Je ne comprends pas

ELECTRICITY SUPPLY
Power sockets are type F, fitting two-pronged plugs. Standard voltage is 230v/50Hz.

Passports and Visas

For entry requirements, consult your nearest French embassy or check the **French-Visas** website. Citizens of the UK, US, Canada, Australia and New Zealand do not need a visa for stays of up to three months but in future must apply in advance for the European Travel Information and Authorization System (**ETIAS**); roll-out has continually been postponed so check website for details.
ETIAS
Ⓦ travel-europe.europa.eu/etias_en
Ⓦ france-visas.gouv.fr

Government Advice

It is important to consult both your and the French government's advice before travelling. The **UK Foreign, Commonwealth and Development Office** (FCDO), the **US State Department**, the **Australian Department of Foreign Affairs and Trade**, and French-Visas website (*above*) offer the latest information on security, health and local regulations.
Australian Department of Foreign Affairs and Trade
Ⓦ smartraveller.gov.au
UK Foreign, Commonwealth and Development Office (FCDO)
Ⓦ gov.uk/foreign-travel-advice
US State Department
Ⓦ travel.state.gov

Customs Information

You can find information on laws relating to goods and currency taken in or out of France on the **Douanes and Droites Indirects** website.
Douanes and Droites Indirects
Ⓦ douanes.gouv.fr

Insurance

We recommend taking out a comprehensive insurance policy covering medical care, theft, loss of belongings, cancellations and delays, and

reading the small print carefully. UK citizens are eligible for free emergency medical care in France provided they have a valid European Health Insurance Card (EHIC) or UK **Global Health Insurance Card** (GHIC).

GHIC

w ghic.org.uk

Vaccinations

No vaccinations are required to visit Corsica.

Booking Accommodation

Corsica offers a wide range of accommodation, from five-star hotels to campsites (known as "refuges") along the GR20 route. Lodgings fill up quickly in the summer, particularly in Bonifacio and Ajaccio, so it's worth booking ahead.

Money

Corsica's currency is the euro. Major credit and debit cards are accepted by most businesses, while prepaid currency cards and American Express are accepted in some. Contactless payments are increasingly common, but it's always a good idea to carry some cash for smaller items, just in case. In rural areas, particularly if you are hiking the GR20, you may find smaller shops that do not take card.

Cash machines (ATMs) can be found every-where. It is customary to tip 5–10 per cent, and when buying a beer at a bar, to round up to the nearest euro.

Travellers With Specific Requirements

Visiting Corsica with specific requirements can be a tough task, particularly if you plan on leaving the larger towns. The terrain is steep and mountainous, and old villages typically have cobbled streets which may pose a challenge to wheelchair users. That said, many of the most beautiful attractions in and around Bonifacio and Ajaccio, including the beaches, are wheelchair accessible, and larger towns are generally well equipped for wheelchair users. Most ferries and boats from the mainland are also wheelchair accessible, though smaller boats to outlying islands may not be.

HandiOasis Corsica offers useful tips on accessible travel on the island. Individual museum websites also typically have information on accessibility.

HandiOasis Corsica

w handioasis-corsica.com

Language

The official language is French, though many Corsicans also speak Italian. The standard of English varies, with fewer English speakers away from the main towns. In rural villages, you will often hear the Corsican language (Corsu) spoken – there are well over 200,000 native speakers and the language is thought to be growing again for the first time in decades.

Opening Hours

Situations can change quickly and unexpectedly. Always check before visiting attractions and hospitality venues for up-to-date opening hours and booking requirements.

Sundays Many rural shops are closed, and public transport services are reduced.
Mondays Many museums and tourist attractions and some restaurants are closed for the day.
Public holidays Schools, post offices, shops and banks are closed.

PUBLIC HOLIDAYS	
1 Jan	New Year's Day
Mar/Apr	Easter and Easter Monday
1 May	Labour Day/May Day
8 May	VE Day
14 Jul	Bastille Day
15 Aug	Assumption Day
1 Nov	All Saints' Day
11 Nov	Armistice Day
25 Dec	Christmas Day
26 Dec	Boxing Day

GETTING AROUND

Whether you're planning on a hiking trip, a cycling tour, a coastal break or all of the above, here's all you need to know to navigate Corsica.

AT A GLANCE

PUBLIC TRANSPORT COSTS

BUS JOURNEY

€2.40

A single bus journey

TRAIN JOURNEY

€2

A single train ride

RAIL TRAVELCARD

€50

Unlimited rail travel for seven days

TOP TIP
Tickets can be bought from machines at most stations on the island.

SPEED LIMIT

HIGHWAYS

110 km/h (70m/h)

RURAL ROADS

90 km/h (55m/h)

URBAN AREAS

60 km/h (40m/h)

CAMPER-VANS

50 km/h (30m/h)

Arriving by Air

The island has four international airports: Calvi and Bastia in the north, and Figari Corse du Sud and Ajaccio in the south. Air Corsica (formerly CCM Airlines) flies from the island to many regions in France, including Aquitaine, Auvergne, Rhône-Alpes, Jura and Île-de-France, as well as Austria, Belgium, Italy, Portugal and Switzerland. Flights from European cities are less frequent in the winter months, when fewer passengers are looking to travel.

As the island's economy relies heavily on seasonal tourism, flight prices tend to be inflated in the summer season, so many visitors opt to arrive by sea from mainland France or Italy, instead.

Arriving by Sea

Corsica has direct sea connections with major Mediterranean ports in France, mainland Italy and the Italian island of Sardinia, with numerous year-round crossings assuring fast travel between these destinations. Sailings can be expensive, however, and fares fluctuate depending on the route. Both day and longer overnight ferry trips are available with most operators.

The island can be accessed by a 50-minute journey from Sante Teresa di Gallura in Sardinia. A boat to the Italian ports of Livorno, Savona, and Genoa, or Nice and Toulon in France take 4.5–6 hours. The port of Marseille is reached in 10 hours. Trips carried out at night such as the crossing to Marseille with Corsica Linea can last around 12 hours.

Corsica Ferries are a popular choice for travel between the island, the mainland, Italy and the island of Sardinia. **Corsica Linea** also has a range of options. If travelling between Corsica and Sardinia, **Ichnusa Lines** are worth exploring.
Corsica Ferries
w corsica-ferries.co.uk
Corsica Linea
w corsicalinea.com/eng
Ichnusa Lines
w ichnusalines.com/en

Boats and Cruises

Many of Corsica's best natural attractions are only reachable by sea, including the Scandola Nature Reserve and the Lavezzi archipelago *(p137)*. Corsica's seven main ports – Bastia, Calvi, Ajaccio, Bonifacio, Porto-Vecchio, L'Île-Rousse and Propriano – each offer regular short trips or day-long excursions, some with planned activities, guided hikes or nature tours.

Some of the most popular excursions by boat include the short trip from Calvi through the Scandola Nature Reserve, Ajaccio to Propriano, or Bonifacio to the outlying Lavezzi islands. The best agencies include **Croisière Exclusive** in Porto-Vecchio and Ajaccio, **Calvi Evasion** in Calvi and **Corse Nautic Escape** in Bonifacio.

For those who prefer to charter their own boat, there are a number of companies, including **Corsica Nautic** and **Locanautic**.

Calvi Evasion
W calvi-evasion.com
Corsica Nautic
W corsica-nautic.com
Corse Nautic Escape
W corse-nautic-escape.com
Croisière Exclusive
W croisiere-exclusive.fr/en
Locanautic
W location-bateau-propriano.com

MAJOR FERRIES TO CORSICAN PORTS

Ferry Route	Distance	Weekly Crossings	Journey Time
Livorno - Bastia	130 km (80 miles)	5	5 hrs
Livorno - Ile Rousse	180 km (110 miles)	3	7 hrs
Toulon - Ajaccio	340 km (210 miles)	3	8 hrs
Toulon - Bastia	400 km (245 miles)	2	9 hrs
Toulon - Ile Rousse	300 km (185 miles)	2	8 hrs
Toulon - Porto Vecchio	410 km (255 miles)	2	15 hrs
Genoa - Bastia	200 km (125 miles)	5	6 hrs
Savona - Bastia	200 km (125 miles)	2	5 hrs
Savona - Ile Rousse	185 km (115 miles)	5	5 hrs
Santa Teresa di Gallura - Bonifacio	15 km (10 miles)	10	1 hr
Marseille - Ajaccio	400 km (250 miles)	6	10 hrs
Marseille - Porto Vecchio	475 km (300 miles)	4	14 hrs
Marseille - Propriano	430 km (265 miles)	4	13 hrs
Marseille - Ile Rousse	405 km (250 miles)	2	13 hrs
Nice - Bastia	260 km (160 miles)	4	5 hrs
Nice - Ile Rousse	215 km (135 miles)	3	5 hrs
Nice - Ajaccio	250 km (155 miles)	6	7 hrs
Nice - Porto Vecchio	320 km (200 miles)	2	13 hrs
Marseille - Bastia	450 km (285 miles)	3	10 hr
Piombino - Bastia	125 km (75 miles)	4	2.5 hrs
Portoferraio - Bastia	100 km (60 miles)	1	1.5 hrs
Porto Torres - Ajaccio	125 km (80 miles)	2	4 hrs

Public Transport

Though the majority of visitors to the island bring their own car, a private vehicle is by no means essential when exploring Corsica. Many of the largest towns are served by bus and train, with the bus network extending to remote, mountainous destinations.

The "U Trinighellu" (Little Train)

Train travel in Corsica may not be the most direct or fastest mode of transport, but it's among the most scenic. The most popular train route is known simply as "U Trinighellu" (little train): a gondola mounted on tracks, its small carriages make their way across the island's mountainous interior, with the main line running between Ajaccio, Corsica's capital, and Bastia, its second city. The railway line was originally planned in 1855 as part of a route to cross both Corsica and the island of Sardinia, but today the route is primarily used as a shuttle service for Corsica's beaches, with stunning views of the island's landscapes. Trains between Bastia and Ajaccio run three to six times daily in each direction in the summer season, with fewer departures in winter. A one-way ticket from Bastia to Ajaccio starts from €21.60. For more information on prices and timetables, visit the **Train Corse** website.

Train Corse
🔲 train-corse.com/fr/tarif-de-base

Other Train Routes

In addition to the little train, Chemin de Fer de la Corse (Corsican Rail) is a metre-gauge railway network that interconnects Corsica's four main towns: Calvi, Corte, Ajaccio and Bastia. The network is not extensive, only serving 16 stations across the island, but it's a great way of seeing the main sights. One of the most frequented train stations is Vizzavona, which many visitors use as a departure point for the GR20 long-distance hiking path.

Note that ongoing efforts to modernize the railway network on the island mean some stations may be closed, even in the high season. For more information on rail travel on the island and for a full list of timetables, visit the **Corsican Rail** website.

Corsican Rail
🔲 cf-corse.corsica/horaires

Bus Travel

Corsica's bus network provides a cheap and reliable way of navigating the island. Buses run between Bastia and Ajaccio (via Corte), Ajaccio and Porto Vecchio (via Sartène, Propriano, and Bonifacio), and Porto Vecchio and Bastia, with a connection to Macinaggio in Cap Corse. The island's bus operators also service several routes in Alta Rocca (south Corsica) and the remote region of Porto.

The best place to consult frequently updated schedules and fares is on the **Corsica Bus** website. The island has various bus, mini-bus and coach operators – including **Autocars Corse-Méditerranée (ACM)**, **Muvistrada** and Eurocorse Voyages – and there is little integration between service routes, times or tickets, which can make travel a struggle.

Bus tickets can be purchased from the driver on board, though it's a better option to buy tickets in advance from bus stations in most towns and cities.

Autocars Corse-Méditerranée
🔲 autocarscorsemediterranee.fr
Corsica Bus
🔲 corsicabus.org
Muvistrada
🔲 mobilite.muvitarra.fr

Taxis

There are a number of taxi companies in most towns and villages across Corsica – most of their vehicles have a "Taxi" sign on the roof. Private taxi companies typically reveal journey prices on request. As with most forms of public transport on the island, prices are inflated during the busy tourist season. Popular options include **Taxi Yellow Cab** and **Taxi Porto Vecchio.**

Taxi Porto Vecchio
🔲 taxi-portovecchio.com
Taxi Yellow Cab
🔲 taxiyellowcabcorsica.com

Driving

The easiest and most convenient way to get around Corsica is by car. Traveling on four wheels gives you access to the majority of the island's tourist attractions, as well as the freedom to plan your own adventures. Driving on the island is often an experience in itself, with some of France's most dramatic and scenic roads.

Driving to Corsica

If you travel to the island in your vehicle, you will arrive in one of Corsica's seven passenger ferry ports *(p175)*. The majority of ferry companies who make the crossing from mainland France, Italy or Sardinia also take personal vehicles for an extra charge.

Driving in Corsica

The Corsican roads are narrow and often incredibly winding, except for the eastern T10 stretch that connects Bastia and Bonifacio. Navigating the precipitous zig-zags requires care and attention, as well as low driving speeds. Often, distances between destinations may seem short, but you are advised to leave ample time to navigate the treacherous roads. Leaving plenty of time should never pose too much of a problem, as the island's twisting labyrinths offer some of the finest views.

In summer, the roads can become very congested, with long queues forming behind slow-moving coaches and tour buses. If at all possible, leaving your car and taking public transport is recommended in the height of the season.

Car Rental

Most of Europe's rental companies are found on the island, with agencies located at airports and in major towns and cities. To rent a car you must be 21 or over and have held a valid driver's licence for at least a year. Note that booking in advance gets you a better deal and ensures you get a car that will meets your needs.

Rules of the Road

The minimum driving age in France is 18, even if your licence qualifies you to drive at a younger age in your home country. Motorists in France drive on the right and overtake on the left. Traffic approaching from the right has priority at crossroads and junctions unless otherwise indicated. In heavy motorway traffic, vehicles are permitted to overtake on either side – just don't use the hard shoulder to do so. Do not indicate when entering a roundabout, only when you see your exit.

Cars must not enter an intersection in heavy traffic unless there's a clear path to exit the junction. This applies regardless of whether the driver has priority or there's a green traffic light. Buses have priority when leaving stops and drivers must give way when one is signalling to re-join the carriageway. Helmets and protective gloves are mandatory for motorcyclists and scooter riders. There must be a first aid kit in your car.

Using a mobile phone while driving can result in an immediate loss of licence. France strictly enforces a blood alcohol content limit of 0.05 per cent. Corsican police can demand on-the-spot payment of traffic fines, and drugs tests can be enforced even for minor infractions.

Cycling

Corsica's mountainous terrain offers some of the finest cycling in France, though the steep ascents and rapid descents demand experience, fitness and confidence.

Corsica's interior is a haven for mountain biking enthusiasts. Some stretches of the GR20 hiking trail can be adapted for off-road cycling, with routes leading down rugged mountain paths and through dense forests. The Grande Traversée (GT20 – the cyclist's equivalent of the GR20) crosses Corsica from north to south. Departing from Bastia and Cap Corse, the route reaches Bonifacio in 12 stages, taking in some of the island's best roads. Familiarizing yourself with designated cycling routes is always recommended, as heading off of permitted routes can incur fines or damage the island's delicate flora and fauna.

Drivers are generally considerate of cyclists in Corsica, but some of the roads with sharper bends can pose a problem. Some drivers are still unaccustomed to seeing cyclists on mountain roads, which can lead to dangerous driving.

One of the best ways to see the island on two wheels is to book a guided cycling holiday. Companies like **Marmot Tours** offer tailored cycling experiences taking in many of the island's best routes.

Marmot Tours
🅦 marmot-tours.co.uk

Bike Rental

There are a number of premium bike rental companies across Corsica. For the best road bikes, gravel bikes or e-bikes, **CCT Bike Rental** is a popular option. Note that bookings must be made at least three days in advance; the company can deliver your chosen bike to numerous towns across Corsica. **BCyclet** offers bike rentals throughout Corsica and the French and Swiss Alps, with a particular focus on quality road bikes. For the best mountain bikes, bike shop **Wild Machja** in Calvi is a good choice, with a range of bikes to buy or rent.

BCyclet
🅦 bcyclet.com/bike-rental/corsica-bike-rental
CCT Bike Rental
🅦 cctbikerental.com
Wild Machja
🅦 wildmachja.com

Walking

Corsica is a hiker's paradise. Many people are aware of the notoriously challenging but richly rewarding GR20 long-distance route (p60), which is among Europe's most popular hikes. The official **GR20** website has a wealth of information on walking the route. While this route is deservedly famous, the island is also home to a network of shorter mountain trails and undulating coastal walks. Most towns have a tourist office with information on local routes. The **Parc Naturel Régional de la Corse** (p44) maintains many of the island's best trails, and the park's website is an excellent resource for hiking inspiration.

GR20
🅦 le-gr20.fr/en
Parc Naturel Régional de la Corse
🅦 pnr.corsica

PRACTICAL
INFORMATION

Things change, so plan ahead to make the most of your trip. Be prepared for all eventualities by considering the following points before you travel.

AT A GLANCE

EMERGENCY NUMBERS

EMERGENCY OPERATOR	POLICE
112	**17**

AMBULANCE	FIRE SERVICE
15	**18**

TIME ZONE
CET/CEST. Central European Summer Time runs from the last Sunday in March to the last Sunday in October.

TAP WATER
Unless stated otherwise, tap water is safe to drink.

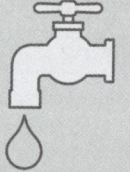

WEBSITES

France Tourism
Find inspiration and information on France's official tourism website (www.france.fr).

Visit Corsica
The official Corsican tourism website (www.visit-corsica.com) has a wealth of information and ideas to help you make the most of your visit to the island.

Corsican Places
The Corsican Places website (www.corsica.co.uk) has advice on hotels.

Personal Security

Corsica is generally a safe place for visitors, but it is always a good idea to take sensible precautions and be aware of your surroundings. Pickpockets are known to operate in busy tourist areas, particularly on public transport in larger towns and cities.

If you have anything stolen, report the crime as soon as possible to the nearest police station. Get a copy of the crime report in order to claim on your insurance. Contact your embassy if you have your passport stolen, or in the event of a serious crime or accident.

Corsicans are generally accepting of all people, regardless of their race, gender or sexuality. Same-sex marriage was officially legalized in France in 2013. In larger towns and cities like Ajaccio, you'll find dedicated LGBTQ+ nights, events and venues. Despite all the freedoms that the LGBTQ+ community enjoy, however, acceptance is not always a given, especially in more rural areas where locals may be unaccustomed to tourists. Rural Corsicans in particular are noted for their traditional outlook, but this rarely gives rise to hostility. If you do at any point feel unsafe, the **Safe Space Alliance** pinpoints your nearest place of refuge.
Safe Space Alliance
w safespacealliance.com

Health

France has a world-class health service. EU citizens are eligible to receive emergency medical treatment in France free of charge. If you have an EHIC or GHIC (p174) present this as soon as possible. For visitors from outside the EU, payment of medical expenses is the patient's responsibility. It is important to arrange comprehensive medical insurance before travelling. Pharmacies are indicated by green crosses and can be used for help with minor ailments or prescriptions. You may need a doctor's prescription to obtain certain pharmaceuticals, and the pharmacist can inform you of the closest doctor's practice. Pharmacies are usually open 8am–6pm, and details of the

nearest 24-hour service are posted in all pharmacy windows or can be found online. For a serious illness or injury, visit a hospital or call an ambulance. All emergency rooms are part of the public health system, so your EHIC, GHIC or insurance will cover you.

Smoking, Alcohol and Drugs

France has a smoking ban in all public places, including bars, cafés, restaurants and hotels. However, many establishments circumvent these laws. The possession of narcotics is prohibited and could result in prosecution and a prison sentence. Unless stated otherwise, it is permitted to drink alcohol on the streets and in public parks and gardens. France has a limit of 0.05 per cent BAC (blood alcohol content) for drivers.

ID

There is no requirement for visitors to carry ID, but in the event of a routine check you may be asked to show your passport. If you don't have it with you, the police may escort you to wherever your passport is being kept.

Local Customs

Etiquette is very important to Corsicans, just as it is to the French more generally. On entering and leaving a store, you are expected to say *"bonjour"* and *"au revoir"* to staff.

France has strict laws on hate speech. Disrespectful behaviour in public places can warrant a fine, or even prosecution. Pay close attention to signage indicating when photos aren't allowed and think carefully about how you compose your shots. Visitors have come under serious criticism for posting inappropriate photos taken at sites of national significance on social media.

Responsible Travel

Overtourism is having a stark impact on many of Corsica's most scenic spots. In areas under the contol of Parc Naturel Régional de Corse (*p44*), a number of rules have been designed to minimize the effects on delicate ecosystems; these fines for those who leave designated trails

and bans on wild camping. Ensure you stick to marked routes and refrain from swimming in forbidden spots. To offset the region's heavy traffic in summer, make use of the good public transport options and cycle paths. When hiking, always deposit rubbish in the available receptacles, or take it with you. Familiarize yourself with fishing and sailing laws if you take to the seas around the island.

Mobile Phones and Wi-Fi

Visitors travelling to Corsica with EU tariffs can use their mobile phones abroad without being affected by data roaming charges; instead they will be charged the same rates for data, SMS and voice calls as they would pay at home. Visitors from other countries should check their contracts before using their phone in Corsica in order to avoid unexpected charges.

Post

Stamps (*timbres*) can be bought in post offices, newsagents, tobacconists and most super-markets. There are usually self-service stamp machines placed outside post offices.

Taxes and Refunds

VAT is around 20 per cent in France. Non-EU residents are entitled to a tax refund subject to certain conditions. In order to obtain this, you must request a tax receipt and export papers when you purchase your goods. When leaving the country, present these papers, along with the receipt and your ID, at customs to receive your refund.

Discount Cards

Many towns and cities have a discount card giving cheaper access to public transport plus free or discounted admission to local attractions for a short period of time. These discounts and benefits are listed on individual town websites. For more information, visit the **Ajaccio** or **Bonifacio** websites.

Ajaccio
w ajaccio-tourisme.com/en
Bonifacio
w bonifacio.co.uk

INDEX

Page numbers in **bold** refer to main entries.

A

Acciaghju, Plage d' 141
Accommodation
    booking 173
    GR20 68
    see also Hotels
Action Régionaliste Corse (ARC) 56, 59
A Cupulatta turtle and tortoise sanctuary 31, **109**, 120
Adventure activities
    for families 31
    on land **26-7**
    on water **40-41**
Adventure parks
    Parc Aventure de Porto-Vecchio 31
    Parc Aventure de Solenzara 31
Aiguilles de Bavella 30, 42, 45, 66, 129, **138-9**
Air travel 174
Aïtone, Forêt d' 30, 42, 45, **125**
Ajaccio **108-115**
    beach 112
    history 105, **108**
    hotels 110
    itinerary 20-21
    map 109
    Napoleonic 47, 48
    restaurants 110
Ajaccio Cathedral **108-9**
Ajaccio and the West Coast 17, **104-127**
    hiking tour 126-7
    hotels 110, 122
    itinerary 20-21
    map 102-3
    restaurants 110, 119
Albertacce 168
Alcohol 179
Aléria 37, 52, **163**, 166
Algajola **97**
Altiani 46, 162
Ancient sites 11, **36-7**
    Aléria 37, 52, **163**, 166
    Casteddu of Araggio 36, 141
    Casteddu of Cucuruzzu 37, **145**
    Casteddu de Tappa 36, **140**
    Cauria 36, 148-9
    Filitosa 11, 31, 36, 37, 129, **147**
    Île Lavezzi 137
    Mariana **81**, 166
    Palaggiu 129
    Renaggiu 129
    Stantari 129
    torri 36

Angling 27
Anglo-Corsican Kingdom 55
Anse de Ficajola 123
Araggio 36, **141**
Aragonese 135, 151
Archaeology **145**
Archery 31
Aregno **98-9**
Arrighi di Casanova, Jean-Toussaint 157
Arts and crafts **32-3**
Asco 167
Asco Stagnu refuge 63
Asinao refuge 66, 67
Asinao river 142
ATMs 173
A Vacca Morta 141

B

Balagne 13, 27, 97, 98
    arts and crafts 33
Balzac, Honoré de 113
Bandits 120
Barbary pirtes 121
Barghiana 125
Bars
    Bastia and the North 85, 95
    Calvi 85
    wine 39
Bastelica 120
Bastia 73, **76-83**
    map 77
    restaurants 80
    shopping 76
Bastia and the North 16, **72-103**
    bars 85, 95
    driving tour 100-101
    itinerary 24-5
    map 74-5
    restaurants 80, 91
    shopping 76, 99
    walking tour 102-3
Bastion de l'Étendard (Bonifacio) **133**
Bavella massif 42
Beaches 12
    family 30
    near Porto-Vecchio 141
    seafood 29
Belvedere (Corte) **156**
Bergeries de Ballone 62
Bergeries de Capannelle 65, 66
Bergeries de Grottelle 160
Bibliothèque Patrimoniale (Ajaccio) **112-13**
Bike rental 177
Birds
    Île Lavezzi 137
    Réserve Naturelle de Scandola **117**
Black Death 54

Boat trips 12, 31, **175**
Bocca di l'Arinella 168
Bocognano 120
Bonaparte, Charles 157
Bonaparte family 48
    see also Napoleon I, Emperor; Napoleon III, Emperor
Bonaparte, Joseph 155
Bonaparte, Letizia 122, 157
Bonaparte, Lucien 112, 114
Bonifacio 12, 40, **132-9**
    cliffs 43, 135, 136-7
    history 129, 132
    hotels 133
    map 133
Bonifacio and the South 18, **128-49**
    driving tour 148-9
    hotels 133, 143
    itinerary 22-3
    map 130-31
    restaurants 146
Bosco (Bonifacio) **135**
Botticelli, Sandro, Virgin Mary and Child with Angel 115
Boulevard du Roi Jérôme (Ajaccio) **111**
Bozio **160**, 164
Brêche de Castillo 64
Bridges, Genoese **123**, 124
Brill, Matthijs 115
Bus travel 175
Byzantine Empire 53

C

Calacuccia **168**, 169
Calanques de Piana 43, 116, 121, 123
    hiking tour 126-7
Cala Rossa promontory 142
Calcatoggio 121
Calenzana 61, 62, 63, **98**
Calvi 73, **84-7**
    beach 30, 85
    history 53
    map 85
Campbell, Miss Thomasina **111**
Camping 45, 68
Campomoro 30, 46, 125, **146**
Canari **93**
Canoeing 40
Canyoning 31
Cap Corse **90-91**
Cape Girolata 116, 121
Capo Chiostro 161
Capo di Feno 119, 122
Capo d'Orto 123
Capo Pertusato 43, **136-7**
Capo Rosso 121, 123
Capo Tafonato 168
Capula castle **145**

Carbini 144
Carbuccia 120
Cardo (Bastia) **80**
Cargèse **122**
Carozzu refuge 63
Car rental 177
Carrington, Dorothy **164**
Cars, heritage, Tour de Corse
  Historique 34
Cartalavonu 141
Carthaginians 146, 163
Casamaccioli 168, **169**
Casa Musicale (Pigna) 96
Cascades see Waterfalls
Castagniccia 160, 164
  driving tour 170
Casteddu of Araggio 36, 141
Casteddu of Cucuruzzu 37, **145**
Casteddu de Tappa 36, **140**
Castel de Verghio 62, 64
Castirla 160
Castles and fortifications 46, 47
  Algajola citadelle 73, 97
  Bastia Citadelle 47, 73, **82-3**
  Bastion de l'Étendard
    (Bonifacio) **133**
  Calvi Citadelle 47, 73, **86-7**
  Capula castle **145**
  Casteddu of Araggio 36, 141
  Casteddu of Cucuruzzu 37, **145**
  Castello della Rocca (Olmeto)
    147
  Citadelle (Ajaccio) 105, **108**
  Citadelle (Corte) 47, 151,
    158-9
  Fort Matra (Aléria) 163
  Genoese watchtowers 46,
    125
  St-Antoine battery
    (Bonifacio) 135
  Tour de Campomoro 146
Cateau-Cambresis, Treaty of
  108
Cauria 36
  Megaliths of Cauria driving
    tour 148-9
Caves, Grotte du Sdragonatu
  133, **136**
Cavu River 27
Centuri **92**
Ceramics 33
Cervione **165**
Chapel/Chapelle see Churches
  and cathedrals
Cheese 28, 29, 34
Chestnuts 29
Chiavari, Forêt de **121**
Children's activities **30-31**
Churches and cathedrals 12, 46
  Ajaccio Cathedral **108-9**
  Chapelle de la Scala Santa
    (Bastia) 12, **80-81**

Churches and cathedrals (cont.)
  Chapelle des Grecs (Ajaccio)
    119
  Chapelle Impériale (Ajaccio)
    113
  Chapelle Ste-Croix (Corte)
    155
  Chapelle St-Roch (Bastia) **77**
  Église de l'Annonciation
    (Corte) **154-5**
  Église St-Jean-Baptiste
    (Bastia) 46, **76-7**
  La Canonica **166**
  Oratoire de l'Immaculée
    Conception **79**
  Oratoire St-Antoine (Calvi)
    84, 86
  Oratoire Ste-Croix (Bastia) 82
  Oratoire St-Théophile (Corte)
    156-7
  San Michele de Murato 12, 46,
    88-9
  Santa Maria Assunta
    (St-Florent) 95
  Santa Maria di e Nevi
    (Erbalunga) 90
  St-Charlesé (Bastia) **78**
  St-Dominique Haute Ville
    (Bonifacio) 35, **134-5**
  Ste-Lucie (Ste-Lucie de
    Tallano) 145
  Ste-Marie cathedral (Bastia)
    82
  Ste-Marie-Majeure
    (Bonifacio) **134**
  Ste-Marie-Majeure (Calvi) **85**
  St-Erasme (Ajaccio) **109**
  St-Jean-Baptiste (Calvi) 87
  St-Jean-Baptiste (La Porta)
    46, 164-5
Cirque de Bonifatu 63
Cirque de la Solitude 62
Cirque de Trimbolocciu 167
Citadelle (Ajaccio) 105, **108**
Citadelle (Bastia) 47, 73, **82-3**
Citadelle (Calvi) 47, 73, **86-7**
Citadelle (Corte) 47, 151, **158-9**
Ciuttulu di Mori refuge 169
Clan warfare 53
Cliffs 43
  Bonifacio **136-7**
Climbing 42
Coastline 43
Col de Bavella 27, 144
Col de Cricheto 120
Col de Marcuggio 120
Col de Mercuju 120
Col de Scalella 120
Col de Teghime 73, 94
Col de Verghio 168, **169**
Col de Vizzavona **161**
Columbus, Christopher 84, 87

Conca 61, 66, 67
Conservation 44, 45
  marine habitats **134**
Coral 32
Cork industry 140
Corniche de la Castagniccia 165
Corsica Libera 57
Corsican language 57, 58, 59,
  188
Corso, Sampiero 108, 120, 140,
  146
Corte 13, 37, **154-9**
  history 54
  hotels 155
  map 155
Corte and the Interior 19,
  150-71
  driving tour 170
  history 151
  hotels 155, 163
  map 152-3
  restaurants 168
Côte des Nacres 142
Côti-Chiavari 121
Cours Napoléon (Ajaccio) **112**
Cowen, William 111
Credit/debit cards 173
Crime 178
Cruises 175
Cucuruzzu 37, **145**
Currency 172
Customs information 172
Cycling 27, 177
  GT20 27
  La Serra loop 27

D

Dame de Bonifacio 52, 144
Daudet, Alphonse 118
Deer, Corsican 11, 45
Della Rocca, Arrigo 147
Departure of Rebecca, The
  (Solimena) 115
Désert des Agriates 41, **96**
Devota, St 94
Disabled travellers 173
Discount cards 179
Diving 41
Domaine des Milelli (Ajaccio) **113**
Doria, Andrea 124
Driving 176-7
Drugs 179
Dumas, Alexandre 113

E

Eau d'Orezza **166**
Eccica-Suarella 120
Église see Churches and
  cathedrals
Electricity supply 172

Index

Emergency numbers 178
Emigration 56
Erbajolo 162
Erbalunga **90**
Érignac, Claude 57
Escalier du Roi d'Aragon
(Bonifacio) **135**
Étang de Biguglia (Bastia) **81**
Etiquette 179
Etruscans 53, 146, 163
Evisa 42, 124, 125

F

Family activities **30–31**
Fango river 124–5
Favalello 160
Femu a Corsica 57
Fesch, Cardinal Joseph 111, 113,
114, **115**
Festivals and events
A Fiera di l'Anandului (Aregno)
28
A Fiera di u Casgiu (Venaco)
28, 34
A Fiera di u Vinu 38
A Year in Corsica **50–51**
Calvi on the Rocks 35
Catenacciu Procession
(Sartène) 144–5
Festivoce (Pigna) 35
Holy Week (Calvi) **84**
In Aleria festial 38
Jazz in Aiacciu 35
Les Nuits de la Guitare
(Patrimonio) 33, 35
Polyphonic Song Festival
(Calvi) 35
Tour de Corse Historique 34
wine 38
Feudal lords 53
Figari 63
Filitosa 11, 31, 36, 37, 129, **147**
Fishing 27
Flag, Corsican 59
Fontaine des Quatre-Canons
(Corte) **156**
Food and drink 10
aziminu **78**
Corsica by the Glass **38–9**
Corsica for Food Lovers **28–9**
Eau d'Orezza **166**
Épicerie Ghionga Jean Marie
(Corte) 157
festivals 28, 34
on GR20 68, 69
Maison Mattei (Bastia) **79**, 91
Forests 42
Forêt d'Aïtone 30, 42, 45, **125**
Forêt de Carozzica 167
Forêt de Chiavari **121**
Forêt de Pineta 120
Forêt de Valdu Niellu **169**
Forêt de Vizzavona 45, **161**
Forêt du Fango 124
Franks 47

French Revolution 48, 49
French rule 54, 55–6, 108
Front de Libération Nationale
de la Corse (FLNC) 56, 57, 59
Front Régionaliste Corse (FRC)
56

G

Gaffori, Jean-Pierre 54, **156**
Galéria **124-15**Evisa 124
Genoese 46, 47, 53–4, 58
Ajaccio and the West Coast
105
Bastia 82
Bastia and the North 73
Bonifacio and the South
129
bridges **123**, 124
Calvi 86
Corte and the Interior 151,
158
watchtowers 46, **125**
Ghignu beach 41
Ghisonaccia 145
Ghisoni 161, 162
Girolata 46, 116, **124**, 125
Golfe d'Ajaccio 118, 120, 121
Golfe de Galéria 124
Golfe de Girolata 40, 116
Golfe de Liscia 121
Golfe de Porticcio 119
Golfe de Porto 123
Golfe de Porto-Vecchio 141
Golfe de Propriano 41
Golfe de Roccapina 146
Golfe de Sagone 118, 122
Golfe de Valinco 121, 145,
146
Gorges de la Restonica 43,
160-61
Gorges de l'Asco 45
Gorges de Spelunca 43, 45,
124
Gorges du Prunelli **120**
Gorges du Tavignano 41,
165
Goths 53
Government advice 172
GR20 10, 26, 30, 44–5, **60–69**
Aiguilles de Bavella 138
Le GR20 restaurant
(Calenzana) 98
planning your hike 68–9
reaching the trailheads 63
stages 1-5 62–3
stages 6-10 64–5
stages 11-15 66–7
Grain de Sable **137**
Grande Sanguinaire
(Mezzumare) 118
Grape varieties 39
Greeks, ancient 52, 146, 163
Grotte du Sdragonatu 133,
136
Guagno Les Bains 122

H

Haut-Asco 167
Health 178–9
Hiking 26, 177
Calanques de Piana hiking
tour 126–7
Campomoro to Tizzano 146
Chemin des Crêtes 26
for children 30
Forêt de Valdu Niellu 169
Gorges de la Restonica
160–61
Gorges du Tavignano 41, **165**
GR20 10, 26, 30, 44–5,
60–69, 177
Mare e Monti path **66**, 124, 125
Mare a Mare path 26, **66**, 125
Monte Cinto 167
Monte Renoso **161**
Sentier de la Sittelle 125
Sentier de Myrte 121
Sentier des Condamnés 125
Sentier des Douaniers (Cap
Corse) **125**
Historic buildings
Bibliothèque Patrimoniale
(Ajaccio) **112-13**
Domaine des Milelli (Ajaccio)
113
Maison Colombe (Calvi) 87
History **52–9**
Corsica for History Buffs **46–9**
Holy Week (Calvi) **84**
Hotels
Ajaccio and the West Coast
110, 122
Bonifacio and the South 133,
143
booking 173
Corte and the Interior 155,
163
Hot springs
Guagno Les Bains 122
Pietrapola 162
Hundred Days War 55

I

ID 179
Île Cavallo **137**
Île de la Giraglia **92-3**
Île Lavezzi **137**
Îles Cerbicale 141
Îles Lavezzi 13, 133, 134, **137**
Îles Sanguinaires **118**, 119
Independence movement 54,
56–7, 58–9
Industrial Revolution 55
Insurance 172–3
Itineraries
2 Days in Ajaccio 20–21
5 Days in Southern Corsica
22–3
7 Days in Northern Corsica
24–5

J

Jacobins 55
Jardin Romieu (Bastia) **78**
Jazz 35
Jesus and the Samaritan Woman (Parrocel) 115
Jewellery 32
Julia, St 94

K

Kayaking 31, 40
Knife-making 33

L

La Canonica **166**
Lac de Bastani 161
Lac de Creno 122
Lac de Nino 64, 65, 169
Lac de Tolla 27, 31
Lac du Capitellu 160-61
La Cinarca 121
La Foce 162
Lakes 27
L'Aldilonda (Bastia) **79**
Lama **98**
Language 173
  Corsican 57, 58, 59, 188
  essential phrases 172
  phrasebook 188-91
La Porta **164-5**
Lear, E Wdward 111
Levie **144**
LGBTQ+ community 178
Lighthouses, Capo Pertusato Lighthouse **137**
L'Île Rousse **96-7**
Liqueurs 79
Liscia river 120, 121
Local customs 179
Lomellini, Leonello 82
L'Onda refuge 65

M

Macinaggio 40, **91**
Maison Bonaparte Museum (Ajaccio) 10, 47, 49, **110**
Maison Colombe (Calvi) 87
Maison du Grand Site de France Conca (St-Florent) 95
Maison Mattei (Bastia) **79**, 91
Manganu refuge 64
Maps
  Ajaccio 109
  Ajaccio and the West Coast 106-7
  Aléria ruins 163
  Bastia 77
  Bastia and the North 74-5
  Bonifacio 133
  Bonifacio and the South 130-31
  Calanques de Piana hiking tour 126

Maps (cont.)
  Calvi 85
  Cap Corse walking tour 102-3
  Castagniccia driving tour 170
  Corsica 14-15
  Corte 155
  Corte and the Interior 152-3
  GR20 stages 1-5 62-3
  GR20 stages 6-10 64-5
  GR20 stages 11-15 66-7
  Megaliths of Cauria driving tour 148
  sea journey planner 175
  Strada di l'Artigiani driving tour 101-2
Maquis, Mediterranean **97**
Mare e Monti path **66**, 124, 125
Mare a Mare path 26, **66**, 125
Mariana **81**, 166
Marina (Ajaccio) **110**
Marina (Bonifacio) **132-3**
Marina (Calvi) **84**
Marine d'Albo 93
Marine habitats **134**
Marinella cove 119
Massif de l'Osédale **141**, 142
Master of Castelsardo 145
Medical treatment 178
Medieval period **47**
Megalithic sites 52
  Megaliths of Cauria driving tour 148-9
  see also Ancient sites
Meloria, Battle of 53
Menhirs 31, **36**, 52, 147
Mobile phones 179
Mohammed V of Morocco 142
Monasteries and convents
  Monastère de Assunta Gloriosa de Sari-Solenzara **143**
  St-François de Caccia **168**
Money 173
Monte Castello 165
Monte Cinto 42, 45, 63, 151, 166-7, 168, 169
Monte d'Oro 43, 120, 161, 162
Montée Rastello (Bonifacio) 132
Monte Renoso 120, **161**, 162
Monte Rotondo 43, 45, 160, 161
Mouflon 11, 45, 66
Mountain biking 27, 45, 177
Mountains 42
Museums and galleries
  Casa di a Natura (Vizzavona) 45
  Eco Museum du Fortin (Bastia) 81
  Maison Bonaparte Museum (Ajaccio) 10, 47, 49, **110**
  Maison du Grand Site de France Conca (St-Florent) 95
  Musée d'Archéologie Jérôme Carcopino 163

Museums and galleries (cont.)
  Musée de Bastia 77
  Musée de la Corse (Corte) 37, 151, 158, 159
  Musée Départemental d'Alta Rocca (Levie) 144
  Musée Departmental de Préhistoire Corse et d'Archéologie (Sartène) 145
  Musée Marc Petit-Lazaret Ollandini (Ajaccio) **112**
  Palais Fesch – Musée des Beaux-Arts (Ajaccio) 49, 111, 113, **114-15**
  Salon Napoléonien (Ajaccio) **110**
Music **34-5**
  Casa Musicale (Pigna) 96
  festivals 33, 35
  musical instruments 33
Mussolini, Benito 56

N

Napoleonic Wars 48
Napoleon I, Emperor 10, **48-9**, 55
  Ajaccio Cathedral 109
  Domaine des Milelli (Ajaccio) **113**
  lighthouses 137
  Maison Bonaparte Museum (Ajaccio) 10, 47, 49, **110**
  Napoleonic Ajaccio 47, 48, 105
  Salon Napoléonien (Ajaccio) **110**
  statues (Ajaccio) 10, 47, 49
Napoleon III, Emperor 113
Nationalism 57, **58-9**
Natural wonders **42-5**
Nature reserves
  Bouches de Bonifacio Nature Reserve 41
  Étang de Biguglia (Bastia) **81**
  Îles Cerbicale reserve 141
  Parc Naturel Régional de la Corse 11, **44-5**, 61, 123, 177
  Réserve Naturelle de Scandola 40, 105, **116-17**
Nebbio **95**
Neolithic era 52
  see also Ancient sites
Neuhof, Baron Theodor von 54, 164
Nonza **94**

O

Oletta **96**
Olmeto 147
Omessa 160
Opening hours 173

Oratoire see Churches and cathedrals
Ortu di u Piobbu refuge 62, 63
Ospédale 141
Ostrogoths 47
Ota 124
Outdoor activities
    on land **26-7**
    on water **40-41**
Overtourism 45

P

Paesolu d;Aïtone 125
Paintballing 31
Palaces
    Palais des Gouverneurs (Bastia) 77, 83
    Palais des Gouverneurs (Calvi) 86
    Palais Fesch – Musée des Beaux-Arts (Ajaccio) 49, 111, 113, **114-15**
    Palais National (Corte) 157
Palaggiu 129
Palais Fesch – Musée des Beaux-Arts (Ajaccio) 49, 111, 113, **114-15**
Paliri refuge 67
Palombaggia, Plage de 12, 41, 141
Paoli, Pascal 48, 49, 54-5, **58**, 91, 105
    Corte 151, 154, 157, 158
    Ponte-Novo 167
Parachuting 26
Paragliding 26
Parc Naturel Régional de la Corse 11, **44-5**, 61, 123, 177
Parks and gardens
    Domaine des Milelli (Ajaccio) **113**
    Jardin Romieu (Bastia) **78**
    see also Adventure parks; Nature reserves
Parrocel, Étienne, Jesus and the Samaritan Woman 115
Passports 172
Patrimonio **94**
Pè a Corsica 57
Penta-di-Casinca **167**
Perelli 164
Peri 120
Personal security 178
Pharmacies 178-9
Phoenicians 52, 163
Photography 179
Phrasebook 188-91
Piana 43, **122-3**
Pianella 124
Piedicorte di Gaggio 162
Pietracorbara **91**
Pietra Piana refuge 64, 65, 69
Pietrapola 162
Pigna 13, 33, 35, **96**

Pinarello, Plage de 141, 142
Pinarellu 12
Pino **93**
Pisan Romanesque 88, 89
Pisans 46, 47, 53
Pius VII, Pope 115
Place Christophe Colomb (Calvi) **84**
Place d'Austerlitz (Ajaccio) 49, **111**
Place du Marché (Bastia) **76**
Place du Poilu (Corte) **157**
Place Foch (Ajaccio) 49, **111**
Place Gaffori (Corte) **154**
Place Padoue (Corte) **157**
Place Paoli (Corte) **154**
Place St-Nicolas (Bastia) **79**
Plage d'Arone 123
Plage de Calvi 30, **85**
Pointe de la Parata **119**
Pointe de Porto-Pollo 147
Police 178
Political heritage 13, 37, 56-9
Polyphonic music **35**
Pont du Muricciolu 168
Ponte-Novo **167**
Ponte-Novo, Battle of 55, 167
Port de Toga(Bastia) **80**
Porte de France (Bonifacio) **134**
Porte de Gênes (Bonifacio) **134**
Porticcio **119**
Porto **123**
Porto-Pollo **147**
Porto-Vecchio 129, **140-41**
    beaches near 141
Portrait of a Man with a Glove (Titian) 115
Postal services 179
Pozzine 64
Pozzines 120
Prati refuge 66, 67
Prehistory 52
    see also Ancient sites
Prices
    average daily spend 172
    public transport 174
Propriano 129, **146-7**
Prunelli-di-Fiumorbo **162**
Ptolemy 73
Public holidays 173
Public transport 176
    prices 174
Punic Wars 37, 53
Punta Fautea **142**
Punta Minuta 167
Punta Mucchilina 116
Punta Palazzo 116

Q

Quai des Martyrs de la Libération (Bastia) **78-9**

Quai Landry (Calvi) **84-5**
Quenza **144**

R

Reasons to Love Corsica **10-13**
Refuges, GR20 68, 69
Refunds, VAT 179
Renaggiu 129
Réserve Naturelle de Scandola 40, 105, **116-17**
Responsible travel 179
Restaurants 28
    Ajaccio and the West Coast 110, 119
    Bastia and the North 80, 91
    Bonifacio and the South 146
    Corte and the Interior 168
Roccapina **146**
Romans 37, 47, 52-3
    Ajaccio 108
    Aléria 163
    Corte 151
    Mariana **81**
    Propriano 146
    see also Ancient sites
Rondinara 12
Route des Sanguinaires **118-19**
Rue Bonaparte (Ajaccio) **109**
Rue de la Loggia (Bonfacio) **134**
Rue du St-Sacrement (Bonifacio) **134**
Rue du Vieux Marché (Corte) **157**
Rules of the road 174, 177

S

Safety
    government advice 172
    GR20 68
    personal security 178
Sagone **122**
Sailing 40
Salon Napoléonien (Ajaccio) **110**
Salt production 140
San Michele de Murato 12, 46, **88-9**
Santa-Giulia, Plage de 12, 141
Sant'Antonino 13, **99**
Saracens 47
Sari d'Orcino 121
Sari-Solenzara 142, 143
Sartène **144-5**
Scala Brocciu (Canari) **93**
Scala di Santa Regina **168**
Scandola peninsula 31
Scandola, Réserve Naturelle de 40, 105, **116-17**
Scudo 119
Seafood 29
Sea travel 174-5

Sea travel (cont.)
  sea journey planner map 175
Sémillante memorial (Île
  Lavezzi) 137
Sentier des Douaniers (Cap
  Corse) **91**
Sermano 160
Shells 32
Shepherd huts 137
Shipwrecks 137
Shopping
  Bastia 76
  Bastia and the North 99
  Bonifacio and the South 144
  Épicerie Ghionga Jean Marie
    (Corte) 157
  GR20 68, 69
Simeoni, Edmond 59
Skiing 120, 167
Smoking 179
Snorkelling 13, 41
Soccia 122
Solenzara 129, **142**
Solenzara valley 41
Solimena, Francesco, *The
  Departure of Rebecca* 115
Sovéria **164**
Spada "the Tiger of Cinarca" 120
Spasimata footbridge 63
Specific requirements,
  travellers with 173
Speed limit 174
Speloncato **99**
Stantari 129
St-Charlesé (Bastia) **78**
St-Dominique Haute Ville
  (Bonifacio) 35, **134-5**
Ste-Lucie de Tallano **145**
Ste-Marie-Majeure (Bonifacio)
  134
Ste-Marie-Majeure (Calvi)
  85
St-Erasme (Ajaccio) **109**
St-Florent 26, 30, 73, **94-5**
St-François beach (Ajaccio) **112**,
  118
St-François de Caccia
  168
Strada di l'Artigiani 33
  driving tour 100-101
Swimming 41

Tap water 178
Tavera 120
Tavignano river 162, 165
Taxes 179
Taxis 176
Terrorism 57
Theft 178
Tighjiettu refuge 167
Time zone 178
Tipping 173
Titian, *Portrait of a Man with a
  Glove* 115

Tiuccia **121**
Tizzano 146
Tolla 27
Torrean civilization 36
Torri 36
Tortoises
  A Cupulatta turtle and
    tortoise sanctuary 31,
    109, 120
  Hermann's 45
Tour de France 57
Tourism 55, 57
  Ajaccio 111
  infrastructure **57**
  overtourism 45, 179
  responsible travel 179
Train travel **176**
  "U Trinighellu" (Little Train) 11,
    176
Travel
  getting around **174-7**
  government advice 172
  responsible 179
Treasure hunt (Corte) 156
Trou de la Bombe (Aiguilles de
  Bavella) **138**
Turtles, A Cupulatta turtle and
  tortoise sanctuary 31, **109**,
  120

Ucciani 120
Urban V, Pope 144
Usciolu refuge 66
"U Trinighellu" (Little Train) 11,
  176

Vaccinations 173
Val d'Ése 120
Valdu Niellu, Forêt de **169**
Vallée d'Alesani **164**
Vallée de la Gravona **120**
Vallée de l'Asco 31, 42, 164,
  166-7, 168
Vallée de Niolo 124
Vallée du Cavu **141**
Vallée du Golo 164, 168
Valléé du Tavignano **162**
Vandals 47, 53, 163
Vendettas **113**
Verghia 121
Vescovato **166**
Vico 122
Vieux Port (Bastia) **78**
Vignola beach 119
Vineyard tours 38
*Virgin Mary and Child with
  Angel* (Botticelli) 115
Visas 172
Vizzavona 65, 69, 161, 162
Vizzavona, Forêt de 45,
  161
Vultures, bearded 45

W

Walking 177
  see also Hiking
Watchtowers, Genoese 46, **125**
Waterfalls 42
  Cascade des Anglais 43, **162**
  Cascade du Voile de la Mariée
    120
  Cascade Piscia di Ghjaddu
    142-3
  Cascades d'Aïtone 42, 125
  Cascades de Radule 169
Water parks, A Tyroliana (Vallée
  du Cavu) 141
Websiotes 178
Wi-Fi 179
Wild camping 45
Wildlife 11
  A Cupulatta turtle and
    tortoise sanctuary 31, **109**,
    120
  conservation 44, 45
  Île Lavezzi 137
  protecting marine habitats **134**
  Réserve Naturelle de
    Scandola **117**
  see also Nature reserves
Wild swimming 41
Wine **38-9**
  festivals 38
World War I 56
World War II 56, 167

Z

Zonza **142**

PHRASE BOOK

IN EMERGENCY

Help!	Au secours!	oh sekoor
Stop!	Arrêtez!	aret-ay
Call a doctor!	Appelez un médecin!	apuh-lay uñ medsañ
Call an ambulance!	Appelez une ambulance!	apuh-lay oon oñboo-loñs
Call the police!	Appelez la police!	apuh-lay lah poh-lees
Call the fire brigade!	Appelez les pompiers!	apuh-lay leh poñ-peeyay
Where is the nearest telephone?	Où est le téléphone le plus proche?	oo ay luh tehleh-fon luh ploo prosh
Where is the nearest hospital?	Où est l'hôpital le plus proche?	oo ay l'opee-tal luh ploo prosh

COMMUNICATION ESSENTIALS

Yes	Oui	wee
No	Non	noñ
Please	S'il vous plaît	seel voo play
Thank you	Merci	mer-see
Excuse me	Excusez-moi	exkoo-zay mwah
Hello	Bonjour	boñzhoor
Goodbye	Au revoir	oh ruh-vwar
Good evening	Bonsoir	boñ-swar
Morning	Le matin	motañ
Afternoon	L'après-midi	l'apreh-meedee
Evening	Le soir	swar
Yesterday	Hier	eeyehr
Today	Aujourd'hui	oh-zhoor-dwee
Tomorrow	Demain	duhmañ
Here	Ici	ee-see
There	Là	lah
What?	Quel, quelle?	kel, kel
When?	Quand?	koñ
Why?	Pourquoi?	poor-kwah
Where?	Où?	oo

USEFUL PHRASES

How are you?	Comment allez-vous?	kom-moñ talay voo
Very well, thank you.	Très bien, merci.	treh byañ, mer-see
Pleased to meet you.	Enchanté de faire votre connaissance.	oñshoñ-tay duh fehr votr kon-ay-sans
See you soon.	A bientôt.	abyañ-toh
That's fine.	Voilà qui est parfait.	vwalah kee ay parfay
Where is/are...?	Où est/sont...?	oo ay/soñ
How far is it to...?	Combien de kilomètres d'ici à...?	kom-byañ duh is keelo-metr d'ee-see ah
Which way to...?	Quelle est la direction pour...?	kel ay lah deer-ek-syoñ poor
Do you speak English?	Parlez-vous anglais?	par-lay voo oñg-lay
I don't understand.	Je ne comprends pas.	zhuh nuh kom-proñ pah
Could you speak slowly, please?	Pouvez-vous parler moins vite, s'il vous plaît?	poo-vay voo par-lay mwañ veet seel voo play
I'm sorry.	Excusez-moi.	exkoo-zay mwah

USEFUL WORDS

big	grand	groñ
small	petit	puh-tee
hot	chaud	show
cold	froid	frwah
good	bon	boñ
bad	mauvais	moh-veh
enough	assez	assay
well	bien	byañ
open	ouvert	oo-ver
closed	fermé	fer-meh
left	gauche	gohsh
right	droite	drwaht
straight on	tout droit	too drwah
near	près	preh
far	loin	lwañ
up	en haut	oñ oh
down	en bas	oñ bah
early	de bonne heure	duh bon urr
late	en retard	oñ ruh-tar
entrance	l'entrée	l'on-tray
exit	la sortie	sor-tee
toilet	les toilettes, les WC	twah-let, vay-see
unoccupied	libre	leebr
no charge	gratuit	grah-twee

MAKING A TELEPHONE CALL

I'll try again later.	Je rappelerai plus tard.	zhuh rapeleray ploo tar
Can I leave a message?	Est-ce que je peux laisser un message?	es-keh zhuh puh leh-say uñ mehsazh
Hold on.	Ne quittez pas, s'il vous plaît.	nuh kee-tay pah seel voo play
Could you speak up a little please?	Pouvez-vous parler un peu plus fort?	poo-vay voo par-lay uñ puh ploo for
local call	la communication locale	komoonikah-syoñ low-kal

SHOPPING

How much does this cost?	C'est combien s'il vous plaît?	say kom-byañ seel voo play
Do you take credit cards?	Est-ce que vous acceptez les cartes de crédit?	es-kuh voo zaksept-ay leh kart duh kreh-dee
Do you take travellers' cheques?	Est-ce que vous acceptez les chèques de voyage?	es-kuh voo zaksept-ay leh shek duh vwayazh
I would like ...	Je voudrais...	zhuh voo-dray
Do you have?	Est-ce que vous avez?	es-kuh voo zavay
I'm just looking.	Je regarde seulement.	zhuh ruhgar suhlmoñ
What time do you open?	A quelle heure vous êtes ouvert?	ah kel urr voo zet oo-ver
What time do you close?	A quelle heure vous êtes fermé?	ah kel urr voo zet fer-may
This one	Celui-ci	suhl-wee-see
That one	Celui-là	suhl-wee-lah
expensive	cher	shehr
cheap	pas cher, bon marché	pah shehr, boñ mar-shay
size, clothes	la taille	tye
size, shoes	la pointure	pwañ-tur
white	blanc	bloñ
black	noir	nwahr
brown	brun	bruñ
red	rouge	roazh
yellow	jaune	zhohwn
green	vert	vehr
blue	bleu	bluh

TYPES OF SHOP

antique shop	le magasin d'antiquités	maga-zañ d'oñteekee-tay
bakery	la boulangerie	booloñ-zhuree
bank	la banque	boñk
book shop	la librairie	lee-brehree
butcher	la boucherie	boo-shehree
cake shop	la pâtisserie	patee-sree
cheese shop	la fromagerie	fromazh-ree
chemist	la pharmacie	farmah-see
dairy	la crémerie	krem-ree
department store	le grand magasin	groñ maga-zañ
delicatessen	la charcuterie	sharkoot-ree
fishmonger	la poissonnerie	pwasson-ree
gift shop	le magasin de cadeaux	maga-zañ duh kadoh
greengrocer	le marchand de légumes	mar-shoñ duh lay-goom
grocery	l'alimentation	alee-moñta-syoñ
hairdresser	le coiffeur	kwafuhr
market	le marché	marsh-ay
newsagent	le magasin de journaux	maga-zañ duh zhoor-no
post office	la poste, le bureau de poste, les PTT	pohst, booroh duh pohst, peh-teh-teh
shoe shop	le magasin de chaussures	maga-zañ duh show-soor

supermarket	le super-marché	soo pehr-marshay		glass	le verre	vehr
tobacconist	le tabac	tabah		bottle	la bouteille	boo-**tay**
travel agent	l'agence de voyages	l'azhoñs duh vwayazh		knife	le couteau	koo-**toh**
				fork	la fourchette	for-**shet**
				spoon	la cuillère	kwee-**yehr**

MENU DECODER

l'agneau	l'anyoh	lamb		breakfast	le petit déjeuner	puh-**tee** deh-**zhuh**-nay
l'ail	l'eye	garlic		lunch	le déjeuner	deh-**zhuh**-nay
la banane	banan	banana		dinner	le dîner	dee-nay
le beurre	burr	butter		main course	le plat principal	plah prañsee-**pal**
la bière	bee-**yehr**	beer		starter, first course	l'entrée, le hors d'oeuvre	l'oñ-tray, or-duhr
le bifteck, le steak	beef-**tek**, stek	steak		dish of the day	le plat du jour	plah doo zhoor
le boeuf	buhf	beef		wine bar	le bar à vin	bar ah vañ
bouilli	boo-**yee**	boiled		café	le café	ka-**fay**
le café	kah-**fay**	coffee		rare	saignant	say-**noñ**
le canard	kanar	duck		medium	à point	ah **pwañ**
le citron pressé	see-**troñ** press-**eh**	fresh lemon juice		well done	bien cuit	byañ **kwee**
les crevettes	kruh-**vet**	prawns				
les crustacés	kroos-**ta**-say	shellfish				
cuit au four	kweet oh foor	baked				
le dessert	deh-**ser**	dessert				
l'eau minérale	l'oh meeney-ral	mineral wate*r*				
les escargots	leh zes-kar-**goh**	snails				
les frites	freet	chips				
le fromage	from-**azh**	cheese				
les fruits frais	frwee freh fresh	fruit				
les fruits de mer	frwee duh mer	seafood				
le gâteau	gah-**toh**	cake				
la glace	glas	ice, ice cream				
grillé	gree-**yay**	grilled				
le homard	omahr	lobster				
l'huile	l'weel	oil				
le jambon	zhoñ-**boñ**	ham				
le lait	leh	milk				
les légumes	lay-**goom**	vegetables				
la moutarde	moo-tard	mustard				
l'oeuf	l'uf	egg				
les oignons	leh zonyoñ	onions				
les olives	leh zoleev	olives				
l'orange pressée	l'oroñzh press-**eh**	fresh orange juice				
le pain	pan	bread				
le petit pain	puh-**tee** pañ	roll				
poché	posh-ay	poached				
le poisson	pwah-**ssoñ**	fish				
le poivre	pwavr	pepper				
la pomme	pom	apple				
les pommes de terre	pom-duh tehr	potatoes				
le porc	por	pork				
le potage	poh-**tazh**	soup				
le poulet	poo-**lay**	chicken				
le riz	ree	rice				
rôti	row-**tee**	roast				
la sauce	sohs	sauce				
la saucisse	sohsees	sausage, fresh				
sec	sek	dry				
le sel	sel	salt				
le sucre	sookr	sugar				
le thé	tay	tea				
le toast	toast	toast				
la viande	vee-yand	meat				
le vin blanc	vañ **bloñ**	white wine				
le vin rouge	vañ roozh	red wine				
le vinaigre	veenaygr	vinegar				

STAYING IN A HOTEL

Do you have a vacant room?	Est-ce que vous avez une chambre?	es-kuh voo-zavay oon shambr
double room	la chambre pour deux personnes, avec un grand lit	shambr ah duh pehr-**son**, avek un groññ lee
with double bed		
twin room	la chambre à deux lits	shambr ah duh lee
single room	la chambre pour une personne	shambr ah oon pehr-**son**
room with a bath, shower	la chambre avec salle de bains, une douche	shambr avek sal duh bañ, oon doosh
porter	le garçon	gar-**soñ**
key	la clef	klay
I have a reservation.	J'ai fait une réservation.	zhay fay oon rayzehrva-**syoñ**

EATING OUT

Have you got a table?	Avez-vous une table libre?	avay-**voo** oon tahbl leebr
I want to reserve a table.	Je voudrais réserver une table.	zhuh voo-**dray** rayzehr-**vay** oon tahbl
The bill, please.	L'addition, s'il vous plaît.	l'adee-**syoñ** seel voo **play**
I am a vegetarian.	Je suis végétarien.	zhuh swee vezhay-**tehryañ**
Waitress waiter	Madame, Mademoiselle/ Monsieur	mah-**dam**, mah-dem wah zel/muh-**syuh**
menu	le menu, la carte	men-**oo**, kart
fixed-price menu	le menu à prix fixe	men-**oo** ah pree feeks
cover charge	le couvert	koo-**vehr**
wine list	la carte des vins	kart-deh vañ

SIGHTSEEING

abbey	l'abbaye	l'abay-**ee**
art gallery	la galerie d'art	galer-**ree** dart
cathedral	la cathédrale	katay-**dral**
church	l'église	l'ayg**leez**
garden	le jardin	zhar-**dañ**
library	la bibliothèque	beeblee**oo**-tek
museum	le musée	moo-**zay**
railway station	la gare (SNCF)	gahr (es-en-say-ef)
bus station	la gare routière	gahr roo-tee-**yehr**
tourist information office	les renseigne-ments touristiques, le syndicat d'initiative	roñsayn-**moñ** too-rees-**teek**, sandee-ka d'eenee-sy**ateev**
town hall	l'hôtel de ville	l'oh**tel** duh veel
private mansion	l'hôtel particulier	l'oh**tel** partikoo-**lyay**
closed for public holiday	fermeture jour férié	fehrmeh-**tur** zhoor fehree-**ay**

NUMBERS

00	zéro	zeh-**roh**
01	un, une	uñ, oon
02	deux	duh
03	trois	trwah
04	quatre	katr
05	cinq	sañk
06	six	sees
07	sept	set
08	huit	weet
09	neuf	nerf
10	dix	dees
11	onze	oñz
12	douze	dooz
13	treize	trehz
14	quatorze	ka**torz**
15	quinze	kañz
16	seize	sehz
17	dix-sept	dees-**set**
18	dix-huit	dees-**weet**
19	dix-neuf	dees-**nerf**
20	vingt	vañ
30	trente	tront
40	quarante	karoñt
50	cinquante	sañk**oñt**

60	soixante	*swa*so**ñt**
70	soixante-dix	*swa*so**ñt**-**dees**
80	quatre-vingts	*katr*-**vañ**
90	quatre-vingts-dix	*katr*-*vañ*-**dees**
100	cent	*so**ñ***
1,000	mille	*meel*

TIME

one minute	une minute	*oon* mee-**noot**
one hour	une heure	*oon urr*
half an hour	une demi-heure	*oon* **duh-mee** *urr*
Monday	Lundi	*luñ*-**dee**

Tuesday	**Mardi**	*mar*-**dee**
Wednesday	**Mercredi**	*mehrkruh*-**dee**
Thursday	**Jeudi**	*zhuh*-**dee**
Friday	**Vendredi**	*voñdruh*-**dee**
Saturday	**Samedi**	*sam*-**dee**
Sunday	**Dimanche**	*dee*-**moñsh**

CORSICAN WORDS AND PHRASES

Although French is spoken everywhere, a few Corsican phrases can come in handy. Corsican is closer to Italian, in fact to medieval Tuscan, both in its vocabulary and its pronunciation, but also shows a few other Mediterranean influences. Geographical terms appear in many sight names, and on the bilingual signs.

BASICS

A'ringraziavvi: Thank you
Fate u piacè: Please
Ié: Yes
Nò: No
Và bé: OK
Induve: Where
Quandu: When
Chì: What, who, which
A'vedeci: Goodbye
A dopu: See you
Buona notte: Goodnight
Buona sera: Good evening
Buonghjornu: Hello
Cumu sì?: How are you?
Me dispiace: Sorry
(Nò) Capiscu: I (don't) understand
Parla inglese?: Do you speak English?

GEOGRAPHICAL TERMS

a marina: beach
anse/cala: cove
boca/foce/col: mountain pass
calanca: gorge, ravine
casa: house
casatorre: stronghold
castellu/casteddu: fortified settlement
fiume: river
fiumicellu: stream
lau/lavu: lake
licettu: oak forest
muntagna: mountain
orriu: shelter under a large stone or boulder, sometimes bricked in
pianu: plateau
piscia: waterfall
ponte: bridge
stagnu: pool or pond
torre: tower
u paese: village
vignale/vignetu: vineyard

DIRECTIONS

dritta: right
sempredrittu: straight on
sinistra: left
Induv'é...?: Where is...?

SHOPPING

aperta/apertu: open
Avetene...?: Do you have...?
basta: enough
buonu mercatu: cheap
chiusu: closed
grande/maio: big
Hè troppu caru: It is too much
menu: less
nulla/nunda/nudda: nothing
piccola/chjucu: small
pui: more
Quantu costa/Quanto hè?: How much does it cost/is it?
Vogliu...: I want...

TIME, DAYS AND MONTHS

Chi ora hè?: What is the time?
oghje: today
ieri: yesterday
dumane: tomorrow
ghjurnu: day
simana: week
meze: month

Monday:	**luni**
Tuesday:	**marti**
Wednesday:	**mercuri**
Thursday:	**ghjovi**
Friday:	**venneri**
Saturday:	**sabatu**
Sunday:	**dumenica**
January:	**Ghjennaghju**
February:	**Febbraghju**
March:	**Marzu**
April:	**Aprile**
May:	**Maghjiu**
June:	**Ghjiugnu**
July:	**Ghjugliu**
August:	**Aostu**
September:	**Sittembre**
October:	**Ottobre**
November:	**Novembre**
December:	**Dicembre**

SEASONS

auturnu: autumn
estate: summer
imbernu/ingnernu: winter
veranu: spring

ACKNOWLEDGMENTS

The publisher would like to thank the following for their kind permission to reproduce their photographs:

Key: a-above; b-below/bottom; c-centre; f-far; l-left; r-right; t-top

Adobe Stock: agaglowala 159t, Dynamoland 134, e55evu 13t, familie-eisenlohr.de 24-25t, John 147b, roberto 11br, Rokas 44-45b, Alexandre Rosa 142cla, ValerioMei 44cra, zicksvift 84, ZoltanJozsef 172-173

Alamy Stock Photo: Action Plus Sports Images 57cb, Afripics 33cl, All Canada Photos / Ian Cook 19, 150, Delmarty / Andia 126, Mari / Andia 26b, Archive Images 55crb, Hans-Joachim Aubert 140, blickwinkel / P. Royer 31bl, 40b, Pascal Boegli 62, 69tr, Christophe Boisvieux 145, Ian Bottle 112tr, 115tl, Benoit Cappronnier 47cr, Chronicle 53tl, 54crb, Classic Image 53clb, Helmut Corneli 8cla, 41br, Julien Cruciani 60, 68bl, Janos Csernoch 141, Danita Delimont / Walter Bibikow 87cra, DPPI Media 50crb, Jacques Dreano 27ca, Greg Balfour Evans 38bl, 111t, Andrew Fare 52t, France Pictures Agency 119, David Gabis 167b, Julia Gavin 100, Brusini Aurélien / Hemis.fr 11t, Cavalier Michel / Hemis.fr 40-41t, 42tl, Giraudou Laurent / Hemis.fr 103, Guiziou Franck / Hemis.fr 67, Lansard Gilles / Hemis.fr 13cr, 50clb, 83, 111b, 156t, Lemaire Stéphane / Hemis.fr 16, 72, 114-115b, Moirenc Camille / Hemis.fr 28tl, 33crb, 101, Montico Lionel / Hemis.fr 6-7, 8cl, 144, Rieger Bertrand / Hemis.fr 25tr, 32br, 80cr, 159cra, Stephen Hughes 164-165b, Ian Dagnall Commercial Collection 39br, Image Professionals GmbH / OOK-foto 117crb, Image Professionals GmbH / TravelCollection 46bl, 50cr, 116-117t, 142-143t, Imagebroker / Arco / F. Scholz 93b, imageBROKER / Daniel Schoenen 97b, imageBROKER / Raimund Franken 20crb, 37cl, 78, 88clb, 88bc, 92, 102, imageBROKER.com GmbH & Co. KG / . / . 51crb, imageBROKER.com GmbH & Co. KG / BAO 53cla, imageBROKER.com GmbH & Co. KG / Bildverlag Bahnmüller 66, imageBROKER.com GmbH & Co. KG / Martina Katz 51tl, imageBROKER.com GmbH & Co. KG / Otto Stadler 121b, Jon Ingall 34b, Ivy Close Images 115bc, Eric James 50cl, Jean Schweitzer energy pictures 35cla, Jon Arnold Images Ltd / Walter Bibikow 138-139, Izzet Keribar 24cla, Heitz Lucas 26-27t, Magite Historic 58cra, mauritius images GmbH / ClickAlps 160-161t, mauritius images GmbH / Walter Bibikow 37br, Paul McErlane 135, Nature Picture Library / Pascal Pittorino 117clb, Nature Picture Library / Wild Wonders of Europe / Pitkin 13br, Sérgio Nogueira 87tl, North Wind Picture Archives 54bc, 54-55t, M. Timothy O'Keefe 20t, Old Images 55cra, Loic Colonna / Onlyfrance.fr 36br, parkerphotography 12-13b, Photo12 / Fondation Napoléon 55tr, piemags 56tl, Prisma Archivo 53bc, robertharding / Eleanor Scriven 28-29b, robertharding / Yadid Levy 51clb, De Rocker 112bl, Peter Schickert 46-47t, Shootpix / Abacapress.com 50cla, 51cl, Witold Skrypczak 37t, 52crb, 88-89, 166, Richard Sowersby 10clb, 47bl, The Print Collector / Heritage Images 55bc, David Tomlinson 136, travelstock44.de /

Juergen Held 20cr, 94b, UtCon Collection 115tr, WBC ART 115cr, Westend61 22clb, Westend61 GmbH / Manuel Sulzer 138bc, 165tr, 168-169, WireStock 80-81b, Jan Wlodarczyk 12t, 122-123, 157, Robert Wyatt 85

AWL Images: Davide Camesasca 2-3, Hemis 24tl, 63, 64, Francesco Riccardo Iacomino 18, 38-39t, 90-91, 127, 128, Doug Pearson 4

Bridgeman Images: Tallandier 56bl, © The Holbarn Archive 54tl

Depositphotos Inc: bimka1 39cl

Dreamstime.com: Eva Bocek 41cla, Dorinmarius 22t, 124-125b, 167t, Eugenesergeev 49bl, 57tr, Freesurf69 43tr, Jon Ingall 11cr, 22cl, 36tl, 43cl, 79, 99, 123br, 132, 149, 161b, 162, Jojjik 24-25ca, 76-77, 137, Milosk50 154-155, 171, Grondin Franck Olivier 42-43b, Nancy Pauwels 108-109t, Kovalenkov Petr 59tl, Pierrelarcher 98tr, Pkazmierczak 146-147t, Rndmst 170, Goran Šafarek 97t, Vampy1 12clb, 110

Getty Images: Simon Massicotte / 500px 94-95t, AFP / Pascal Pochard-Casabianca 34t, 35br, Pascal Pochard-Casabianca / AFP 29tr, 32-33t, 57bc, Toussaint Canazzi / AFP 56crb, Studio Borlenghi / ALeA 93t, De Agostini / DEA / Biblioteca Ambrosiana 53tr, De Agostini Picture Library 52bc, Hulton Archive / Fototeca Storica Nazionale / Fototeca Gilardi 48-49t, Moment / © Pascal Boegli 65, Moment / Francesco Riccardo Iacomino 17, 104, 118, Moment / Marius Roman 90b, Moment / Massimo Ravera 50cra, Moment / Pakin Songmor 70-71, Moment Unreleased / Roberto Moiola / Sysaworld 22br, Jean Tesseyre / Paris Match 56-57t, Photodisc / Alex Treadway 10-11b, 30bl, Jean-Marc Zaorski / Gamma-Rapho 51tr, Alexis Rosenfeld 117br, François Desjobert / Sygma 58-59b, The Image Bank / John Elk III 98bl, The Image Bank / Marc Dozier 113, The Image Bank Unreleased / Izzet Keribar 8clb

Getty Images / iStock: alxpin 8-9, helovi 10ca, Corrado Morale 30-31t

Shutterstock.com: Axel LDQ 120-121t, Besides the Obvious 87tr, bikemp 27br, givi585 156b, Andrii_K 45br, Rozenn Leboucher 51cr, Panumas Nikhomkhai 29cl, p2n Media 20bl, PhotoArtStudio29 143b, Ondrej Prochazka 68-69b, Tatyana Soares 31cr, Dennis Wegewijs 138clb, Jeff Whyte 108br, Wirestock Creators 96t

Cover images:
Front and Spine: **Shutterstock.com:** Zoltan Szabo Photography; Back: **Alamy Stock Photo:** Jan Wlodarczyk tr; **AWL Images:** Francesco Riccardo Iacomino cla; **Dreamstime.com:** Jojjik c; **Shutterstock.com:** Zoltan Szabo Photography b; Front Flap: **Alamy Stock Photo:** Westend61 GmbH / Manuel Sulzer cb, Jan Wlodarczyk cra; **Dreamstime. com:** Eva Bocek br, Jon Ingall bl, Jojjik t; **Getty Images:** Alexis Rosenfeld cla

Contributors Fabrizio Ardito, Cristina Gambaro, Jon Bryant, Anna Richards

Senior Editors Zoë Rutland, Dipika Dasgupta

Senior Designers Vinita Venugopal, Laura O'Brien

Project Editor Alex Pathe

Editor Nandini Desiraju

Designers Vidit Vashisht, Sulagna Das

Proofreader Elizabeth Dowsett

Indexer Helen Peters

Picture Research Team Nishwan Rasool, Virien Chopra, Manpreet Kaur

Illustrators Modi Artistici, Anna Mucciarelli, Tiziano Perotto

Publishing Assistant Simona Velikova

Jacket Designers Laura O'Brien, Vidit Vashisht

Project Cartographer Ashif

Senior Cartographic Editor James Macdonald

Cartography Manager Suresh Kumar

Senior DTP Designer Tanveer Zaidi

Image Retouching Vijay Kandwal

Senior Production Controller Samantha Cross

Managing Editor Beverly Smart

Managing Art Editor Gemma Doyle

Senior Managing Art Editor Priyanka Thakur

Editorial Director Hollie Teague

Art Director Maxine Pedliham

Publishing Director Georgina Dee

First edition 2003

Published in Great Britain by
Dorling Kindersley Limited,
20 Vauxhall Bridge Road, London SW1V 2SA

The authorised representative in the EEA is
Dorling Kindersley Verlag GmbH. Arnulfstr.
124, 80636 Munich, Germany

Published in the United States by DK Publishing,
1745 Broadway, 20th Floor, New York, NY 10019, USA

Copyright © 2003, 2025 Dorling Kindersley Limited
A Penguin Random House Company

24 25 26 27 10 9 8 7 6 5 4 3 2 1

The publishers cannot accept responsibility for any consequences
arising from the use of this book, nor for any material on third
party websites, and cannot guarantee that any website address in
this book will be a suitable source of travel information.

A CIP catalog record for this book
is available from the British Library.

A catalog record for this book is available
from the Library of Congress.

ISSN: 1542 1554
ISBN: 978 0 2417 2168 1

Printed and bound in China.

www.dk.com

MIX
Paper | Supporting
responsible forestry
FSC™ C018179
www.fsc.org

This book was made with Forest
Stewardship Council™ certified
paper – one small step in DK's
commitment to a sustainable future.
Learn more at **www.dk.com/uk/
information/sustainability**

A NOTE FROM DK

The rapid rate at which the world is changing is
constantly keeping the DK Travel team on our toes.
While we've worked hard to ensure that this edition
of Corsica is accurate and up-to-date, we know that
opening hours alter, standards shift, prices fluctuate,
places close and new ones pop up in their stead. So,
if you notice we've got something wrong or left
something out, we want to hear about it.
Please get in touch at travelguides@dk.com

002 18